Sandra Winlow

655 - 4416
656 - 7639

RESOLVING
SEXUAL ABUSE

By the same author

A Path With a Heart:
Ericksonian Utilization With Resistant and Chronic Clients

A NORTON PROFESSIONAL BOOK

RESOLVING SEXUAL ABUSE

*Solution-Focused Therapy and
Ericksonian Hypnosis for
Adult Survivors*

Yvonne M. Dolan, M.A.

W.W. NORTON & COMPANY • *NEW YORK* • *LONDON*

Library of Congress Cataloging-in-Publication Data

Dolan, Yvonne M., 1951–
  Resolving sexual abuse : solution-focused therapy and Ericksonian
hypnosis for adult survivors / Yvonne M. Dolan.
    p. cm.
  "A Norton professional book"—
  Includes bibliographical references.
  ISBN 0-393-70112-3
  1. Adult child abuse victims—Rehabilitation. 2. Problem-solving
therapy. 3. Hypnotism—Therapeutic use. I. Title.
RC569.5.A28D65 1991   616.85′83—dc20   90-25384

W. W. Norton & Company, Inc., 500 Fifth Avenue, New York, N.Y. 10110
W. W. Norton & Company, Ltd., 10 Coptic Street, London WC1A 1PU

1 2 3 4 5 6 7 8 9 0

*Dedicated with love and gratitude to
the memory of my grandmother,
Yvonne Marie Chartrand Dolan
(1906–1989), and to my father,
William James Dolan (1929–1951)*

CONTENTS

FOREWORD

YVONNE DOLAN BRINGS a wide repertoire of knowledge and tools to her work with clients. She carefully situates her work within a larger context involving the treatment of sexual abuse survivors and the pertinent research. Notice the word choice: "survivors" and not "victims." This word, survivors, implies that (as Dolan points out) these clients—and indeed all clients—have what it takes to survive, i.e., persistence, strengths, skills, resources, etc. (None of this is implied in the alternate word choice: victim.) And, as Dolan shows us, these tools, useful for survival, can also be useful in building a new, more satisfactory life.

Dolan's work reminded me of the soundness of John H. Weakland's first principle of effective therapy: Go slow. The therapist needs to pace therapy so that it fits the client's pace. Sometimes even one step at a time is too fast and it needs to be just a half-step at a time. Do as Dolan does: Be directed in this by the client.

In one of the later chapters, Yvonne Dolan tells us that she is frequently asked if she is doing "brief therapy" since she uses a solution-focused approach that includes various "solution-focused" techniques. Her answer is: "I work with my clients for as long as it takes for them to experience relief from symptoms, resolution of the intrusive traumatic memories, and acquisition of a hopeful and nonsymptomatic orientation toward the future. The resulting therapy process is definitely 'briefer' than it would be without solution-focused . . . techniques." This is somewhat similar to what I say to my clients: "'Brief therapy' simply means therapy that takes as few sessions as possible, not even one more than is necessary, for you to develop a satisfactory solution." The term "solution-focused therapy" is not (and is not meant to be) synonymous with, or the same as, or a substitute for, the term "brief therapy," even though the ideas involved developed within the brief therapy tradition.

"Brief therapy" is a relative term, typically meaning: (a) fewer sessions than standard, and/or (b) a shorter period of time from intake to termination, and/or (c) a lower number of sessions and a lower frequency of sessions from start to finish. In contrast, as Dolan puts it, "solution-focused therapy" means therapy that includes and strongly emphasizes "an active utilization of the client's present life resources and images of future goals and possibilities" and that "assumes that the construction of a solution is a joint process between client and therapist, with the therapist taking responsibility for empowering the client to create and experience her own uniquely meaningful and effective therapeutic changes." I could not have put it better.

According to Yvonne Dolan, solution-focused therapy "is based on the respectful assumption that clients have the inner resources to construct highly individualized and uniquely effective solutions to the problems that bring them to therapy." This respectful attitude Dolan has toward clients comes through loudly and clearly throughout the course of this book and is particularly clear in her admonition that clients do "only what is necessary for healing."

And what you will find in this book is: "only what is necessary for healing." Could or should one ask for more?

Steve de Shazer

ACKNOWLEDGMENTS

FIRST OF ALL, I want to thank my clients for the honor of their trust, for allowing me to learn from them, and for the joy of witnessing their healing and empowerment.

My husband, Charlie Johnson, lovingly encouraged and generously supported me through the process of writing this book. My relationship with him continues to be a wonderful reminder that there is goodness, laughter and love in the world, and life beyond recovery from trauma. I don't think I would have even started the book if he hadn't provoked me with his characteristic combination of loving and outrageous humor.

I am especially grateful to my dear friends and colleagues, Steve de Shazer and Insoo Berg, who have so graciously allowed me to learn from them in many different and very meaningful contexts over the years. Their encouragement inspired me to follow through with the writing.

Writing a book on the treatment of sexual abuse while maintaining a full-time private practice and teaching weekend workshops became, at times, an overwhelming experience. I appreciated the warm support of my wonderful sisters, Margaret Buhk and Lisa Schultz. Among the friends and colleagues who really made a difference for me during this process are David Bice, Linda Mraz, Gene Combs, Jill Freedman, Brigitte Schluger, Manfred and Liselotte Georg, Richard Schaub, Mara Prestia, Stephen Gilligan, Denise Ross, Susan Van Scoyk, Lynn Johnson, Denny Webster, Mark and Julie Disorbio, Gigi Payne, Karen and Michael Dudelcyzk, Chris Duran, Kerry Golden, Jane Wingle, Janet Wright, Debra Gaburo, and early on, Edie Israel, Bill and Evelyn Braithwaite, Eve Lipchik, Pat O'Hanlon Hudson, and Bill Hudson O'Hanlon. I would also like to thank the members of the Adams County and Jefferson County Intensive Family Treatment teams, and the students in our six-month intensive training in Ericksonian hypnosis and psychotherapy.

My grandma, to whom this book is dedicated, died several months before it could be completed. She was very supportive in the early writing stages, despite the ravages of her cancer. I am so thankful to her for being in my life as long as she was and continue to draw comfort and strength from the memories. She always told me to "light a little candle" instead of cursing the darkness. That metaphor made writing this book very meaningful.

Very special thanks to my excellent editor, Susan Barrows for her patient and perceptive editing. Without her, this book could not have been completed.

INTRODUCTION

SEXUAL ABUSE IS among the most potentially damaging traumas a person can sustain. Nevertheless, people can and do heal. Repeatedly witnessing that healing as a therapist has been one of the most profoundly meaningful experiences of my life.

My purpose in writing this book is to help therapists empower clients to resolve experiences of sexual abuse. Some people may question whether sexual abuse can ever "really" be resolved. In many cases it can, and perhaps this would be true in many more cases if treatment occurred sooner. By resolving sexual abuse, I am referring to accomplishing the following three goals:

1. Providing stabilization and relief for the client from symptoms stemming from or related to the sexual abuse trauma.
2. Altering feelings associated with memories of trauma, so that the memories and/or flashbacks are no longer intrusive or painfully prevalent in the client's daily life.
3. Developing a positive, practical, and healthy future orientation that results in nonsymptomatic patterns and, more importantly, in the client's living what she would consider a "satisfying" life.

Resolving sexual abuse is generally a demanding process for both the therapist and the client, but it is nevertheless possible.

However, if the therapist thinks that sexual abuse trauma absolutely cannot be resolved, that is certainly going to make the process of trying to do so a lot more difficult! This book is respectfully dedicated to making the treatment process more effective and less stressful for both the therapist and the client.

The combination of solution-focused therapy and Ericksonian hypnosis is ideally suited to the treatment of sexual abuse survivors. The Ericksonian techniques address the unconscious source of the symptomatology, while the solution-focused therapy provides the client with more conscious control over the symptoms themselves. The client is thereby empowered to resolve or at least mitigate existing symptomatology, and to identify and gradually reclaim healthy patterns of perceiving and behaving in the future.

Treating survivors of sexual abuse was not my original choice as a caregiver. Rather, my caseload has naturalistically and gradually evolved in that direction over the course of the past 15 years, as I have sought to assist the growing number of victims of sexual abuse who have presented themselves for treatment. My experience has encompassed not only treating these survivors in my own caseload but also learning from staff and clients as part of ongoing consultation at various social service, mental health, and women's treatment agencies.

Throughout the book, I have used the female pronoun to designate survivors of sexual abuse. This usage is not intended to imply that all victims of sexual abuse are female. Rather, it reflects current statistics, which suggest that the majority are female (Finkelhor, 1986; Russell, 1986). Recent researchers suggest that there are probably more male victims of childhood sexual abuse than current statistics show (Courtois, 1988). My own clinical experience with ratio of male to female clients would support this.

In all case examples, details have been changed to make clients unrecognizable. The clinical interventions, however, remain factually accurate. My clinical descriptions are not intended as examples of "perfect" ways to intervene with survivors of sexual abuse, but are instead offered as illustrative examples of ways to use solution-focused and Ericksonian techniques. In order to be effective, therapy techniques must be creatively reinvented by the therapist each time so as to constitute a truly personalized and sensitive response to the client.

A Personal Note

During the course of writing the book, I experienced my own traumatic events. My grandmother, to whom the book is dedicated, died after a long and painful struggle with cancer. It was my privilege to care for her in her home during the last two months she was alive. Parts of this book were begun while I kept vigil in the middle of the night, sitting at her old oak dining room table.

As a child I had always used the concept of a guardian angel for comfort when hurt or frightened. Watching Grandma, with her very intelligent mind still well intact, struggle with the excruciating ravages of cancer on her frail, old body was a heartbreaking experience for me. The angel again came to mind. Late one night, when I went to give Grandma her medicine, I asked her if she still believed in angels. She looked right into my eyes with a beatific and peaceful smile that I will never forget, gently saying, "I've been riding on the tips of their wings." Even during times of intense trauma, there can be moments of comfort and peace. Creating and therapeutically using those moments comprise the essence of this book.

My grandmother was one of the first social workers in the United States and successfully ran a social service agency for over 30 years. Upon "retirement," she did a variety of volunteer work with various human service agencies until the last months of her illness. She and I used to joke that perhaps she should go back to work so that she could get a "rest"!

Her attitude of "full sail to the wind" was evident to the very last hours of her life, and her inspiration made abandonment of this book, even during my subsequent period of intense grief, unthinkable. Throughout her career, she demonstrated a willingness to "get involved" with people in a way that was respectful and empowering and yet left no doubt that they—not she—were in charge of their lives. I hope that I have succeeded in embodying this same posture in my own work with clients. She will always remain for me a role model of a strong, competent, and deeply caring woman dedicated to making a positive difference whenever possible.

I offer the information in this book to readers in the same spirit that I present material in my workshops. Good therapy goes beyond any "technique" and is a personalized, compassionate, and very human response to the client. The reader is asked to consider what he or she is already doing that has a helpful and healing effect on individual clients and to take in all information presented through this filter. There is no substitute for each therapist's unique expression of human compassion and respect.

RESOLVING
SEXUAL ABUSE

1

THE LEGACY OF ABUSE

THIS CHAPTER GIVES an overview of the symptomatology likely to
be experienced by adult survivors of sexual abuse and provides a
general orientation to the Ericksonian and solution-focused techniques presented throughout this book.

Definition of Terms

In using the term *sexual abuse*, I am referring to any form of
coerced sexual interaction between an individual and a person in
a position of power over that individual.

I use the term *incest* to refer to sexual contact with anyone who
could be considered an inappropriate sexual partner because of
blood ties or social ties to the individual and her family (Benward
& Densen-Gerber, 1975). In addition to "blood relatives," this
would include relatives by marriage, members of parents' social
circle such as family friends, and parents' sexual partners. The
research definition of incestuous sexual child abuse generally requires an age difference between victim and perpetrator of at least
five years and requires that the victim be 14 or 15 years of age
or younger (Briere, 1989). Sibling incest is not always abusive
(Finkelhor 1980; Kempe & Kempe, 1984; Trepper & Barrett
1989); this is most likely to be true in cases involving little age
difference between siblings and no violence or coercion.

Child incestuous sexual abuse as used in this book refers to any sexual involvement between a child or adolescent and an individual who is in a position of power over her and from whom the child would traditionally expect protection and affection. In further defining incestuous sexual child abuse, Christine Courtois (1988) points out:

> The inability of the child to give informed consent to sexual involvement is implicit in this definition even in those cases where the child or adolescent might argue that she consented or appears to have consented. (p.13)

Abusive sexual contact can be defined by degrees from exhibitionism to intercourse (Courtois, 1988) to include progressively (Sgroi, Blick, & Porter, 1982): nudity, disrobing and genital exposure in front of the child, observation of the child (in a manner so as to make the child uncomfortable), kissing, fondling, masturbation, fellatio, cunnilingus, digital penetration of the anus or rectal opening, penile penetration of the anus or rectal opening, digital penetration of the vagina, penile penetration of the vagina, and intercourse. The level of intrusion implied in the above progression of abusive behaviors does not necessarily correspond to the degree of psychological damage likely to result.

Many complex factors are involved in determining the degree of trauma likely to be sustained by the sexual abuse victim. The effects of sexual abuse are subject to many variables, such as the frequency, duration, relationship to the offender, age of the victim when it occurred, reactions of significant others to the disclosure of the abuse, and resources and nurturing relationships, if any, available to the victim.

The degree and duration of debilitating post traumatic-symptoms vary. However, research has rarely found sexual abuse to be without damaging consequences for the victim (Briere, 1989). It appears that victimization involving violence and coercion and perpetrated by highly valued and trusted family members over extended periods of time is likely to cause the most damaging consequences. Conversely, the traumagenic factors may be somewhat lessened if the sexual abuse is of short duration, if the victim is given strong familial support upon disclosure, and particularly if responsibility is placed clearly on the perpetrator by the perpetrator's acceptance of responsibility (Dolan, 1989) and/or through the extended family's social and legal means.

Sadly, the responses from immediate family members most desirable for mitigating the degree of trauma suffered by victims of sexual abuse are all too rarely available. As a society, we still tend to minimize the extent of the abuse and its consequences and even to blame the victim, who as a consequence of her victimization is often all too ready to accept the blame.

In family systems typical of incestuous sexual abuse, there is a tendency for the immediate family to minimize the extent and effects of the sexual abuse, to deny that it in fact happened, and, most disturbingly, to actually protect the perpetrator by blaming or not believing the victim, causing the victim either to tolerate further victimization or to suffer expulsion from the family. Tragically, for many victims, the people who are most in a position to protect and support them are those who further victimize them through explicit or implicit denial, blaming, and rejection. It is no wonder that these victims are at risk for developing severe, enduring, debilitating symptoms.

This is not to deny that there are some survivors of sexual abuse who escape with less trauma than others. Browne and Finkelhor (1986) point out that sexual abuse does not inevitably produce severe and extreme psychological problems. Briere (1989) observes that "there are many survivors in the general population who appear to have 'gotten past' their victimization and who report few (if any) long term consequences" (p.50). However, my experience in working with survivors of sexual abuse is that even those who appear to have "gotten past" their victimization remain vulnerable to regression to symptomatic responses in times of severe stress or following experiences that either are reminiscent of or symbolically represent the original sexual abuse trauma. One of the goals of this book is to provide the therapist with a number of ways to effectively lessen the client's potential vulnerability to future stress.

How the Post-Traumatic Stress Disorder Applies to Sexual Abuse

Sexual abuse fits the criteria outlined in *DSM-III-R* (American Psychiatric Association, 1987) for events which cause post-traumatic stress disorder, subsequently referred to as PTSD. PTSD refers to the psychological reactions that typically occur as a result of a disaster or other extreme psychological stressor. Examples of such traumagenic experiences include war, floods, hurricanes, airplane and automobile accidents, tornadoes, earthquakes, and most significantly for our purposes, physical and sexual assault.

According to *DSM-III-R*, a combination of the following criteria must be present in order to form a diagnosis of PTSD (p.250):

1. The existence of a "psychologically distressing event" that would evoke significant disturbance in almost anyone.
2. Later reexperiencing of the trauma in one's mind, for example, through recurrent dreams of the stressor, or "flashbacks" (intrusive sensory memories) to the original traumatic situation.
3. "Numbing of general responsiveness" to avoid the external world, for example, dissociation, withdrawal, restricted affect, or loss of interest in daily events.
4. A wide variety of other reactions or symptoms, such as sleep disturbance, difficulty concentrating, memory problems, irrational guilt, extreme alertness to danger in the environment, and an intensification of symptoms upon exposure to situations that resemble the original event.

While some researchers in the past attempted to downplay the aversive qualities and destructive impact of sexual abuse (Briere, 1989), most contemporary writers emphasize that, for most children, sexual victimization is a very frightening, harmful, and psychologically destructive experience (Finkelhor, 1979; Herman, Russell, & Trocki, 1986; Russell, 1986) and therefore presumably quite capable of producing post traumatic stress. For example, in one community study of 930 women, it was found that 80% of those who had been sexually abused were "somewhat" to "extremely" upset by the event and 78% reported long-term negative effects (Russell, 1986). Sexual abuse during childhood, particularly within the family, may produce chronic or delayed post traumatic stress disorders later in life (Blake-White & Kline, 1985; Briere & Runtz, 1987; Courtois, 1988; Donaldson & Gardner, 1985; Gelinas, 1981, 1983; Goodwin, 1984; Lindberg & Distad, 1985; Van der Kolk; 1987).

The Advantages of Using a PTSD Diagnosis

A PTSD diagnosis is helpful for survivors of sexual abuse because the definition not only has a normalizing effect for clients but also is clinically accurate. When symptoms of childhood sexual abuse are explained as initially reasonable, and in many cases valuable, efforts to survive extreme psychological stress, they become less stigmatizing in clients' eyes. Many clients have expressed relief when told that their symptoms are common to many different causes of PTSD. Seeing themselves in the same group as victims of natural disasters, airplane and car accidents, and random criminal assaults can be helpful in overcoming a tendency to blame themselves rather than the perpetrator.

In addition, knowing that many PTSD reactions are common and even predictable gives the client a sense of being in control. As one client said, "It's been really important to hear that I'm having these reactions for a reason, and to know that a lot of other people who went through this sort of thing [sexual abuse] have the same kind of feelings. It makes me feel like I'm not just some sort of jerk—there's a reason I've been having trouble." Conversely, if adult survivors of childhood sexual abuse are not given some sort of map to understand their current symptoms, they may fear that they are going crazy. This is particularly true when the PTSD includes intrusive and regressive symptoms (these symptoms will be referred to in this book as PTSD symptoms).

Symptomatology

How does PTSD translate specifically for adult survivors of sexual abuse? Classic symptoms of PTSD characteristic of this population include dissociative responses (Brickman, 1984; Butler, 1978; Gelinas, 1983; Herman, 1981; Shengold, 1979, 1989; Summit, 1983), sleep disturbances , flashbacks, concentration difficulties (Briere, 1989), memory problems (Gelinas, 1983; Herman, 1985; Herman & Schatzow, 1987; Maltz, 1988), hyperalertness (Briere, 1989), irrational guilt (Briere, 1989; Courtois, 1988; Janoff-Bulman & Frieze, 1983; Miller & Porter, 1983), and an intensification of symptoms when exposed to experiences that even symbolically resemble the original trauma (Briere, 1989). These symptoms are similar to those found in rape victims (Burgess & Holmstrom, 1974).

Other symptoms may include sexual dysfunction (Meiselman, 1978), eating disorders, substance abuse (usually involving amphetamines or alcohol), compulsive sexuality (Courtois, 1979; de Young, 1982; Herman, 1981; Maltz, 1988), self-destructive behaviors (Briere, 1988; Briere & Zaidi, 1988), self-mutilation (de Young, 1982; Goodwin, Simms, & Bergman, 1979; Lindberg & Distad, 1985b), socially maladaptive behaviors such as truancy (De Francis, 1969; Reich & Gutierres, 1979; Runtz & Briere, 1986), inappropriate aggression toward others (Bagley, 1984; Briere & Runtz, 1987), and a tendency toward isolation (Briere, 1989). On an interpersonal level, the post-traumatic reaction is likely to result in difficulties with trust and, in cases involving female victims, an overvaluing of men resulting in a tendency to fluctuate between overidealization (Herman, 1981) and inevitable disappointment. Further symptoms include cognitive reactions, such as impaired self-esteem (Briere, 1989; Courtois, 1979, 1988; Herman, 1981; Jehu, Klassen, & Gazan, 1985–1986), and negative perceptions of the self, others and the future (Briere, 1989; Courtois, 1979, 1988; Herman, 1981; Jehu, Klassen, & Gazan, 1985–1986).

Depression is the most frequently reported symptom identified in research on adults molested as children (Browne & Finkelhor, 1986). Related to the depression is the fact that sexual abuse survivors are twice as likely to attempt suicide as those without a history of sexual abuse (Briere & Runtz, 1986; Sedney & Brooks, 1984).

The remainder of this chapter will explore the sexual abuse victim's symptomatology in greater detail, with reference to techniques derived from solution-focused therapy and Ericksonian hypnosis and psychotherapy.

The Dissociative Response Developed
by Recovering Trauma Victims

In the attempt to survive an overwhelming and potentially psychologically destructive event such as sexual or physical abuse, the victim is likely spontaneously to resort to a variety of unconscious dissociative devices. Unfortunately, such dissociative attempts as amnesia, numbing, and "spacing out" are rarely, if ever, fully successful in the original situation. They are, however, understandable in the context of the victim's desperate need to survive situations of extreme stress and trauma. Long after the original traumatic experience has passed, the survivor of childhood sexual abuse may spontaneously and unconsciously reactivate these dissociative defenses in times of stress.

The unconscious nature of the above responses makes them ideal for hypnotic intervention, since they exist as part of the survivor's highly developed repertoire of unconscious dissociative abilities. The Ericksonian techniques in subsequent chapters will describe how to mitigate existing dysfunctional dissociative responses and to utilize the client's dissociative abilities as a therapeutic resource rather than as a constriction of personality.

Amnesia

Memory disturbance among sexual abuse victims has been well documented (Briere, 1989; Courtois, 1988; Gelinas, 1983; Herman, 1985; Herman & Schatzow, 1987; Maltz, 1988), particularly in reference to partial or even complete amnesia for the original abuse experience. In more extreme cases, the result of the client's attempt to defend herself from devastating memories of abuse memories is a complete lack of memories for extended periods of childhood. Given the pain and trauma inherent in memories of the sexual abuse, this amnesia can be understood as an unconscious attempt to defend against reexperiencing the victimization through memories. In some cases, it seems apparent that amnesia was the victim's only alternative for psychological survival, as illustrated by the words of one former victim. Here she describes the process of beginning to recover memories of dissociated sexual abuse:

> I saw myself [in the first memory retrieved from those previously blank years in childhood] sitting in a chair looking out the window on a summer day. I was sitting at the table in my grandparents' kitchen, and in the memory I was about 10 years old. I had just realized, as the 10-year-old sitting at that table, that what my uncles, my stepfather, and my grandfather did to me wasn't normal— it didn't happen to other little girls. Somehow I had connected

some things the nuns had said that day (in the Catholic school I went to at the time) with the idea that I had been under some kind of a moral test. Sitting there at that table I suddenly had the realization that what had happened to me with my uncles not only wasn't normal or right but, worse yet, it was all my fault because the nuns had said in religion class that it was up to the girl to say no. They had specifically said that women are stronger than men and it was up them to stop men from committing sins of impurity.

Sitting there in the kitchen, 10 years old, I started crying because—I know this may sound silly—but the one thing I really wanted when I was a little girl was to be a saint, and in order to be a saint they said that you should try never to commit a mortal sin so that you would have a spotless soul. I remember feeling so bad because I knew that I had somehow, without even meaning to, committed very bad sins and I felt that nothing could completely take it away, that even after confession there would always be a sort of "stain" on this white thing I imagined to be my soul.

I remember actually thinking, I can't live with this, I can't go on, I'm going to have to die, I'll have to find a way to die. And then I panicked, because I remembered also hearing at school that it was a sin to kill yourself, and even thinking these thoughts was probably a sin. Being suicidal at 10 years old is pretty scary. I just remember at this point sort of rocking in my chair with my arms wrapped around my legs, thinking, I can't go on, I can't go on. It never occurred to me to discuss this with my mother. I had told her about it more than once and she had even witnessed it once— and her response left no doubt in my mind that she thought what was happening was just something that happened, and she had no intention of making them stop it. And she had told me not to mention it again, to just put it out of my mind. Her exact advice, I recall, was to "Pretend it never happened."

I remember thinking, I can't go on, I can't go on, and then I very thoroughly forgot all about it for many, many years.

And strangely, the first memory about the childhood abuse I recovered as a 30-plus-year-old adult was this one . . . almost like it got remembered in the order of the last thing forgotten. I have never been able to recover all the specific memories of the abuse at the hands of my stepfather, uncles and grandfather, but I have been able to remember in great detail sitting at the kitchen table thinking about it having happened in the past on that day. I have a strong feeling, however, that there will always be some details that

I just won't be able to remember. I know there's more because when I really push and try hard to remember I get this palpable feeling of dread, like this very young part of me deep inside is screaming *no, no, no*! It's really strange how I can remember remembering the abuse, almost as if it happened yesterday, but instead of directly remembering past events, I remember them as part of remembering at that kitchen table. When the memory first came it was really, really scary. I felt so filled with shame and disgust that I was truly in danger of committing suicide. I just sat there for several hours on the couch, crying and crying until finally I told my husband. That seemed to sort of break the spell.

For some victims of childhood sexual abuse, the memory of the abuse seems to come back rather spontaneously. Sometimes it appears to be triggered by events that are symbolically or literally similar to the events of the actual abuse, such as being manipulated and overpowered in the politics of the work setting, seeing a movie about sexual abuse, or more tragically, being raped as an adult. In other cases, the memories of the abuse seem to come back for no obviously discernible reason.

The amnesia may not be limited to memories of the abuse. As another adult survivor of childhood sexual abuse complained to me in therapy:

How can I get insight into my life when I can't even remember my childhood? I really resent that I can't learn from my past because I can't even remember it for years on end. It's as if somebody stole it from me, and in fact somebody did, that bastard [perpetrator]. And I know it's not just the bad things I can't remember—it's the good things, too, the best parts of being a child. He stole my childhood and I'll never get it back.

Fortunately, with the use of hypnosis, the survivor may be empowered to remember some of the "good things" about childhood, as well as recovering and addressing in a safe environment the trauma that occurred in the past. Specific instructions for helping the sexual survivor to remember events from the past without painfully and unnecessarily reliving the victimization will be offered in Chapter 9.

Amnesia and Concentration Problems in Everyday Life

Oftentimes, with survivors of sexual abuse, amnesic tendencies are not limited just to events from childhood, but also show up in memory problems in everyday life, such as difficulty concentrating on assigned reading material and problems retaining what is heard or read. As one client to me, "If I don't read the whole novel in one or two sittings over a day or so, I forget what happened in the first half of the book." Obviously, the concentration problems and spontaneous amnesia for stored material can pose severe problems for adult survivors of sexual abuse who are trying to succeed in school.

These same dissociative abilities suggest that the client has highly developed idiosyncratic autohypnotic abilities that can be utilized to improve recall of material for tests and other situations. This technique, called state-dependent memory scaling, is described in Chapter 7. The technique improves both concentration and recall of learned material.

Numbing, "Spacing Out," and Related Dissociative Responses

Briere (1989) describes numbing as a psychological withdrawal from the outside world, wherein the individual experiences a loss of reactivity, detachment from others and/or constricted emotionality (p.50). Many researchers have observed numbing symptoms in sexual abuse survivors (Butler, 1978; Courtois, 1988; Gelinas, 1983; Herman, 1981).

The constriction of affect inherent in the "numbing" response can impair the survivor's ability to forge much-needed emotional bonds, since others may experience her as "cold" and "unfeeling." Ironically, the survivor is most likely to become "numb" as a spontaneous defense when her own strong emotions are present; yet, this is precisely the time when she is likely to come across to others as "unfeeling."

While the degree of dissociation varies from person to person, the "spacing out" response (Briere, Evans, Runtz, & Wall, 1988; Lindberg & Distad, 1985a) is basically a shutting down of emotional and sensory experiences in the immediate environment. It can be understood in the context of victimization as a learned response originating in the client's attempts to escape from the traumatic sensations and feelings during the abuse. Unfortunately, this dissociative reaction may then become an automatic generalized response to other anxiety-provoking experiences in later life to such a degree that it becomes pervasive and constricting (Briere & Runtz, 1987).

Tragically, the spacing-out response may prevent victims from acting in their own behalf to escape additional victimization in the future, since they shut off the perceptions that could and should function as danger signals. Significantly, "spacing out" and numbing responses may also prevent mothers of future incest victims from recognizing danger and acting to protect their children. This response may be one reason that sexual abuse sometimes spans generations in families.

Other related dissociative symptoms typical of sexual abuse victims include depersonalization (the feeling of not being in one's body); derealization (the feeling that one's surroundings are not real); out-of-body experiences (the sensation of being disconnected from one's body, such as floating above one's body, particularly during sex); a general disengagement from one's environment into a state of detached observation; and at times inexplicable but temporary memory lapses, in which apparently mundane everyday details are inaccessible.

Dissociative responses may make the survivor of sexual abuse prone to lapses in attention, leading to car accidents and other accidents in situations involving extended periods of attentiveness. For example, a survivor of sexual abuse may not be ideally suited to being an air traffic controller! On the other hand, her advanced dissociative abilities make her well suited to enduring chaos and noise, because she can often simply "separate" from it, as exemplified by the following comment from an abuse survivor.

> I came from a big family and most of the time when I was in school I had to study while in a house with four or five younger kids making a big racket. I would just open my book, and it was like I just didn't hear it anymore. I remember one time I got in big trouble with my mother because apparently she left the house and as she was leaving told me to take the bread out of the oven in 15 minutes. Well, she came home an hour later and the oven timer was going and the bread was burning and I hadn't been aware of a thing except my book. Boy, was she mad, but I just couldn't help

it. Nowadays I can read on trains, buses, planes even when there is a lot of noise going on around me.

While the dissociative response is most likely to occur during periods of high stress, it can become an almost pervasive response for some victims of sexual abuse. Later (Chapter 7) I will give detailed instructions for helping clients turn the symptoms of highly developed dissociation into a healing resource. I will also provide techniques for helping the overly dissociated sexual abuse survivor strengthen her awareness and responsiveness to the present.

Dissociative Abilities as Resources

The highly advanced dissociative abilities commonly found in survivors of sexual abuse should not be viewed solely in the context of symptomatology, but should be appreciated as a valuable autohypnotic skills learned under severe duress.

It is my belief that the sex abuse survivor's ability to develop an optimal level of dissociation may all make the difference in her ultimate psychological survival. For example, it may be those victims who were unable to develop adequate dissociative abilities at the time of the abuse who are most likely to become the psychotic patients seen in hospital back wards and community settings for the chronically mentally ill. Conversely, those clients who dissociated "too well" may develop multiple personalities. Researchers have linked a history of sexual abuse trauma to the development of multiple personality (Bliss, 1984; Coons & Milstein, 1986; Putman, Post, Guroff et al., 1983). In my work with homeless chronically mentally ill clients, I have seen a disproportionately high number of former victims of sexual abuse who are too dissociated to navigate the work world successfully.

Flashbacks, Nightmares, and Other Intrusive Symptoms

It is common for survivors of childhood sexual abuse to describe recurring nightmares, intrusive memories, and flashbacks of the abuse (Briere, 1989; Courtois, 1988; Herman & Schatzow, 1987). In treating survivors of sexual abuse, one should remember that the intrusive and very vivid reexperiencing of the abuse during the flashback, as if it were actually happening, is not a psychotic experience. Rather, it is an unconscious response to a stimulus relating directly or indirectly to the original abuse trauma. Briere (1989) suggests that flashbacks may be viewed as "classically conditioned associations to the original abuse event triggered by stimuli in the survivor's current environment" (p.7). Flashbacks may be evoked by participation in an incest therapy group (Courtois, 1988), watching movies or television shows depicting sexual abuse, non-abusive sexual experiences, massage or sensate focusing exercises, or other experiences in which the survivor experiences feelings similar to those she experienced during the abuse, such as fear, powerlessness, anger, betrayal, and feeling "used."

Sometimes flashbacks or nightmares appear to come "out of nowhere" until the feelings associated with the experience are examined. For example, a woman who felt betrayed by a coworker who failed to stand up for her when she was unfairly criticized by her boss subsequently "flashed" on a vivid memory of her mother passively ignoring her when she disclosed that a neighbor had molested her. This client did not immediately connect the flashback to any stimulus in the environment until I asked, "Is there something going on in your life right now that reminds you of how you felt during this flashback?"

Similarly, another survivor had a severe fight with her husband when he sided with her girlfriend rather than her in an argument. She realized at the time that she was "over-reacting," but she could not help feeling powerless and enraged. That night she vividly recalled an image of her mother and father enjoying the company of the uncle who had raped her, and later in a disturbing "daydream" she watched her mother eating dinner with the perpetrator while she was locked out of the house.

A flashback may involve all or just some of the senses. If misunderstood by the therapist, flashbacks can be misdiagnosed as hallucinations or psychosis (Gelinas, 1983), particularly if the survivor reports fragments of previously dissociated memories of sexual abuse. For example, one client described a "creepy sensation" of someone touching her genitals and only later began to connect these sensations to memories of the actual sexual abuse.

Flashbacks may come in the form of smells, tastes, sensations, sights, and sounds, and may at times be so vivid that the victim temporarily becomes unaware of her actual surroundings.

Flashbacks can be seen as an unconscious attempt to desensitize through repetition; however, this apparent desensitization attempt is, like the defenses of amnesia and partial repression, rarely successful. Instead, the survivor needs additional help and support from external rather than just internal sources. In Chapter 6, techniques will be presented for assisting clients in reorienting from the flashback into the safety of the external environment.

If the survivor is able to identify the stimulus that triggered the flashback, she is likely to feel more secure. Of course, this is more difficult with flashbacks that may have been triggered by subtle olfactory or auditory cues that are hard to consciously identify. For example, one woman objected to skiing in an area where there were snowmobiles because she found the noise very upsetting. Her companions ignored her request and she reluctantly accompanied them because she had no car of her own. She then began to experience "inexplicably strong" feelings of powerlessness, rage, and sadness. She sobbed for the remainder of the afternoon, overwhelmed by the frightening feeling of "not knowing why" she was sobbing.

Later, assisted by autohypnotic techniques, she realized that the snowmobile sounds resembled the sounds of a jackhammer going on outside a building where she had been brutally raped as a child. Her assailant had relied on the jackhammer noise to cover up her screams for help. Knowing that her seemingly "hysterical and childish" response was not simply a "crazy" reaction to not getting her way about a choice of a ski area was very important to this woman and enabled her husband to respond supportively rather than simply viewing her behavior as disruptive and obnoxious.

An advantage to using autohypnotic techniques is that survivors may gain access to understandings unavailable on an everyday conscious level. Understanding the source of a flashback or other intrusive symptoms will make the experience less frightening to the victim. If sexual abuse survivors are not warned about flashbacks, nightmares, and other intrusive reexperiencing related to their sexual abuse, they may think they are losing their minds, becoming psychotic, or "imagining things."

Common themes in the recurring nightmares of adolescents and adults abused as children include threatening figures by one's bed, attacks by coiling snakes and horrifying monsters, experiences of being endlessly chased down dark corridors, violent disfigurement, mutilation, and of course, replaying of the actual scenes from the abuse similar to flashbacks. Typically, in these "posttraumatic nightmares" (Briere, 1989; Hartmann, 1984), the victim experiences extreme terror and helplessness and is apt to be paralyzed or in some other way unable to find any kind of help. Hypnosis or guided imagining with the active support of the therapist can provide a way for the sexual abuse survivor to alter or experience the nightmare in a less traumatic and more satisfying manner. Chapter 7 will detail the above technique and will also teach the therapist how to limit the flashbacks through dissociative strategies.

While flashbacks and other intrusive symptoms are probably not completely preventable (Courtois, 1988), the survivor can be assisted considerably by learning to identify what sorts of experiences are most likely to trigger them, knowing how to best limit the duration and intensity of the experience when it begins to occur, and learning ways to recover more quickly afterwards.

Sleep Disturbances

Given the traumatic nature of the sexual abuse survivor's nightmares, it is not surprising that chronic sleep disturbance is common among this client population (Briere, 1989; Sedney & Brooks, 1984). Since the sexual abuse probably occurred at night, in the dark, in bed, that is where the sexual abuse survivor may, unfortunately, feel most vulnerable and afraid. As one survivor expressed this:

> The one place where I should be able to count on feeling really safe is in bed in my own house with the doors locked, and that's where I always feel most afraid. There is no place in the whole world where I feel completely safe because I always feel that something could happen, but at night in bed it's the worst.

· 15 ·

The externally focused self-hypnosis technique described in Chapter 7 is useful for inducing sufficient relaxation for the client to sleep and in overcoming anxiety following nightmares or other stressors that interfere with sleep.

Irrational Guilt and Other Perceptual Distortions

The survivor of childhood sexual abuse is likely to suffer negative effects in the way she perceives and understand herself, others and the future (Briere, 1989; Jehu, Klassen, & Gazan, 1985–1986; McCann, Pearlman, Sackheim, & Abramson, 1985; McCord, 1985). These perceptual distortions, also knows as "cognitive effects" (Briere, 1989), include distrust of others, guilt and negative self-evaluation, perceived helplessness, and hopelessness about the future.

Many clinicians have reported that sexual abuse survivors demonstrate impaired self-esteem (Courtois, 1979, 1988; Herman, 1981; Jehu et al., 1985–1986). Regardless of the reality of the actual abuse situation, the victim is likely to blame herself for having been victimized (Janoff-Bulman & Frieze, 1983; Miller & Porter, 1983).

Some researchers suggest that perhaps self-blame functions to enable victims to avoid feelings of powerlessness, in that, if they feel that they did something to deserve the abuse, they can then believe that they had and therefore have some control in their life. A currently popular "New Age" view, sometimes interpreted to mean that each person somehow voluntarily "creates" her life experiences, unfortunately reinforces the victim's painful and irrational guilt. She is all too willing to believe that she somehow "caused"—and therefore deserved and is "responsible"—for her abuse. Another possible explanation for the sexual abuse victim's irrational self-blame is that this perception is related to a desire to believe in a "just world" (Lerner, 1980), in which the victim "deserved" the abuse, as opposed to the potentially terrifying idea that such violence can be random and is therefore unpreventable.

The family secrecy that characteristically surrounds incestuous sexual abuse (Butler,1978) may also serve to indirectly but effectively communicate to the victim that she was somehow to blame for being involved in a shameful act. The result of the learned perception of guilt and shame transmitted perhaps by the perpetrator or in some cases by the family is that victims may tend to experience chronic self-hatred and self-destructiveness (McCann et al., 1988). It is therefore not surprising that sexual abuse survivors, when compared to those individuals who have not been abused, have twice the likelihood of committing suicide or seriously contemplating suicide (Bagley & Ramsay, 1986; Briere & Runtz, 1986; Sedney & Brooks, 1984). Questions and rituals helpful for overcoming chronic self-blame and self-hatred will be discussed in Chapters 2 and 8.

Self-Destructive Behaviors

Given the negative self-perceptions described above, it is not surprising that many survivors of sexual abuse engage in self-destructive behaviors. These symptoms range from socially maladaptive behaviors to dramatic self-mutilation. Sexually abused individuals are likely to have school problems, including truancy (De Francis, 1969; Reich & Gutierres, 1979; Runtz & Briere, 1986) and concentration problems, which may result in later difficulties in the work world. Aggression (Bagley, 1984; Reich & Gutierres, 1979), drug and alcohol abuse (Bagley, 1984; Briere & Runtz, 1987; Briere & Zaidi, 1988; Herman, 1981), and self-mutilation (Briere, 1988; Briere & Zaidi, 1988; de Young, 1982; Goodwin, Simms, & Bergman, 1979; Lindberg & Distad, 1985b) have been reported as prominent among sexual abuse survivors.

Self-mutilation refers to deliberate self-injury, such as cutting or drawing with knives or razor blades on one's limbs, burning the body with matches or cigarettes, tearing out hair, and biting nails and fingers until they are bleeding or infected. These self-mutilating behaviors have been described by clients as ways to reorient from flashbacks, end dissociative experiences (Briere, 1989), reconnect to a feeling of being "real," and "express how bad it [the memories of sexual abuse] really hurts me." As one of my clients said:

> People can't see the memories of what he did that I carry inside me all the time, but they can see the scars on my arm. It makes it more real to other people. . . .

Other survivors may try to hide signs of their self-mutilation by wearing long-sleeved shirts and hurting themselves in less visible areas of the body.

Another client, when asked why she was burning her arm said simply:

> I hate myself. I burn my arm because sometimes I just need to feel and that's how I stop feeling empty. It makes me feel something. I hate my body. If I didn't have a body none of this would have happened.

My experience is that "insight" into the etiology of these behaviors is usually not sufficient in and of itself to enable the client to cease self-destructive patterns. Rather, in addition to receiving a compassionate explanation for the behavior, clients need to identify something to substitute for these patterns. Chapters 2, 6, 7, and 10 offer various ways to empower the client to find meaningful and nonsymptomatic alternative behaviors.

Eating Disorders

Sexual abuse does not in and of itself produce an eating disorder, but it can certainly be a strong factor in the development of one. Courtois (1988) points out, "A history of sexual abuse has been most frequently associated with bulimia, but it seems to have a relationship with compulsive overeating and anorexia as well" (p.314). The eating disorder can be viewed in the same context as other symptoms of post-traumatic stress that are likely to intensify during periods of high stress and abate or be more under control as the sexual abuse issues are resolved. Chapter 11 will offer ideas for helping prevent relapse into compulsive eating and other related symptoms, while empowering the client to control eating disorder symptoms during the course of treatment through community support and substitution of alternative "self-nurturing" activities.

Sexual Compulsions

Sexual compulsions can be viewed as a form of learned self-destructive behavior that was elicited and reinforced by the sexual victimization. Sexually compulsive behavior can be described as the victim's inability to identify, avoid, or refuse potentially abusive sexual partners and self-destructive sexual practices. In some cases, the sexual abuse victim will, in later years, appear to seek out self-destructive sexual liaisons in an apparently unconscious reenactment of the abuse. The survivor of sexual abuse is likely to associate exploitation and trauma with sexual relationships (Briere, 1989). Yet, ironically, she may be particularly vulnerable to exploitation because she instinctively craves an intimate relationship to provide the nurturance and caring she missed in childhood.

Since in childhood self-worth was associated with sexuality in relationship to the abuse perpetrators, it is not surprising that many sexual abuse survivors experience periods of sexually compulsive behavior (Courtois, 1979; de Young, 1982; Herman, 1981; Maltz, 1988; Meiselman, 1978), in which they engage in frequent though temporary and emotionally unsatisfying sexual relationships with many different partners.

Because of the abuse survivor's dissociation, she is likely to go through periods when she is unable to assess potential partners realistically. This makes her particularly vulnerable to predatory partners, who will continue to further erode her self-esteem by complying all too readily with her learned belief that men value her for "just one thing" (sex).

Since seductive behavior may have been repeatedly elicited and reinforced as part of early childhood sexual abuse, the adult survivor may behave in a seductive manner at times without having any conscious awareness that she is doing so. Or she may deliberately behave flirtatiously because of the message she received through her victimization that her sexuality is all that she has to offer "in exchange" for the potential nurturing of a relationship.

The notion that she could be loved intrinsically for her self rather than for what she has to offer is likely to be a foreign concept. She is likely to see herself as needing to "barter" something in return for a relationship. Since sex is commonly what sex abuse survivors believe they have to barter, it is not surprising that among prostitutes there is a high percentage of former victims of sexual abuse (Bagley & Young, 1987; James & Meyerding, 1977; Silbert & Pines, 1981).

Manipulation and "Personality Disorders"

The sexual abuse survivor has learned early in life that "nothing comes without a price" and that she cannot assume that people have her best interests in mind. She has been taught through her victimization that she cannot expect people to be good to her unless she offers something in return, and her low self-esteem makes it likely that she will see her sexuality as her only possession of value to trade. This perception and resulting behaviors may cause the sex abuse survivor to behave in ways that are seen as manipulative and that clinicians are likely to label as "personality disorder."

The survivor of incest is at risk for being diagnosed as a "borderline personality disorder" (Wheeler & Walton, 1987) and may display many of the characteristics of this diagnosis, particularly the splitting and hysterical features. The reader is referred to two books that offer excellent discussions of the borderline personality disorder in reference to sexual abuse survivors: *Healing the Incest Wound* by Christine Courtois and *Therapy for Adults Molested as Children: Beyond Survival* by John Briere.

Admittedly, the survivor of sexual abuse may be likely to display all or some of the symptoms of a borderline personality disorder (Briere, 1984) and "diagnostic shorthand" can be valuable when trying to communicate descriptive information about a client quickly and effectively to another therapist. However, I am philosophically biased against labeling survivors of sexual abuse as "borderline personality disorders," because this label does not provide an understanding of the symptoms in specific relationship to the victimization, thereby making it more difficult for corrective therapeutic changes to occur. I believe that the manipulative behaviors and other symptoms that may cause the client to be labeled as a "personality disorder" are more appropriately viewed in the context of learned survival responses that were once adaptive and reasonable but are no longer appropriate in the client's current environment. As Christine Courtois (1988) observes, "Many of the difficulties associated with treating borderlines might be alleviated by providing therapy which focuses on the trauma" (p.161).

Furthermore, the borderline personality disorder label may be experienced as very demoralizing and therefore counterproductive for both client and therapist if they believe that the label implies a negative or severely limited ability to respond successfully to treatment. For example, a client I saw became suicidal after reading literature on borderline personality in response to a former therapist's diagnosing her as "borderline." If the therapist feels that this diagnosis must be presented to the client, it should be done so with sensitivity and careful preparation. Most important-ly, the context should be adjusted to provide for the client's history of trauma, so that the diagnosis actually counteracts despair and self-blame by providing a compassionate and meaningful under-standing of the client's current predicament and leads to a practi-cal description of useful therapy directions. When it is necessary to introduce a potentially distressing diagnosis, the therapist should counteract the client's potential distress by specifically mentioning the ways that therapy may be helpful in reference to the diagnosis. In this way, the diagnosis helps the client and therapist to identify what needs to happen to allow the client to experience under-standing, comfort, and eventual symptomatic relief. For example, the therapist might explain that, given a diagnosis of borderline personality, it can be expected that therapy techniques that en-hance comfort and security are likely to be very helpful. This manner of explanation offers the client hope. As a result of creat-ing this practical and hopeful context in identifying the client's unique therapeutic needs, there will be the understanding that therapy is progressing in a hopeful direction, and that the client can ultimately expect an easing of difficulties. This hopeful con-text should, of course, also be used in cases where it is necessary to make other potentially distressing diagnoses such as multiple personality disorder. Above all, the therapist should guard against needlessly pathologizing the client's symptomology in ways that are not helpful for treatment, but that are merely upsetting to the client.

In Chapter 12, practical techniques will be described for assisting the survivor of sexual abuse in identifying and carrying out healthy behaviors in sexual and nonsexual relationships with others.

Sexual Dysfunction

Given the distorted messages regarding sexuality associated with abuse, it is not surprising that sexual abuse survivors are at high risk for suffering from sexual dysfunction. Meiselman (1978) reports that 87% of the group of sex abuse survivors she studied suffered from serious sexual problems, as opposed to only 20% of those who had not been sexually abused in childhood. Many other researchers report findings that substantiate the greater likelihood of sexual dysfunction among abuse survivors (Becker, Skinner, Abel, & Treacy, 1982; Briere & Runtz, 1988; Courtois, 1979; Finkelhor, 1979; Herman, 1981; Langmade, 1983; McCord; 1985; Tsai, Felman-Summers, & Edgar, 1979). In a study by Maltz and Holman (1987), nearly half (46%) of a group of incest survivors were anorgasmic and 60% reported pain during intercourse.

Sexual contact as an adult, even with a loving and reassuring partner, can inadvertently trigger physical flashbacks for the adult survivor of childhood sexual abuse. Chapter 10 will offer suggestions for empowering the client to reduce the intrusiveness and frequency of these sexually debilitating and emotionally disturbing flashbacks, and two cases will be described illustrating an indirect approach to resolution of anorgasmia.

Hopelessness

For many of the reasons described above, survivors of sexual abuse tend to suffer from a sense of hopelessness and powerlessness to influence their own life. I sometimes suggest to my sexual abuse survivor clients that they have learned to behave as if they are from Missouri, the "show me state," because of their understandable attitude of "I'll believe it when I see it."

In terms of positive future planning and goals, the learned cyni-

cism may be helpful in empowering the survivor of abuse to tena-
ciously carry out her objectives. Yet, without help in redirecting
her lack of trust, this same cynicism, when carried to the extreme,
can severely constrict the client in developing rewarding goals and
expressing herself in meaningful ways. Without a positive sense
of the future, the client is still living in relationship to the abuse,
rather than meeting her own needs in the context of a healthy
personality.

Among survivors of sexual abuse I have consistently seen a
poignantly and subtly expressed need for a positive future orientation, something that many clients initially describe as "impossible
to imagine." A positive future orientation provides clients with a
much-needed sense of hopefulness and a "map" for creating a
nurturing, meaningful life beyond their victimization. It enables
them to, as one client said, "move into our own lives."

Chapters 2 and 12 offer techniques for overcoming hopelessness
in gradual but effective ways, as demonstrated by empowering the
client to take an active rather than passive role in the creation
of her desired future. Hypnosis and solution-focused therapy are
helpful in overcoming the apparent block of "not being able to
imagine anything good."

While the extent of symptomatology and corresponding treatment needs of adult survivors of sexual abuse are extensive, often
the symptoms are intertwined in such a manner that treatment of
one aspect seems to have a helpful effect on related symptoms.
This is beneficial for both therapist and client and yet often requires the therapist to be cognizant of many of the above treatment issues simultaneously. The subsequent chapters in this book
will seek to address both the treatment of the client's symptomatology and the resolution of its source.

2
SEEDING HOPE:
UTILIZING THE CLIENT'S
RESOURCES

THIS CHAPTER WILL address the client's treatment needs in the first interview. Included are techniques to facilitate the client's disclosure of the sexual abuse to the therapist, suggestions for client education, and practical techniques for initiating the therapy process. Emphasis is placed on solution-focused strategies that are particularly effective and well suited to this phase of treatment (Berg, 1990; de Shazer, 1982, 1984, 1985; de Shazer, Berg, Lipchik, Nunnally, Molnar, Gingerich, & Weiner-Davis, 1986; Lipchik, 1988; Lipchik & de Shazer, 1986; O'Hanlon & Weiner-Davis, 1989). Interventions include a "symbol for the present" (Dolan, 1989), "pre-treatment changes" (Weiner-Davis, de Shazer, & Gingerich, 1987), the "miracle question" (de Shazer, 1988), the solution-focused recovery scale, the "first session formula task" (de Shazer et al., 1986), and various forms of solution-focused questions tailored to the needs of the sexual abuse survivor.

The client with a history of sexual abuse may come to treatment with hardly any or a great deal of awareness about the details of her sexual victimization. In this chapter we assume that the client is aware of her victimization and is actively seeking assistance in recovering from its effects. Suggestions for working with clients suffering from severe dissociation and traumatic amnesia are provided in later chapters.

First Priorities

The seasoned clinician will not need to be reminded that initially it is very important that the client be given an opportunity to tell the therapist the details of her victimization in a context of warmth and support and that her disclosure be treated compassionately and respectfully. To fail to have the client adequately share the details of the abuse may not only play into the secrecy and stigmatization so often characteristic of sexual abuse, but also lead to the client's feeling discounted and inadequately supported.

However, it is equally important that therapy not be limited to the tasks of recounting the details of the abuse and sorting out and acknowledging the resultant feelings. In order to respectfully and effectively address the client's treatment needs, therapy needs to include and strongly emphasize an active utilization of the client's present life resources and images of future goals and possibilities.

Trepper and Barrett (1989) caution therapists about the danger of focusing solely on the trauma in treating adult survivors of incest:

> It is very important for adult survivors to confront their own childhood abuse openly and understand the impact it may have on their current life. However, the abuse was not the only event in the adult survivor's life, and all her existent adulthood behaviors are not a function of that abuse. Each of the client's systems must be taken into account when developing a treatment plan lest she be forced to remain in the role of the victim, this time not of her father but of the institution of therapy. (p.243)

It is also important that the therapist provide the client with information regarding symptoms commonly experienced by survivors of sexual abuse, such as those described in Chapter 1. It should be stressed that sexual abuse affects different people in different ways, so that symptoms and severity vary from person to person. This can prevent the client from misinterpreting the information as a suggestion that she should experience all the symptoms mentioned.

Rather than demoralizing the client, knowledge that other survivors have experienced various symptoms she is experiencing reassures the survivor that the symptoms she is experiencing are not signs that she is "going crazy." Indeed, she is likely to feel relieved to hear that she has been experiencing understandable post-traumatic stress symptoms—symptoms that can be identified and treated. As one insightful client said early in therapy, "It feels good to know that this territory has been traversed before by other people and that there are guidelines for what to expect."

Helping the Client Tell the Details of Her Victimization

In taking the history of a client who was or is suspected of having been sexually abused, the therapist must communicate a state of concerned attentiveness that is neither voyeuristic in its attention to detail nor minimizing or inadvertently dismissive through lack of sufficient exploration of the actual facts of the victimization. I like to begin by gently asking my client to "please tell me everything that you feel I need to know in order for you to know that I understand."

Since flashbacks might be inadvertently evoked as the client tells her story, the therapist needs to provide something for her to focus on in addition to the memories. This technique, which enables part of the client to remain comfortable, was inspired by Erickson's work with a client whose water phobia was caused by a series of traumatic events (Erickson & Rossi, 1989). Erickson provided some comfort for the client while she was remembering a trauma by giving her something else to experience simultaneously—in this case, comfort in her arm. Erickson and Rossi discuss the effect of this technique (p.149):

Erickson: . . . I wanted her hand in comfort.
Rossi: Why?
Erickson: She may be miserable, but one part gets comfortable and at ease.
Rossi: You can initiate and radiate comfort throughout her system by getting one part comfortable . . .

The "comfort in one part" can be provided both consciously and unconsciously. Later chapters will describe some effective ways to provide the comfort unconsciously through hypnosis. Here our focus is on the utilization of conscious processes—in this case, the client's conscious exploration of memories while experiencing some conscious comfort.

If the client becomes overwhelmed during the initial telling of the facts of her victimization and appears to be unconsciously lapsing into a flashback, she should be invited to take a momentary break from her narrative. This can be accomplished in a variety of ways that we will define; however, in all cases, the client should first be respectfully asked, "Would you like to take a break from this for a moment, knowing that we can return to it later when you choose to do so?"

Generally, the client either will tell the therapist that a break is not needed or, more frequently, will agree to a break with obvious relief. The client can then be asked to "take a nice deep breath" and then assisted in employing one of the following conscious dissociative strategies designed to provide comfort.

Reconnecting to the Present

Ideally, the client should be asked, before she begins the narrative of her victimization, to identify something in the room, a "symbol for the present" (Dolan, 1989), that can be used to remind her of the here and now. Clients often choose a personal item such as their purse, a picture of their kids or partner or other significant person, a ring or other piece of jewelry. Others simply focus on some object in the office that reminds them of the present.

In some cases there is no opportunity for the therapist to develop a symbol for the present before the client begins her description of her victimization. The therapist may not know that the client is a victim of sexual abuse, or the client may be in too much pain in the first session to stop and set up a specific "symbol for the present." As one client told me, "Once I got here, I knew I had to start talking right away before I got scared and clammed up." In such cases, the client's intuition about what she needs to do should, of course, be respected.

If no symbol for the present has been chosen and the client appears to be reexperiencing the trauma to a degree that is overwhelming, the therapist may simply say, "Look around the room, and tell me what you see here and now." Or the client may be directed to look around the room and locate, identify, and describe an object, such as a plant, a pleasant decorative item, or perhaps a detail of the view outside the window.

This external focus on a visual and then verbal descriptive task provides a conscious break from the memory of the trauma and reduces the emotional impact of talking about the abuse. Later, when the therapist is ready to provide therapeutic assistance and intervention, the feelings associated with the original abuse can and should be explored. However, during initial history-taking, the client should be protected from needless revivifying of the trauma. Allowing a client intensely to reexperience a trauma over and over again without providing a corrective therapeutic experience not only is ineffective but also revictimizes her.

After reconnecting with the present, the client may be engaged in casual conversation for a moment or two. This provides further comfort and relief from any premature elicitation of unconscious feelings associated with the abuse. In addition or as an alternative, some of the constructive, solution-focused questions described later in this chapter can be employed to strengthen the conscious focus while providing a context of hope.

When the client obviously exhibits a sense of comfort, the therapist may ask if she feels ready to go back to relating the facts of her victimization, while reassuring her that "we can take as many breaks as you need." These little breaks during the initial session can help the client begin to experience some control over her symptoms from the very beginning of treatment.

If a break is unnecessary, the client may refuse it. However, one should be politely offered whenever the therapist has even a slight suspicion that the client is beginning to relive the trauma. Reexperiencing the trauma should be allowed only if the therapist is prepared to provide practical interventions. Abreaction simply for the purpose of desensitization is unethical. If the client were going to achieve desensitization simply by reliving the trauma, she would not be in a therapy office requiring assistance, nor would she be exhibiting obviously overwhelming terror and physical discomfort. Moreover, if an event is sufficiently traumatic, retelling it over time is not, in and of itself, going to desensitize and relieve the client of all of the pain and fear evoked by the experience. Erickson (Erickson & Rossi, 1989) tells the following anecdote describing his 30-year-old mother coming into the house to find her baby daughter sitting on the floor with a rattlesnake coiled up right in front of her:

> And my mother said: "So I grabbed up the broom and I swept Mr. Rattlesnake out of the cabin so fast he never knew what happened." Forty years later, 50 years later, 60 years later, she still said she swept "Mr. Rattlesnake" out of that cabin. She always put in the respectful "Mr." And her voice got more rigid as she talked about grabbing that broom. This was a traumatic experience and she never entirely desensitized from it. (p.155)

Having a victim of sexual abuse tell and retell the tale of her victimization for the sole therapeutic purpose of desensitization is like removing a bullet slowly and painfully, one tiny millimeter of metal at a time, reopening the wound each time. This form of desensitization is not always dependable; even in the cases where it does succeed over time, it is often an inefficient and unnecessarily painful method of treatment that prolongs the client's suffering and revictimizes her over and over again.

This is not to deny the helpful effect of telling one's story in supportive group therapy sessions. Hearing another's story of victimization can be a powerful way—sometimes the only way—for a client to recognize that the abuse was not her fault. Furthermore, realizing that she is not alone in having this history can help to counteract feelings of stigmatization and isolation. However, storytelling should not be the only focus of the group, lest it simply reinforce the trauma rather than assisting clients in moving beyond the constrictions of the past.

Solution-Focused Therapy

The solution-focused (de Shazer, 1985, 1988; de Shazer et al., 1986) techniques presented here provide a realistic map of recovery while implicitly offering hope to the client.

Basic to this approach is the concept of co-creation of solutions by client and therapist (O'Hanlon & Weiner-Davis, 1989). This is based on the respectful assumption that clients have the inner resources to construct highly individualized and uniquely effective solutions to the problems that bring them to therapy. Solution-focused therapy assumes that the construction of a solution is a joint process between client and therapist, with the therapist taking responsibility for empowering the client to create and experience her own uniquely meaningful and effective therapeutic changes.

Before undertaking therapy focused specifically on the resolution of the past trauma, the client needs to acquire some physical and emotional stability, to feel somewhat "in control." Solution-oriented techniques are offered as an effective means to provide some realistic hope and stability for the client during the therapy process and to enable her to replace negative, self-destructive expectations with a healthy and positive, yet realistic, vision of the future. These techniques can be used throughout therapy and will provide a useful way for the client to acknowledge her progress and set goals for the future even when she is no longer actively in treatment.

The posture of respect, pragmatism, and hopefulness is uniquely suited to the survivor of sexual abuse, who, because of a history of victimization, may be unable to respond to other more intrusive and less personalized therapy approaches. Shifting from the present not only to the past but also to a hopeful future makes dealing with the trauma less overwhelming for the client and makes the treatment process more manageable for the therapist.

Once the therapist has learned the facts of the client's victimization, treatment planning should begin. Solution-focused therapy provides five important tools ideal for this task: pretreatment changes (O'Hanlon & Weiner-Davis, 1989), the Solution-Focused Recovery Scale, the miracle question (de Shazer, 1988), the first session formula task (de Shazer, 1985), and constructive individual and systemic questions (Lipchik, 1988), I have also included in this section a related technique, the "older, wiser, self."

Pre-Treatment Changes

Identified by Michele Weiner-Davis, a "pretreatment change" (Weiner-Davis, de Shazer, & Gingerich, 1987; O'Hanlon & Weiner-Davis, 1989) is an improvement in the situation for which the client is seeking therapy that occurs between scheduling the appointment and coming to the first session. To identify a useful pretreatment change, the therapist can mention this phenomenon to the client and ask if she is already aware of any such changes that she would like to have continue. This question leads easily into the solution-focused recovery scale, a further way of emphasizing and utilizing the sexual abuse survivor's natural ability to experience change in helpful ways.

The Solution-Focused Recovery Scale

Inspired by the Solution Identification Scale developed by Ron Kral at the Milwaukee Brief Family Therapy Center in 1988, the Solution-Focused Recovery Scale for Survivors of Sexual Abuse (Figure 1) was developed as an external device to help the client begin to identify and talk about the ways she has already begun to heal and the signs that will convince her that she is healing in the future. The items on the scale were derived from my clients' most frequent responses to questions about their individual signs of healing from sexual abuse.

The purpose of the Solution-Focused Recovery Scale is to provide a context of hope and to shift the focus toward healing. As it appears in this book, it is designed to be read aloud to the client, with the client responding verbally, although it could easily be adapted and adjusted for the purpose of having clients fill it out themselves in group or individual settings. The therapist can then show the client what areas she marked as already existing signs of healing and/or pretreatment changes and ask the client to speculate about what she thinks will be the signs of healing she (and in some cases, significant others) will notice next.

Once the client has identified a healing sign, she can be assigned the task of noticing (de Shazer, 1988) when it happens and to notice any other healing signs as they occur. Noticing signs of healing rather than just signs of trauma lays the groundwork for an identity that goes beyond that of victim.

Often the most revealing category on the Solution-Focused Recovery Scale is "Other Signs of Healing." As she identifies her own individual signs of healing, the client is encouraged to develop her own unique map for recovering from the effects of sexual abuse. In addition, pretreatment changes can be identified most readily through this category. Identification of these exceptions to the

Figure 1 SOLUTION-FOCUSED RECOVERY SCALE FOR SURVIVORS OF SEXUAL ABUSE

Name: _____ Date: _____

Please answer all questions. Beside each item below, indicate the degree to which it occurs.

	Not at All	Just a Little	Pretty Much	Very Much
1 Able to think/talk about trauma				
2 Able to think/talk about things other than the trauma.............................				
3 Sleeps OK				
4 Feels part of the family......................				
5 Stands up for self				
6 Maintains physical appearance (nails, hair, etc.)......................................				
7 Goes to work..................................				
8 Engages in social activities outside home				
9 Able to leave the house.....................				
10 Cares for child, loved ones				
11 Cares for pets, plants.........................				
12 Goes out for dinner				
13 Shows healthy appetite......................				
14 Adapts to new situations				
15 Telephones friends and loved ones				
16 Laughs at something funny				
17 Able to look loved ones, friends in the eye				
18 Able to look strangers in the eye				
19 Able to shake hands				
20 Holds hands with loved one				
21 Kisses loved one on the cheek				
22 Kisses husband/wife or boyfriend/girl-friend on the mouth..........................				
23 Enjoys lovemaking............................				
24 Initiates lovemaking				
25 Bathes normally				
26 Interested in the future				
27 Pursues leisure activity				
28 Engages in new recreational activity/new interest....................................				
29 Takes protective measures inside and outside the house				
30 Able to discriminate between support-ive and nonsupportive relationships				
31 Chooses supportive relationships.........				
32 Initiates conversation with family, friends or coworkers...........................				
33 Able to initiate conversations with ac-quaintances and strangers				
34 Able to relax without drugs or alcohol ..				
35 Tolerates criticism well				
36 Accepts praise well..........................				
37 Other signs of recovery				

38 COMMENTS:

client's problem not only fosters hope but also points toward help-ful therapy directions.

Some of the items on the Solution-Focused Recovery Scale may initially constitute "big" signs of healing for some individuals. When asking clients to speculate on their personal signs of future healing, I emphasize identifying the "smallest" signs first. This makes the task more achievable and less overwhelming. As one client responded to my question regarding the "next smallest sign," "It makes it 'doable' when you ask it that way."

In some cases, the traumatic effects of the sexual abuse are so pervasive that attempting to identify everything that would have to happen in order for the client to feel that she had fully recovered may be intolerable early in therapy. The "smallest sign" cuts the task down to a more manageable size.

There are, of course, some instances when the client is so acutely traumatized and demoralized that she is initially unable to identify her own healing signs in response to the scale. This oc-curs most commonly when the client is acutely depressed. In such cases, a systemic constructive question may help, such as "What do you think your [significant other] would say your first small healing sign would be, . . . and your next small sign of healing?" In effect, the client temporarily "borrows" the perspec-tive of someone who cares about her. One extremely isolated client was able to think of a healing sign that she could notice in the future by imagining what her dog would identify if he could talk!

Having the client—and her partner, too, if he or she is involved in treatment—look for any small and gradual signs of healing as therapy progresses can provide a much-needed positive orienta-tion; this balances the effects of dealing with feelings related to victimization. One client told me,

> Noticing how I'm healing even in little ways feels so much better than just thinking about all the bad stuff that happened to me. I'd rather have my husband noticing how I seem to him to be healing from week to week rather than having him just sitting there thinking about what's wrong with me—that [think-ing about what's wrong with her] made me feel like some kind of freak, like a victim.

Many clients have told me that just filling out the scale has had the immediate effect of making them feel more "hopeful." One client said, "When we did that scale I realized that, even though I definitely have some things to work on, I also have a lot of strengths and ways I have already healed that I wasn't even aware of."

The Miracle Question

Developed by Steve de Shazer (1988) at the Milwaukee Brief Family Therapy Center, the miracle question is particularly useful in empowering very demoralized clients to imagine a solved version of their seemingly "hopeless" problems. Based on de Shazer's original, I have tailored the following question specifically to fit adult survivors of sexual abuse:

> If a miracle happened in the middle of the night and you had overcome the effects of your childhood abuse to the extent that you no longer needed therapy and felt quite satisfied with your daily life, what would be different?

In response to this question, some survivors of sexual abuse can be empowered to identify for themselves various therapeutically useful and healthy perceptions and behaviors. For example, one survivor of sexual abuse responded to the miracle question by saying, "I'd be spending more time with my husband and daughter, I'd be taking good care of my body instead of overeating all the time and I wouldn't be thinking about the past all the time. I'd be thinking about my life *now*. I'd really believe what happened wasn't my fault."

Once these perceptions and behaviors have been identified, the client can be asked if any of these useful phenomena are already occurring. These healthy behaviors and perceptions can then be reinforced with a "noticing task" (de Shazer, 1988), in which the client is asked to notice the times that she does these healthy behaviors and has these healthy thoughts (e.g., "It wasn't my fault") between sessions. Noticing these self-identified moments of healthy functioning can help the client realize that she is already in control of her life in some areas. She can then increase those feelings of being in control by doing more of the things that she has identified as helpful and healthy and "telling herself" encouraging thoughts.

In using the miracle question, as well as any other solution-focused techniques, the therapist should take care to avoid inadvertently making the client feel that her traumatic experiences are being trivialized. Again, it is important that the therapist find out the available details of the client's victimization and express accurate understanding, support, and empathy *before* proceeding with treatment.

The First Session Formula Task

The first session formula task (de Shazer, 1985) was developed at the Milwaukee Brief Family Therapy Center as an assignment after the first session to help clients who were initially vague in their description of what they wanted from therapy. The assigned task is: "Between now and the next time I see you I'd like you to think about the things in your life that you would like to have continue." I have altered this slightly by asking the client to "make a written list of those things in your life that you would like to have continue."

For the purposes of treating survivors of sexual abuse, the listing is useful in strengthening clients' awareness of the resources that exist as part of her everyday life in the present. Having the list to "hold onto" is particularly important in the intense early stages of treatment, when focusing on the past trauma may tend to eclipse the client's awareness of the safety, comfort, and support available in her everyday life in the here and now. A typical response to the first session formula task from a sexual abuse survivor might include such items as:

1. my job
2. my relationship with [significant other]
3. my hobbies
4. my friends
5. my habit of taking a bubble bath every night to unwind
6. exercise class
7. my sense of humor

The client should be encouraged to make the list as long as she wishes. Some clients choose to carry the list around with them during the early stages of treatment, particularly if they are suffering from repeated intrusive flashbacks and revivification of the abuse. The list serves as a tangible reminder that they have comfort and security available in their present life. Carrying the list around may also function to counteract the phenomenon of "spontaneous age regression" (Beahrs, 1982) that can occur in survivors of sexual abuse in response to events symbolically reminiscent of their abuse, particularly when long dissociated memories of sexual abuse are just coming into conscious awareness.

The "Older, Wiser Self"

Another useful approach for empowering survivors of sexual abuse is based on the idea that the client will grow older and presumably wiser. For example, I might say to a client,

> Imagine that you have grown to be a healthy, wise old woman and you are looking back on this period of your life. What do you think that this wonderful, old, wiser you would suggest to you to help you get through this current phase of your life? What would she tell you to remember? What would she suggest that would be most helpful in helping you heal from the past? What would she say to comfort you? And does she have any advice about how therapy could be most useful and helpful?

The therapeutic impact of these questions can be enhanced with the following homework task: Ask the client to write a letter to the "older, wiser self" telling her what the client is struggling with right now. Have the client then take the role of the 'older wiser self' and respond with a letter offering comfort, advice, and helpful instructions for getting through this period of life based on what she has learned from old age. This exercise can also be used by having the client imagine a presumably supportive but deceased "old, wise" relative or friend, and write the letter from that viewpoint.

If the client is a multiple personality, some caution is advised with the "older, wiser self" technique, since it might evoke a personality part that is not currently supportive of the client's health and healing.

Constructive Individual and Systemic Questions

Solution-focused questions (Lipchik, 1988; Lipchik & de Shazer, 1986) are carefully formulated queries asked by the therapist to help clients focus on what they are already doing that is working (even to some degree), on imagined solutions, and on ideas about how to make the solutions occur. The client's responses to these questions provide a useful and highly personalized map for therapy, while ensuring that the treatment goals and interventions truly fit the client's current predicament and resources.

Constructive questions (Lipchik & de Shazer, 1986) are a specific form of solution-focused intervention that can be employed both individually and systemically. Individually oriented constructive questions help the client identify the specifics of her own solutions, while systemically oriented constructive questions evoke and utilize the resources of supportive family, friends, and meaningful others.

Here are some examples of constructive individual questions to help the therapist and the client identify a personalized definition of what is needed for the client to overcome the trauma and its constricting effects on her life:

- What will be the first (smallest) sign that things are getting better, that this (the sexual abuse) is having less of an impact on your current life?
- What will you be doing differently when this (sexual abuse trauma) is less of a current problem in your life?
- What will you be doing differently with your time?
- What will you be thinking about (doing) *instead* of thinking about the past?
- Are there times when the above is already happening to some (even a small) extent? What is different about those times? What is helpful about those differences?
- What differences will the above healing changes make when they have been present in your life over extended time (days, weeks, months, years)?

Here are some constructive systemic questions:

- What do your think that your (significant other) would say would be the first sign that things are getting better? What do you think your (significant other) will notice first?
- What do you think your (friends, boss, significant other, etc.) will notice about you as you heal even more?
- What positive differences will these healing changes you've identified make over time in your relationship with (significant other)?
- What differences will these healing changes you've identified make in future generations of your family?

Asking the client to speculate about the positive effects of the healing changes in the future further strengthens the developing solutions and fosters a positive future orientation. In order for this technique to be optimally effective, the therapist and client need to explore the healing changes to their ultimate positive conclusion.

Once the client has begun to identify signs of healing in response to these questions, she can be asked to notice other signs, to notice the times when she succeeds in behaving in ways that she has identified as healthy and positive. She can also be asked to identify and notice the times when she "overcomes" the effects of the trauma. The therapist can guide the conversation in this direction, as in the following:

Client: I'm insecure and I am afraid to go for that job interview because I don't really trust anybody because of what happened to me. If I were over this, it wouldn't bother me so much . . .

Therapist: So the past trauma is getting in your way. How would you know that you had overcome it even a little bit?

Client: Well, I'd at least schedule an interview. . . . I could always cancel it, but scheduling it would mean I had overcome the trauma a little bit . . .

Therapist: So the first little sign that you were overcoming the trauma in that area of your life would be scheduling an interview. What do you think the next little sign would be?

Client: Well, I'd show up.

Therapist: And the next little sign?
Client: I'd have another interview and I would be just a little less nervous.
Therapist: And then what?
Client: Well, I'd probably have another interview and maybe I'd be even just a little more comfortable about being there.
Therapist: And so what would be the next little sign after that?
Client: I'll get a job!

The client can be asked to predict each "little sign" until she can say that, if she did all of those "little signs," she would feel that she had overcome the trauma in that particular area of her life. The frame allows the client to develop an adversarial relationship with the trauma and experience her own progressive success at overcoming and gradually undoing its effects in various areas in her life. "Overcoming the trauma" should be applied as a frame only to behaviors that the client is able to influence and change consciously. While "overcoming" is a concept that can be used to help the client experience her own power, it is not meant to be used as a "should."

With all solution-focused questions, the client is asked to identify the "smallest signs" one by one and then encouraged to attempt the smallest and easiest to do. This allows the client safely and gradually to experience control over symptoms without becoming frightened and overwhelmed by tasks for which she is not ready. These small changes may lead to larger and larger ones, but in a manner which prevents relapses, as in the proverbial "Journey of a Thousand Miles"—one step at a time.

Of course, the client can always surprise herself and the therapist by experiencing and noticing many "small" and "larger" signs of healing in quick succession. I often see this happen in some aspect of the client's life after a few sessions. I believe this is due in part to the growing confidence that the client gains from the early "small" signs. A particular advantage of using the above solution-focused techniques with the client who has been sexually abused is that this approach provides an explicit and implicit context in which she is in control, the exact opposite of her experience of victimization and an important ongoing corrective experience.

Solution-focused questions are particularly helpful in empowering the survivor of sexual abuse to participate in her own treatment planning while also implicitly providing a context of hope. Many clients have told me that this way of looking at their healing process has affected many different aspects of their life in positive ways, in that they develop a habit of noticing what they're doing that is good, healthy, and helpful.

3
UTILIZING SUPPORTIVE RELATIONSHIPS

THIS CHAPTER WILL focus on the therapeutic utilization of the client's supportive relationships. Also addressed will be the needs of those important people in the sexual abuse survivor's life, particularly in reference to prevention and treatment of secondary victimization.

Frequently, the effects of the sexual abuse are so strongly felt by those close to the victim that both they and the victim can benefit from some conjoint therapy sessions. First and foremost, the prerogative to include a significant other in a therapy session should be the client's. When a significant other is included in the sexual abuse survivor's individual therapy process, it should be made clear that the partner, relative, or friend is there primarily for the client. Sexual abuse survivors are all too adept at sacrificing their needs for others. However, the significant others should also receive support and validation for expressions of concern and efforts to help, and they should be provided with resources and practical information about the sexual abuse healing process and ways to best support the loved one who was victimized. Seeing the supportive others with the sexual abuse survivor will help ensure that their expression of caring is focused in a helpful direction.

I do not suggest that significant others be present for the sexual abuse survivor's core individual therapy work, such as disclosure and expression of feelings related to the victimization. This would be needlessly painful for the supportive others and might even slow therapeutic progress, since the survivor might understandably try to protect the loved ones from the pain. Rather, the purpose of supportive others' participation is to emphasize and utilize the resources and strengths inherent in their relationship with the survivor, to provide support and validation, and whenever possible, to prevent "fallout" from the original trauma from contaminating current relationships. If others within the system appear to be exhibiting symptoms of depression or secondary post-traumatic stress, a referral for psychotherapy is indicated.

The Partner

The adult survivor of sexual abuse who is in a committed relationship with a supportive partner has, in that relationship, a potentially powerful resource. Nevertheless, the partner is likely to require some support and guidance from the therapist and may benefit from a referral to a support group or individual therapy.

Entering treatment for sexual abuse generally indicates that the former victim is absorbed with thoughts of the past sexual abuse. The fact that she is bringing up this issue from the past may have powerful consequences for the supportive partner. He or she may learn all too quickly that, in the initial stages of the partner's coming to terms with the sexual abuse, the proverbial road to hell may, indeed, be paved with good intentions. The therapist should provide information to lessen potential difficulties for the partner and spouse. In addition to the therapy session, bibliotherapy may also be a way for the partner to gain understanding.

The partner should be given a practical description of the symptoms of sexual abuse, so that she or he can understand that they are a consequence of victimization and not a personal response. This is particularly important in the vulnerable interpersonal areas of trust and sexual intimacy, where the partner may be most apt to feel hurt and rejected.

Anger at the Perpetrator

In response to disclosures of sexual abuse, the partner may understandably feel rage toward the perpetrator. However, early on, expressing this rage directly to the victim may have the effect of causing the victim to feel guilty and even to defend the perpetrator to her partner. The partner should be warned of this by the therapist, with the explanation that this response may be one of the results of victimization.

Later in treatment the victim may actually find her partner's rage at the perpetrator very appropriate and healing. In response to her husband's rage at her incestuously abusive father, one survivor said:

> When he told me how angry he was and what he'd like to do to him [perpetrator], I felt really good and wanted to cry because it was the first time in my whole life that someone had really stood up for me.

In some cases, clients' difficulty accepting their partners' rage about the abuse appears to continue indefinitely. This seems to be most often the case when the perpetrator was a parent and the victim still harbors mixed feelings about the relationship. Trying to convince the victim that she should feel differently about the perpetrator will probably only lead to fights in which she may feel compelled to defend the parent more aggressively. This can be very frustrating for the partner, who finds himself at the receiving end of the anger that should in all fairness be directed toward the perpetrator.

A similar dynamic may take place regarding the partner's feelings of anger toward parents or other adults who knowingly or unknowingly failed to protect the victim in childhood. The partner is likely to be far ahead of the victim in the ability to place responsibility squarely where it belongs and risks evoking the victim's tendency initially to defend those who overtly or covertly failed to protect her.

The partner should, however, be reassured that feeling angry is legitimate and understandable under the circumstances. If there is a need to process anger about what was done to the sexually abused loved one—and there may well be—it is probably better for the supportive partner to do this with a professional outside of the relationship, such as an individual therapist, or in a support group.

In some cases, an otherwise supportive partner may express

anger that the victim did not prevent or stop her sexual victimization. The therapist must impress upon the partner the nature of sexual abuse, in which the victim is rendered powerless, and to emphasize that "if she could have, she would have." It is inappropriate and potentially very damaging for the partner to blame the victim; it constitutes further abuse.

Anger as a Rescue From Pain

Although I lack formal research backing for these comments, I have repeatedly observed versions of the following phenomenon in couples in which one member is a sexual abuse survivor. The partner, who is otherwise described as accepting and supportive, seems irrationally to "pick" and escalate fights about seemingly inconsequential things during the more acute stages of treatment, particularly when the sexual abuse survivor is experiencing intense pain about the past. I have observed this in couples where both partners subsequently describe such of fighting behavior as atypical of the relationship and afterwards agree that the fights seemed to occur over what they would normally consider inconsequential issues.

It is my hunch that the supportive partner is, on some unconscious level, using the fight in a desperate effort to pull the victim back into the relative safety of the here and now. However, no matter how heroic the presumed unconscious motivation, the partner's initiating or escalating fights about inconsequential issues rarely, if ever, has long-term positive effects for either member of the couple. Alternatives need to be developed!

If the therapist believes that this phenomenon is occurring, he or she should describe it to the couple as something others have experienced. Once they recognize the pattern, they can work together to develop alternative ways for the supportive partner to help the sexual abuse survivor reconnect to the safety and comfort of the present.

Guidelines for the Partner
and the Sexual Abuse Survivor

Once the partner has expressed understanding and validation of the loved one's past experience of sexual victimization, it is important to help the partner and the sexual abuse survivor refocus their shared energy away from the trauma of the past and toward the healing, comfort, and hope inherent in the present and future. Here are some general therapeutic directions that have proven useful for this purpose:

- Reassure the partner that his loved one does have the resources needed to make therapeutic changes.
- Ask the partner to identify what he or she is doing that appears to be most helpful to the sexual abuse survivor. What behaviors on the part of the supportive partner would the survivor be likely to say that she would like to have occur more? Which ones would she like to see less? Which of the partner's attempts to be supportive would the survivor be likely to want to remain the same?
- The partner's guesses about the survivor's responses to above questions can then be compared with the survivor's actual preferences and verified to the degree that they match. Ask the sexual abuse survivor to identify what the partner is doing that is most helpful. What behaviors would she like to have the partner do more? What would she like to have occur less? What are the supportive things that the partner is doing that the survivor wants him or her to keep doing?
- Once these behaviors have been identified, the survivor can be asked to "notice" the times when the partner succeeds in supporting her in the ways she has identified as helpful and in any new ways she identifies as helpful. The partner can be asked to predict which of his behaviors will be identified as helpful.
- The partner can be asked to notice any observable signs of healing in the sexual abuse survivor from week to week, and the sex abuse survivor can be asked to predict which healing signs she thinks the partner will have noticed and which ones may have initially escaped his or her awareness. For example, the partner might be asked, at various times:
  - How will you know that she has healed even more based on what she has told you?
  - What differences will it make for you to observe these signs and know that she is healing?

- How will you know that you, too, are healing from the trauma of knowing that your loved one was abused?
- What will you be doing, experiencing, thinking that will be signs that you, too, are healing?
- What will you be telling yourself?
- What will others be noticing about you that are signs of healing?
- How will your mutual healing affect your relationship with each other and with other important people in your life?
- Ask both partners to identify what their relationship has been like apart from the issue of past sexual abuse. In these areas, what are the things that they both want to have continue?
- In a guided future imagining exercise, ask both partners to imagine the current healing signs continuing and expanding over the next few days, weeks, months, and years. What will things be like for each of them as the healing becomes more and more a part of their lives? How will it affect their relationship to have gone through these adjustments together? How will they know that they have both done everything that would be helpful? What kinds of things will they each appreciate about the other as time goes by?

The above guidelines are, of course, only suggestions. The couple's responses will dictate the specific course of the conjoint sessions. In some cases, despite support from the therapist, the sexual abuse post-traumatic crisis so overloads an already fragile and historically troubled relationship that, over time, it becomes apparent that the couple is no longer able to continue as a couple. When this happens, it is important that the couple not be allowed to fall into the destructive abyss of mutual self-blame, in which the sexual abuse survivor blames herself for not dealing adequately with her victimization and the partner blames him or herself for failing to overcome effects of what happened in the past. Rather, the partners should be compassionately supported in their decision to separate, with the understanding that unfair blaming of themselves or each other is not appropriate or helpful. It is better for both partners to refocus their energy on individually rebuilding their lives. This may eventually allow them to come back together as a couple or to lead a healthy life as part of a different, satisfying couple relationship in the future.

Siblings

When a sibling is proposed as a supportive other, the therapist should be prepared for the fact that he or she may have been sexually abused by the same perpetrator who molested her sister or brother. The sibling may or may be consciously aware of any abuse that she sustained; however, if the sibling suspects that she, too, was victimized, the therapist should provide her with suitable referrals to support groups and individual therapy.

Survivor Guilt

Supportive siblings of adults who experienced childhood sexual victimization may experience "survivor guilt" (Trepper & Barrett, 1989). One version of this that I have observed among siblings, regardless of whether they were themselves victimized, is deep regret and self-blame for not having been able to have protected their sister from the perpetrator. Some siblings have told me that hearing about their sister's or brother's victimization is more painful than remembering their own. The siblings' pain needs to be validated; however, they need to be helped to realize that their guilt about failing to protect the victim is not warranted or fair, because they, too, were children.

A complex situation arises when the currently supportive sibling also has a history of sexual victimization and has engaged in an incestuous relationship with the client. In cases of mutual consent, no coercion, and little age difference, the sibling incestuous relationship should be viewed compassionately within the appropriate context of an understandable response to childhood curiosity, deprivation, parental abuse, and/or sexual victimization. In cases of sibling sexual abuse, where a large age difference, coercion, and/or violence were involved in the incestuous sibling relationship, obviously the sibling is not likely to be a viable choice as a supportive other. An exception might occur if both siblings were victims of abuse and the older sibling has taken responsibility for abusing the client and shown undeniable remorse.

In cases of intrafamilial incestuous sexual abuse, the supportive sibling may experience complex loyalty conflicts. She may waver between supporting her sibling and succumbing to pressures from the other family members to suppress or deny the reality, extent, and/or effects of the sexual abuse. Both the client and her supportive sibling may benefit from hearing that other supportive siblings have experienced this dynamic of split loyalties. In some cases this may empower the sibling to resist the familial pressure to deny the reality of the victim's abuse.

As with the supportive partner, the sibling's feelings about the abuse should be acknowledged. Then the emphasis should be respectfully shifted away from the trauma and toward healing. The following solution-focused questions can be used in conjoint sessions with the sexual abuse survivor and sibling.

For the survivor:

- How will your sister (or brother) know that you are continuing to heal?
- What signs can be looked for to know that your healing is progressing? What will (the sibling) be noticing? What kinds of things will you be mentioning that you are experiencing, thinking, and doing that will be signs of healing?
- What is (the sibling) now doing that is helpful? What would you like her to do more of, less of? What are the things she or he is now doing/saying that you would like to have continue?

For the sibling:

- How will you know that your sister has continued to heal? What will you be noticing in her behavior? What sorts of things will she be saying?
- How will she know that you, too, are healing from this trauma? What will she be noticing about you in terms of your behavior and what you are saying? What will the two of you be talking about instead of the sexual abuse?

Nonoffending Supportive Parents

The parent who was neither a perpetrator nor accomplice in the incest and is supportive of the sexual abuse survivor is a powerful resource. These parents are likely to feel very badly that their child was not protected and harbor feelings of guilt and pain. It is important for the therapist to acknowledge these feelings respectfully and then to refocus understandable sadness and guilt about the past into support that is mutually rewarding for the parent and the adult child. These parents may benefit from referral for supportive counseling to help them deal with feelings evoked by learning of the abuse.

It should also be noted that, as with siblings, sometimes seemingly supportive parents may switch allegiances without warning in apparent response to invisible but very powerful loyalty conflicts. This is most apt to happen if the parent enjoyed a close relationship with the perpetrator and if maintaining secrecy or minimizing the extent and seriousness of the abuse will enable that parent to retain a valued image or relationship rewards, such as inheritances, preservation of a marriage, or social image. Another dynamic to be aware of is the tendency for some seemingly supportive parents to suddenly switch from appropriately seeing the perpetrator as responsible to blaming the child for not telling them about the abuse earlier. Such departures from the supportive stance can happen quickly and without warning. At these times, the therapist needs to be prepared to confront the parent and to support the victim.

The following questions can be employed in conjoint sessions with the supportive parent and the adult survivor of sexual abuse.

Questions for the parent:

- What would you have done differently if you had been aware of the abuse as soon as it happened? How would you have protected your child? What differences, if any, do you think this would make in your current relationship with your daughter (or son)?
- How will you know that your daughter (or son) is healing? What (if any) signs have you already noticed? What do you

suspect the next sign will be? What do you imagine will be different when this is no longer a current problem?

Questions for the sexual abuse survivor:

- What difference does it make to know that your parent feels this way about what happened?
- How will your parent know that you are healing from this experience? What will she or he notice you doing or saying? What will be the smallest signs that your parent is likely to notice first? What will your mother (father) be likely to say you are doing more of, less of, as you heal? What do you suspect she (he) will notice is different when this is no longer a current problem?
- What difference will these healing changes make over time? What do you think your mother (or father) will say the differences are? What will you be saying in the future that will be true of you and your behavior and thoughts when this (trauma) is no longer a current problem?

The above suggestions for working with supportive parents can also be applied to supportive aunts, uncles, stepparents, grandparents, etc.

Friends

Because sexual abuse can destroy family relationships, some survivors of sexual abuse come to therapy without the support of relatives but with the support of significant friends, who may, in essence, have become a second family. Perhaps because they are not in a specific familial relationship with the client, friends seem to be less apt to fall into painful emotions of guilt and rage and more apt to successfully support the client during the treatment process.

Many of the sexual abuse survivors I see feel too afraid to come alone for the first session and bring a friend for support. In some cases, this friend has held the client's hand while she has remembered and disclosed painful details of her victimization. Here are some questions that can be used in conjoint sessions with a sexual abuse survivor and a friend.

To the sexual abuse survivor:

- How will your friend know that you have healed more? What will she notice that you are doing, saying?
- What is your friend currently doing that is helpful in supporting you in this healing process? What would you like her (or him) to do more of, less of? What things that your friend is doing would you like to have continue?

To the friend:

- What will convince you that your friend is continuing to heal?
- What (if any) healing signs have you already noticed?
- How will your shared awareness of your friend's healing changes affect your relationship? What kinds of things will you be talking about more as the healing changes continue over time? What do you think the two of you will be doing differently as time goes by?

Case Examples

The following two case examples illustrate the general process and positive effects of using these solution-focused approaches in conjoint sessions with sexual abuse survivors and supportive significant others.

Judy

Judy was a 29-year-old woman who brought her boyfriend, sister, and friend to treatment sessions at various stages. She brought her boyfriend with her initially because she was seeking therapy at his urging. He was aware of her recurrent nightmares, fearful associations with her sexuality, and very low self-esteem, and he was concerned about her. This session focused on identifying ways that he could be supportive without making her feel, in her words, "like a victim or a mental patient." For example, she wanted him to tell her about what was going on with him as well as asking her about her feelings. She specifically asked him to talk to her about aspects of everyday life besides her abuse.

Subsequently, they stated that as a result of the session they both experienced a sense of hopefulness about the resolution of her pain and about the future of their relationship. He felt relieved to observe directly that her pain was being dealt with, and she felt that he was now able to be more helpful and less "smothering" and angry in his expressions of concern.

Judy asked to bring her sister to a later session because she was worried that her sister had been abused also. Her sister had no memories of abuse; however, she was deeply concerned for Judy and expressed great sadness about how alone Judy must have felt during the time she was being victimized by an uncle. She offered to be with Judy when she confronted the uncle and vowed to do whatever she could to help Judy heal.

Specific therapeutic behaviors were identified during the session. Judy told her sister that, while it was helpful to talk about what happened in the past, it was also very helpful to talk about other things, because that reminded her that life goes on and that she could have a different sort of life in the present. Judy requested that her sister not bring up the past unless Judy initiated it, because she felt that they needed more balance in their conversations—she didn't want the trauma taking over their relationship.

Judy's sister expressed relief at having some specific direction about what was useful and admitted she had been doing a lot of worried "guessing" about what Judy needed. Specific signs of healing were identified by Judy, and she and her sister were given the task of noticing which ones occurred first, with a specific time scheduled for these periodic discussions. Judy and her sister reported that having a specific time set up to discuss the signs of healing seemed to put the pain from the past into a more compact container. This lessened its effects on their everyday life. Focusing on healing instead of only on the trauma made the sister, as well as Judy, more hopeful about the future.

When previously dissociated memories of sexual victimization began to intrude into Judy's dreams and waking states in the form of flashbacks, hypnosis was offered as a way to retrieve the information necessary to heal in a more efficient manner. Judy requested that her friend sit in on the hypnosis sessions as a physical reminder of the safety and the comfort of the "here and now."

During a series of three hypnosis sessions, the friend held Judy's hand and provided a continuous context of support through her physical presence. At the end of each session, both women were given the homework of identifying any healing signs they had noticed in Judy and to speculate on what might be the next small sign of healing. Judy's friend said at the end of the middle session that she felt as if she were watching Judy give birth, "I feel like you're giving birth to your true self, getting back what was taken from you. I am so proud of you."

Judy said that having her sister, boyfriend, and friend attend sessions had eased the strain of the incest trauma on their relationship, brought them closer together, and probably accelerated the healing process. Judy's parents, unfortunately, were not supportive.

Linda

Linda's mother was stricken with grief, rage, and guilt when she found out that a family friend had molested her daughter between the ages of seven and twelve years. She said, "If he was not dead, I think I might go and kill him with my bare hands. He betrayed all of us in our trust in him."

Linda felt supported, but also rather overwhelmed and concerned about her mother's expression of rage and guilt, which seemed as if it might continue indefinitely. She requested that her mother come to her next therapy session. The session focused on the mother's reaction, as we discussed what she would have done differently if she had known and redirected her energy away from a repetitive traumatic imagining toward her own and her daughter's healing. After Linda and her mother identified healing signs, they were assigned the task of noticing new ones as they appeared and how they affected their sense of hope about the future. Linda's mother was given referrals for individual therapy and to a mothers' support group, which she subsequently described as having been helpful. At the end of the session, Linda said to her mother, "I am glad we had this session, because I was feeling that I should be taking care of you, taking care of your hurt, and I didn't know how to fix it for you, and it was interfering with my taking care of me."

Two individual sessions later, Linda explained her rapid succession of healing changes (including increasing control over her compulsive eating, increased confidence and self-esteem, and enrollment in a high school equivalency program), saying, "I have a lot more energy to work on myself now that I'm not trying to take care of my mother all the time." Other healing signs included sleeping through the night and reengaging with friends.

Creating Supportive Others

Tragically, sometimes there are no significant supportive others for the client to bring to therapy. In such cases, the supportive other can be created in two different ways.

First, there may have been, in the past, someone who was at least somewhat supportive but who has died. The therapist can assist the client in accessing memories of that person. In this case the client is asked to notice, "What difference did the supportive person in the past make, even if he (or she) didn't know what you were struggling with?" The client can imagine what that person would say and can write a letter to herself based on the imagined response of that supportive person. The client can then be assigned the task of noticing how this supportive person's helpful influence shows up currently in healing changes and how she reminds herself of that important influence.

The second approach was inspired by an exercise described by Lucia Capacchione in *The Creative Journal* (1979). The client can be asked to choose a symbolic person to identify with, such as a historical person, a religious leader, a current hero or heroine, or even a character from fiction. The client can write a letter to that person describing the issues with which she is struggling and then write an imagined response from that person providing support and solution-focused advice. A symbol of that person may be chosen and carried around as a reminder of the strength and inner convictions that are part of the healing journey. The following two case vignettes illustrate accessing support, courage and healing from a past or imagined relationship.

Grandma and My Father

A survivor of sexual abuse who had been victimized by her maternal grandfather, two uncles, and a stepfather, as well as betrayed by her mother, reconnected with a memory of two supportive people in her past in the following way:

> When I asked myself who was supportive in my past in a significant way, my paternal grandmother came to mind. She never protected me from the abuse, because she didn't know about it. But she was not related to any of the abusers, and my relationship with her was entirely separate from that terrifying, hellish aspect of my life as a child at their mercy and at the mercy of a mother who just pretended nothing was happening and was even pleasant with the people she knew had abused me.
>
> In contrast, with my Grandma, I had the unwavering impression from her that she would do anything for me, and I believe she would have. Looking back on it now, I believe she definitely would have protected me if she had known what was happening to me. If only I could have defied all those sick adults and told her what was being done to me!
>
> She was very intelligent, and that, too, is different from the people on the other side of my family who hurt me so deeply. And it was obvious that she was exceptionally bright, as was her son, my father. And I have been told that I inherited some of her intelligence.
>
> She's dead now, but her influence lives on in my life. Just by being in my life, she taught me that there were some people who weren't cruel and sick in their behaviors and ways of thinking, who would at least try to come through for a vulnerable child. Just knowing her made me see that things could be different in different families, and even now, the memory of how she was gives me some hope for relationships in the future.
>
> If she could talk to me right now, I know what she'd say, "Don't give up." And she'd remind me of my scholastic abilities and the solace that her career gave her with the idea that I, too, can get some comfort and strength from a career. She was the only one who gave me the idea that I could ever do anything. Only Grandma and, to a small extent, an English teacher I had in my freshman year of high school—but mostly Grandma, and on a much more personal level with Grandma. I never knew her son—my father.

He died just before I was born, but I also believe that he would have protected me, supported me if he could have. It may sound funny, but I've started carrying his rosary around, the same one my grandmother carried after he died. It reminds me of both of them, and even when things are feeling pretty bleak for me in my relationships or lack of them with my other family members, and the nightmares from the PTS, just touching that rosary reminds me of my own strengths and my need to carry on for two family members who were good people and left me that legacy of decency, intelligence, and kindness. It is a major strength and has saved my life on many occasions when I was all alone and felt suicidal, and now it is a reminder — no, it's stronger than that — it's an obligation, to have a positive future. When I think of them I get this powerful, "You can do it" feeling.

Sally

Sally could think of no one in her present or past who was really "there" for her other than the therapist. To provide additional support and pave the trail for future relationships, she was asked to write a letter to someone she might be able to imagine, even slightly, as a supportive ally. Here is a synopsis of her response:

> In response to this assignment, I thought and thought about who might be someone I could imagine being able to give me comfort, support, and advice. Of all people, the opera singer Rise Stevens came to mind. I was kind of surprised, but I thought, "Why not, what do I have to lose?" I had read about how she had been such a loving mother to her own family despite various tragedies and difficulties, and yet she was obviously not some kind of sick martyr about it; she maintained her professional work and gave the world the gift of her music. Here is the letter I imagine her writing back to me:

> Dear Sally:
>
> I am very sad to hear of all that you went through as a child and the effects you are still experiencing. You have to realize, however, how far you have come in putting this behind you to the extent you have. I am very proud of you for working so hard and not giving up.
>
> I wonder if you have seen the movie, *The Natural*. In that

movie, the young hero gets shot by a crazy person who takes advantage of his loneliness and vulnerability on a train on the way to a baseball camp. He was all set to become a very successful and famous baseball player, and then he had this terrible stroke of bad luck. He was so badly injured he had to learn even to walk all over again, using all different muscles. Maybe he blamed himself for trusting this woman who later shot him, maybe not, but regardless, he certainly didn't deserve to be hurt so badly like that. Nobody deserves that kind of injury.

It took him years and years to build himself back up to being able to play baseball professionally again, but he did it, and he was a big success. He never gave up until he got himself back as a full baseball player.

You have to remind yourself that, even if it takes a lot of work, you can build yourself back up.

I believe in you and I know you are trying so hard, and I also know that it will all pay off for you in ways that matter inside. I am always here for you if you need my support or caring. I will be your "honorary" mother.

Sincerely,

Rise

The letter was very meaningful to the client and functioned as a future reference for the therapist. Both the image of Ms. Stevens and the movie *The Natural* became useful symbols for the client. There were many possibilities for establishing a tangible symbol to remind her of this resource. For example, she could carry around opera scores, a picture of her heroine, or even a baseball to remind her of that sense of hope and comfort that she accessed in the imagined letter.

Utilization of other supportive relationships as part of the therapeutic process helps implicitly to reassure the client that when therapy ends she will still have the comfort of other supportive relationships in her life. This encourages the client to see the therapy relationship as a special subset on a continuum of various nurturing relationships and to avoid feeling abandoned or disappointed that the therapist is unavailable for relationships that are not appropriately professional.

The most consistent and important result of therapeutic utilization of existing, past, or newly created, imagined, supportive relationships is a strengthening of the client's sense of self-worth and hopefulness about other relationships in the future. This is crucial in order to empower the client to move beyond the constricting and often disastrous pattern of painful isolation that is so often a legacy of childhood sexual abuse. Existing relationships, past relationships, and imagined relationships based on the client's personalized version of meaningful support, comfort, and positive future orientations are all important resources for accessing the hope and courage the client needs to resolve the past trauma and create a rewarding future.

4

DEALING WITH NONSUPPORTIVE FAMILY MEMBERS AND WITH PERPETRATORS

IN RECOVERING from sexual abuse, the client must come to terms with feelings not only about the perpetrator(s) but also about those family members who failed to protect her in the past and may continue even now to participate passively in the abuse through denial and protection of the perpetrator. Calof (1987) uses the term "implied incest" to describe the behavior of family members who do not respond appropriately to abuse perpetrated by an individual who has a close relationship with the family. Sexual abuse survivors need specific tools to deal with the effects of disclosure and confrontation with such nonsupportive family members and with perpetrators. The various techniques described in this chapter are suitable for use in individual or group treatment settings.

Disclosure of Incest

Christine Courtois (1988) writes:

> We now know from available research that approximately half of all incest victims made an attempt at disclosure at the time of the incest and that most responses were unfavorable. (p.326)

So how is the therapist to help the adult survivor disclose past incest? Disclosure should be prepared for in therapy carefully and thoroughly. Generally, the more thoroughly the client has prepared for the disclosure, the more likely she is to experience the resulting interaction as satisfactory or at least not overwhelming and emotionally devastating. The possibility that the client will encounter resistance and denial from family members should be anticipated and predicted, since in most cases disclosure of sexual abuse severely threatens the family status quo.

Family members are apt to react in ways generally characteristic of their style of defensiveness. The client needs to be informed of various patterns of family reactions and assisted in formulating a realistic assessment of how her family is most likely to react. If she or other members have previously attempted disclosure in the past, this should be taken into account and utilized as part of the preparation.

Step 1. Review Any Past Attempts

Courtois (1988) suggests beginning preparation for disclosure by discussing any previous attempts at disclosure, exploring the results of these attempts and the emotional effect they had on the client. The client needs to work through her feelings about any past attempts before attempting another one.

Step 2. Predict Possible Reactions

The way family members reacted to past attempts at disclosure may provide the therapist and client with a map for predicting how they will react now. Even in cases where no known attempts at disclosure have been made, family members can generally be expected to respond in their habitual interactive style. For example, families that tend to react in an emotionally constricted and repressive manner are likely to respond to a disclosure with minimal reaction and then "sweep it under the rug," as if it never happened. Another related scenario is for family members to respond initially with concern and support, only then to rebury the secret as if it had never been disclosed and refuse to discuss it again with the victim. For some victims, this passive denial may be more difficult to deal with than overt revictimization, since it is subtler and harder to identify.

In more emotionally expressive families, particularly those that characteristically use intimidation and guilt to manipulate and control family members, disclosure may evoke hostile reproach. In such cases, the victim may be angrily accused of "cruelty" for attacking the perpetrator, even if the abuse is admitted and recognized. For instance, one family member responded to a victim's disclosure by saying, "I can't believe you are so sick as to deliberately hurt us all by bringing this up after all these years. He [the perpetrator] only has a few more years to live, and we're not going to let you ruin them."

When power and control have been characteristically expressed and maintained through physical violence, the family's response to the disclosure may include outbursts of anger, threats of or actual physical abuse and/or suicide. If the client comes from this sort of family, safety considerations should definitely be addressed.

Also included in predictions of possible reactions should be the fact that upon disclosure the client may learn that siblings, cousins, and other peers have been victimized. Older relatives, too, may respond by disclosing their own victimization in previous generations, since incest is often passed down through several generations.

The client should also be warned that a family member's initial response to the disclosure may not be his or her ultimate response. Even seemingly "supportive" family members may initially respond to the client in a warm and validating manner, only later to deny the truth of her statements and scapegoat her. On a more positive note, in cases where support seems initially unavailable, some members of the family may, with time, become strong and emotionally autonomous enough to respond to the victim in an appropriate and caring manner.

Once the family's probable reaction has been predicted and other responses characteristic of families of sexual abuse victims have been described as potential possibilities, the client needs to be further strengthened so that she can maintain a self-supportive perspective during the disclosure. Before attempting disclosure, much less confrontation, she needs to be far enough along in her therapy to have resolved any ambivalence about her role in the victimization. Specifically, she needs to maintain her awareness that she was a child and undeniably the victim and that she in no way was or is responsible for the abuse she sustained. Even when the client appears to be very strong and solid in her stance, it is a good idea to provide her with a specific way to remain in touch with this inner truth.

Step 3. Developing and Keeping a "Reminder of Truth" in One's Pocket

I have found it particularly effective to have clients write down, on a small piece of paper, their healthy inner truth about their victimization, specifically the facts that it was not their fault and that they are in no way to blame. This truth should be expressed in their own words, rewritten if necessary until the statement is undeniable to them. I ask them to carry this message in a pocket, so they may actually feel it in their hand if needed while disclosing abuse to family members. This approach can also be used for clients who must testify about abuse in court or who choose to confront their perpetrator. This little piece of paper helps the client maintain her connection to the inner resources she evokes while in the therapist's office. Similarly, the symbols she uses as associational cues for comfort and security may also be carried in her pocket to further enhance her connection to inner resources and convictions.

Examples of the reminders my clients have written down and carried in their pockets while disclosing abuse, going to court, or otherwise confronting their sexual abuse perpetrators include:

- "It was not my fault."
- "I am doing this for the little girl I used to be."
- "I need to do this so that little girl inside finally feels really protected."
- "He is the one who did something wrong, not me."
- "I must do this so that he can't hurt anyone else."
- "I'm going to feel a lot better once I get this over with."

Step 4. Healing Letters as Preparation for Disclosure

Derived from a technique described by Ellen Bass and Laura Davis in *The Courage to Heal* (1988), healing letters provide a symbolic way for the client to get the support she requires *before* risking disclosure. In combination with the previously suggested techniques, this step significantly reduces the client's vulnerability to further revictimization by relatives who respond inappropriately or inadequately to disclosures of past sexual abuse.

The client is asked to write a letter of disclosure to a family member and not mail it (at least not immediately). The next step is for her to write an imaginary but realistic response from the relative based on how she would expect the relative to respond. This letter should also reflect any fears the client might have about how the relative will respond. Then she is asked to write a third imaginary letter from the relative expressing in full measure the response the client wants and needs.

When actual verbal disclosure is impossible because the relative is dead or his/her whereabouts are unknown, healing letters can provide a way for the client to experience needed support and symbolically resolve unfinished business with that person. For instance, one client experienced much comfort and relief by writing healing letters to and from a deceased grandmother who would have been protective and supportive.

In cases where direct disclosure is geographically impossible, the client may later choose to actually send the first letter. Regardless of the relative's potential response, the client has already provided herself with some support and further integration.

Disclosures to Distant Relatives

As a general rule, the adult survivor who makes a disclosure about incest that occurred in the nuclear family is more apt to receive support from more distantly related family members and friends than from members of the immediate family. For this reason, some clients prefer to begin the process of disclosure by talking to a more distantly related but obviously supportive relative or friend or to someone who obviously has a much closer relationship with the victim than with the perpetrator and other members of the nuclear family. However, even in the case of distant relatives whom the client expects to be unequivocally supportive, I recommend following all of the steps described above. Since sexual abuse is all too frequently multigenerational, its effects may extend to distant family members in ways that are not recognizable and predictable in advance to the client or the therapist. Unfortunately, the distant relative the client perceives as supportive may not evidence that support following the client's disclosure.

Confronting the Perpetrator

If the perpetrator is available, the client may feel a need to confront him or her in order to put the issue truly to rest. In some cases, in order to prevent further sexual abuse, public disclosure and legal confrontation in court settings may be necessary.

While confrontation can be very traumatic, it also offers many potential advantages. In confronting the perpetrator, the client is doing what should have been done for her in the past; she is putting the responsibility for the abuse where it belongs and, in so doing, giving herself the message that it was not her fault. As one client put it, "By having it out with him once and for all, I felt like I got as much closure as I was ever going to get and afterwards I began to think about it [the abuse and the perpetrator] a lot less."

Even in cases where legal authorities are not already involved, if the statute of limitations has not run out, the client may choose to prosecute the perpetrator. This is particularly important in preventing further abuse and may also provide some symbolic retribution for the client, such as a court ordered settlement to pay for therapy and other expenses incurred as the client works to rebuild her life. The client may also be able to take some solace in the fact that, by bringing charges against the perpetrator, she may succeed in preventing the abuse of others.

Ironically, the client may require some assistance in working through some guilt about confronting the perpetrator, as she is likely, as a consequence of her abuse, to consider the perpetrator's needs before her own.

While the therapist may, understandably, experience feelings of anger toward the perpetrator and unsupportive members of the client's family, expressing these feelings directly to the client is risky. The client is likely to perceive the therapist's anger as threatening and react defensively. She may imagine that the therapist is trying to deprive her of the only family she has. This is particularly true in the early stages of dealing with the reality of the abuse and grieving for the loss of the illusory support of the family. The client's pace in coming to terms with her feelings about the perpetrator and her relationship with unsupportive members of the family needs to be carefully respected.

Preparing for Confrontation

Ideally, confrontation should not occur until the client feels ready; however, when legal authorities are involved for purposes of protection, the therapist must assist the client in getting ready for public disclosure and confrontation before this would have occurred naturally or, in some cases, at all.

As in the case of preparing for disclosure of the abuse to relatives, the client needs to be given support and practical tools for coping with the potential stress and pain of the confrontation. Although in some cases the perpetrator may choose to take responsibility for his crime and show remorse and compassion to his victim (Courtois, 1988; Dolan, 1989), there is a high likelihood that he will defend himself with denial, anger, and blaming of the victim. The survivor of sexual abuse must be carefully prepared for the worst.

In addition to the four steps described above, the following techniques will further strengthen and empower the victim, enabling her to experience control over the confrontive interactions and reduce the risk of further psychological victimization.

Imagine the Worst and Arrange Protection

In addition to examining any past attempts at confrontation and their results, and assessing and predicting the perpetrator's possible responses, I ask my clients to imagine the worst that could happen as a result of confronting the perpetrator. Generally, they mention denial, anger, and blame. Sometimes they fear physical violence or sexual assault. In such cases, the potential for violence should be taken seriously; the client needs to be sure that the setting for the confrontation is physically safe for her. I then ask clients what they would need to do to protect themselves from the possibility of these "worst fears." I divide this protection into psychological and physical protection.

Because of highly developed dissociative abilities resulting from the original abuse, the client is at maximum risk for "splitting" off from her needed resources while under the stress of confronting the perpetrator. Therefore, it is important that in rehearsing the confrontation she repeatedly be directed to identify what she needs to protect herself psychologically while in the situation, e.g., "What do you need to remember to tell yourself in order to feel okay?" The therapist can play the role of the perpetrator for the client, using the client's "worst fear" scenario. The therapist can then stop the role-playing every few minutes to monitor the client's inner state and make sure that she is maintaining her self-support.

The "reminder of truth" described earlier can help significantly in ensuring that the sexual abuse survivor maintains a reliable connection to her inner resources during the confrontation. The client may carry the message in a pocket, where she can reach in and touch it, or even in her shoe, where she can feel it, as a kinesthetic reminder. Similarly, if the client has an object that reminds her of comfort and security, such as a wedding ring or a photo that can be carried in a purse or pocket, that object can be used to elicit security. The reminder of truth and meaningful object should both be utilized in rehearsals of the future confrontation, so that the client can practice reconnecting to her inner resources.

The client cannot feel psychologically safe if she lacks physical protection. A relative or close friend who has been identified as strongly and reliably supportive may be asked to accompany her to ensure physical safety. Another alternative is for the client to ask the perpetrator to attend a therapy session, so that the client can make the confrontation in the safe setting of the therapy office. Under no circumstances should the client put herself at risk by making the confrontation alone in an isolated setting where the perpetrator could conceivably abuse her again. This issue needs to be addressed carefully, because the victim's protective dissociative abilities, which were originally developed to survive the abuse, may interfere with her current ability to recognize potential danger.

The content of the confrontation should include acknowledgment and description of the abuse the client suffered, how it affected her, and what sort of retribution she feels she should have from the perpetrator, such as an apology, paying for her therapy, or providing funds for her to complete her education.

Healing Letters

The three-step healing letter exercise described earlier ensures that the client will experience support and validation regardless of the perpetrator's actual response. The process begins with a letter to the perpetrator in which the survivor describes the details of the abuse and then expresses her feelings about the abuse and how it has affected her life. The letter should also include a request for any form of retribution the client feels would be appropriate.

The client then writes two other letters, similar in form to those written in preparation for disclosure. The second is the letter she thinks the perpetrator would actually write or have actually written if he were available to do so. Or it may be a recapitulation of what the perpetrator said to her during an actual past confrontation. It should reflect the response the client fears.

The third letter, in which the client details the response she wants and needs, is perhaps the most powerful. This is the response that the perpetrator would write if he were willing and/or able to take responsibility for the abuse and respond appropriately with remorse and a desire to make amends. In other words, the third letter is the letter the client needs but hasn't received in the past and is unlikely to get in real life. Writing the third letter can be a significant healing experience for the client, as it empowers her to provide, for herself, important messages of support, apology, and validation that were previously denied her.

The healing letters are especially useful in cases when the perpetrator is permanently absent because of death or other reasons. In addition, they can be used to complete a confrontation that was aborted when the perpetrator refused to take responsibility.

Once all three letters have been written, the client may choose to mail the first one. The fact that the three healing letters have already been written will help her deal with the perpetrator's response or lack thereof.

Working With the "Nonoffending" (Yet Nonsupportive) Mother

While logically it would seem that the nonoffending parent would be a person the victim could count on for support and protection, often dynamics in incestuous family systems severely impair the nonoffending mother's ability to support and stand up for her daughter.

According to research on nonoffending mothers of survivors of sexual abuse, the mother is often not aware that the abuse is going on until she is told (Herman, 1981.) She is likely to be in some way psychologically or physically incapacitated (Finkelhor, 1980). Moreover, if the nonoffending mother is aware of the abuse, there is a likelihood that she herself is a survivor of sexual abuse (Goodwin, McCarthy, & DiVasto, 1981).

Since survivors of sexual abuse are at high risk for a diagnosis of borderline personality (Briere, 1989), and since both sexual abuse and borderline personality are multigenerational, the mother may be suffering from borderline personality symptoms related to her own sexual abuse victimization. Cases where the mother is also a sex abuse victim with borderline personality features present some special difficulties for the therapist seeking to assist the client in receiving support and protection from family members. For instance, I have repeatedly observed situations in which the borderline mother of a sex abuse victim acts out the splitting so characteristic of the borderline diagnosis. In such cases, the mother may initially be supportive of the victim, particularly in the presence of helping professionals, but then suddenly refuse to believe the victim or switch to a blaming, castigating stance. This blaming behavior appears to be especially upsetting to the victim, since it follows directly on the heels of the mother's apparent attitude of support.

When the clinician suspects that the mother has borderline features and has been victimized herself, it may be helpful to warn the client in advance that some mothers who were themselves victimized are not able to maintain a supportive stance toward their victimized children. Instead they "flip" between apparently sincere, healthy support and dysfunctional, blaming behavior. If the victim can view her mother's blaming as inappropriate behavior stemming from the mother's abuse or apparent "mental problems," rather than a solely personal response, it may lessen the traumatic effect.

It should be emphasized that the purpose of gaining this understanding is not to excuse the mother's behavior. Rather, the client is helped to understand possible reasons behind her mother's blaming or rejecting behavior in the hope that this will lessen the client's pain. The blaming reaction can be viewed as a predictable though unfortunate side effect of the mother's own unresolved (and probably untreated) victimization.Sometimes offering this explanation to the mother with reference to other mothers' having similar reactions, has strengthened her ability to be more consistently supportive of her daughter.

Mothers who have themselves been victims of sexual abuse may also minimize their daughter's abuse or current distress. While minimizing is a characteristic and common aspect of denial in dysfunctional families where alcoholism and various kinds of physical and emotional abuse occur, it seems to be particularly destructive when it is personalized by a mother's denying the impact of a type of victimization she shares with her child.

For example, when several daughters disclosed that they had been molested by their stepfather, their mother responded by saying, "Okay, I know it wasn't a good thing to have happen, but there's lots of worse things that could happen. My father did it to me and I got over it. I didn't take it personally, and anyway it's not happening now, so I don't know why you're making such a big deal about it."

The clear implication was that, since it had happened to the mother and she hadn't "made a big deal about it," the daughters should not either. The mother placed no emphasis on her husband's wrongdoing, instead criticizing the daughters for being so "weak" as to let the abuse bother them and to bring it up as a therapy issue years later. It can be very difficult for victims to defend themselves against such criticism when it is from their mother.

To someone unfamiliar with incest cases, this mother's denial may sound extreme. Tragically, in my experience this reaction is not uncommon. Over the past 10 years, in my own practice and as a consultant for family treatment teams at various county social service agencies, I have observed many mothers reacting in this discounting and minimizing manner.

Mothers who were themselves victimized tend not only to discount their daughters' abuse but also to depict themselves as being victimized by the daughters' coming forth with the truth. And the perpetrator is usually all too willing to join the mother in her victim role, giving the actual victim the message that she is being abusive to them! While this may sound ridiculous to those outside the family, the client, already carrying a heavy load of undeserved guilt, is quite susceptible to the mother's and perpetrator's blaming. Especially in cases involving father/stepfather-daughter incest, the mother (and often the perpetrator along with her) may cite the financially devastating consequences of the husband's going to jail, as if the daughter, rather than the father, is responsible for this.

Furthermore, the mother, with or without the perpetrator, may actually succeed in convincing other family members to assist in "defending" them from the victim. In one case, the younger sister of an incest victim cruelly castigated her older sister for "being so cruel as to bring this stuff up to Dad and Mom after all these years." The victim, who had only recently recovered specific and very disturbing memories of being molested by her father, became suicidal and expressed great remorse for "having broken up the family," even though she had already reached the point where, in her own words, "I just can't continue in any kind of relationship with them unless we sit down and talk about this."

The mother and perpetrator (if they are united) may succeed in convincing members of the extended family that the victim is "making it up," persecuting them by "bringing it up after all these years." Because of the horror of sexual abuse, relatives of incest victims are often all too willing to "let sleeping dogs lie," preferring not to believe the victim. Ultimately, the adult victim who finally summons the courage to come forth with the truth about what was done to her may be perceived as persecuting her parents!

Many adult survivors have initially expressed the fantasy that talking about the sexual abuse with family members will suddenly make everything better. This fantasy very rarely has any basis in fact, although, of course, there are exceptional cases where the perpetrator is willing to take responsibility for the crime, to express remorse effectively, and to make at least symbolic retribution. Far more often, however, in disclosures involving mothers who have chosen to support the perpetrator rather than the victim, the victim is placed in the terrible position of losing what familial support (if any) has been available to her up until now.

The Dissociated Mother

The dissociated mother merits special consideration, since assisting her to overcome dissociation regarding her own abuse may empower her to support her daughter while resolving some of her own previously untreated and perhaps even consciously unknown victimization issues. The following case illustrates a pattern of response indicative of a mother who is dissociated from her own childhood victimization and as a result has dissociated from her daughter's victimization.

A young adult client who had confided to her mother that she was being abused by her stepfather, described the following interaction:

> I told my mother that her husband had been fondling me and I was scared. I knew that she would be really angry and I didn't want that, but I knew also that I had no choice but to tell her because it was getting worse and worse and I didn't know what he would try to do to me next. I believed that if I came out and told her there was no way she wouldn't do something to make him stop. Boy, was I wrong!
>
> When I told her, instead of getting mad, she just got real quiet and her face got pale, and she just stood there looking at me for a while and then she asked, "Are you sure?" I got kind of mad and said indignantly, "Of course, I'm sure." She got a kind of faraway look in her eye and just said, "Thank you for telling me," and walked away without saying anything else, as if I had told her we were out of milk or some other thing that really didn't make any difference.
>
> Then I began to feel real crazy, like I didn't know if I was just making a big deal about something that was really minor, even though I was really upset about in a very major way, or maybe I hadn't really told her and just thought I had—because her reaction was just so . . . not there.
>
> A couple days later he started trying it again and I got very

angry at him and he threatened to hit me. Then I went and told her again and it was really horrible. She acted not only as if I hadn't told her before, but also as if I wasn't telling her anything right now . . . she just sort of spaced out, acting kind of bored or preoccupied. She didn't even say anything back to me; she just changed the subject and started talking about nothing things, like what we were going to have for dinner that night.

I got really angry then and she sent me to my room and told me not to come back until I could behave myself. I know this sounds really crazy, but she gave me the feeling, without exactly saying anything, that I was acting really crazy, and I actually started to wonder if I had imagined the whole thing in my mind, until the next time he started to do it again. That's how I found out I couldn't count on my mother for anything.

In the interest of both mother and daughter (as well as any other children still living in the home and potentially at risk), the therapist must assist the dissociated mother in becoming strong enough to deal with current and past issues of abuse. This may be initiated in a conjoint session with the survivor and the mother. However, in the meantime, if the therapist suspects further abuse is occurring, these concerns need to be reported to the local protective agencies.

The most obvious way to begin to empower a presumably dissociated mother is to ask her if she was sexually abused as a child. Of course, even if she was abused, she may or may not be able to remember it consciously. And if she does recall abuse, she may minimize it. In such cases, offering information about how past sexual abuse may subsequently interfere with a mother's ability to perceive danger and protect her children may strengthen the mother. She should be told that mothers with a history of sexual abuse sometimes have difficulty even recognizing evidence of abuse in their children and initially may be completely unable to protect and emotionally support their children without outside help. Victimized mothers frequently feel compelled to deny the reality of the abuse, which may doom the next generation to repeat it. To avoid further arousal of the mother's already active defense system, this information should be conveyed in an objective but caring and definitely nonblaming tone.

In some cases the apparently dissociated mother may respond to the question about whether she was ever sexually abused by hesitantly replying "No," or, "I'm not sure." If abuse is strongly suspected, it may be helpful to mention that former victims of sexual abuse sometimes initially do not remember or are not sure and, in addition, may have difficulty recognizing the signs of abuse in their own families. Because of these dynamics, the therapist has reason to very gently say, "I suspect this may have happened to you."

Even if the mother was not in fact abused, the above frame may make it easier for her to acknowledge that her daughter has been. By being aware of her own victimization (or its likelihood), the mother is empowered to become more supportive and protective of her daughter without losing face and jeopardizing her hierarchical position. If a mother continues to deny her daughter's abuse even in the face of clear and obvious evidence, it may be helpful to ask her how her own mother (or father if relevant) dealt with or would have dealt with abuse of her as a child. If she discloses that her parents failed to protect her, it may be useful to have her imagine what a difference would have been made in her life if her parents had protected her.

This is likely to be a highly emotionally charged subject for the dissociated mother. Yet raising questions about it may empower her to begin to confront the reality of the abuse and its effects. The therapist should be prepared for the mother's anger when such painful feelings are activated; it may be possible to refocus the anger appropriately toward the perpetrator(s). For example, "I know you're angry at me, and that's understandable because I brought up a really painful topic for you, but I wonder if you're also feeling some anger towards the person(s) who initially caused all this pain." If she is able to own her anger, the mother, like the identified sexual abuse victim, is likely to need support in overcoming inappropriate, but nevertheless very common, feelings of guilt for being angry at the perpetrator.

Before the conjoint session ends, a plan should be formulated concerning how the mother and daughter can support each other and how each can receive additional support from the therapeutic community via support groups, family or conjoint mother and daughter therapy, and, if indicated, individual therapy. The risk of suicide should be addressed and care should be taken to ensure that both mother and daughter have adequate support available.

A Metaphor to Break Through Denial: The Sinking of the Titanic

In my consultation work, as well as my private practice, I all too often see cases involving mothers who deny an apparent history of sexual victimization in their own past and aggressively refuse to accept the reality that their daughter has been abused. In fact, some of these mothers have been physically and emotionally abusive to the daughter themselves.

Despite professional distance, this can be painful to watch, and it is presumably far more painful for the young adult daughter and the mother to experience. The following metaphor, "The Sinking of the Titanic," has sometimes been successful in empowering these mothers and occasionally other family members to break through denial and come to the aid of the victim.*

The Titanic was thought to be one of the finest and certainly one of the most beautiful ships of its kind, and the captain was very proud of his position as commander of the ship. He had been especially excited about taking the ship out on its maiden voyage. Imagine his consternation when he realized, late one night, that the ship had hit an iceberg. He was embarrassed by this misfortune and wondered how it might adversely affect his career. Instead of taking immediate safety measures while thoroughly assessing the damage, he, after much contemplation, decided to hide the seriousness of the damage from his crew and passengers. He thought he could have the ship repaired at the next port and no one would ever know the seriousness of the situation they had experienced at sea the previous night.

However, the captain's plan tragically backfired, and the ship sunk in the middle of the night, far from port and before other ships could be summoned to rescue the crew and passengers. Many lives were needlessly lost, because no one would have died if the captain had been willing to admit the seriousness of the situation

---

*Those familiar with the actual historical details of this shipwreck will note that I have taken some liberties with the facts. I contend that the potential therapeutic usefulness of the metaphor justifies the "alterations."

and signal for help. At the time the damage occurred there was still sufficient time for the lifeboats to be activated and measures taken to assure the continued safety of all the passengers until they could be picked up by another boat. Ironically, the captain's stubborn insistence that they continue to run the motors and proceed full steam ahead, as if nothing had happened, may have actually caused the boat to sink faster.

Depotentiating the Victim's Paradoxical Double Bind

Even with a great deal of therapeutic support, clients abused by a mother who refuses to protect them and/or a parent who is explicitly the perpetrator may retreat to a self-blaming mode in which they view themselves as "bad" for causing the parent's pain by disclosing the abuse. This can also happen when the perpetrator is not in the immediate family but is for some reason afforded protection by the parent(s).

When the therapist or other clients in a sex abuse survivors group assert that the parent is being further abusive by blaming the victim for her victimization, the victim may struggle with the pain of finding her parent guilty of such severe charges. As one of my clients said while in the throes of this dilemma, "But she's my mother. I just can't stand to see her as being capable of doing something so wrong and cruel."

This is just one example of the intense and often excruciatingly painful double binds in which the survivor of sexual abuse who encounters nonsupportive family members may find herself. The resolution of such paradoxes, when the conflicting statements are stated in reference to her family rather than herself, depends on responses from the family that are unattainable. Therefore, the survivor's inner conflict is never ending. Specifically, she is unable to resolve these seemingly irreconcilable truths in relation to her parent:

A. I love you.
B. I am very hurt and angry about what you did (or let happen) to me.
C. You deny the truth of what happened to me.
D. You hurt me badly and you continue to hurt me whenever I try to resolve the past so that I can continue to love you.

The client is likely to express these truths in the form of "But" statements, such as:

- "I feel like I'm going crazy because I really love my mother, but am really angry."
- " He's my father and I love him, but he just hurts me more every time I try to talk about what he did to me. . . . We just can't get past it. I try but he won't even admit what happened."

The client cannot resolve this inner conflict unless such statements can be expressed as coexisting, so that the client no longer needs to choose between them or struggle to reconcile them. As the client is assisted in replacing contradictory "but" statements with "and" statements that accurately describe her predicament, she will experience much relief from the inner response to the paradox created by loving someone who has hurt her. While the paradox can be unlocked verbally by reflecting noncontradictory formulations of the client's truths back to her, having it in writing is much more concrete and more powerful. For example, here is a letter I assisted a survivor in writing to her nonsupportive mother. The mother had consistently denied the degree and devastating consequences of the sexual abuse and actively continued to protect her husband (the perpetrator).

Dear Mom:

I am sorry our differences about the past are unresolvable. I love you very much, and I always will, even though I am unable to continue a relationship with you because of these differences. I view you as a victim of the same abuse I suffered, even though I don't expect you to agree with me.

The first sentence acknowledges the fact that the client and her mother are in disagreement about the past and supports the client's truth that something (the abuse) did happen to her in the past. The second sentence, "I love you and always will, even though I am unable to have a relationship with you because of these differences," allows the client to acknowledge and therefore transcend the paradox because it is no longer formulated as self-contradictory. The last sentence provides the client with an explanation of her mother's behavior that the client can live with. Predicting that her mother will probably disagree lessens the risk of the mother's undoing the client's attainment of a model of the situation that she no longer has to reconcile or "solve" for herself or, as is more often the case, for the family.

Other (perhaps more hopeful) versions of the above letter might form the statement slightly differently, "I am sorry that our differences about the past are unresolvable at this time," or "I regret that we are currently unable to agree about the past." The client can choose to mail the letter or not.

Interventions to Help the Client
Deal With the Lost Image of Her Good Parent

Incest and physical abuse perpetrated by members of the nuclear family are especially difficult for victims to resolve since feelings of love are intertwined with sadness and anger toward the perpetrator(s). Often the client would rather see herself as deserving of the abuse than risk losing her "good" image of what many clients have ruefully referred to as "the only parent(s) I'll ever have."

Henry Close (1989), a pastoral counselor and the director of the Milton Erickson Institute in Atlanta, described his work with one client who not only had to come to terms with the fact that her parents had been physically, sexually, and emotionally abusive, but had also lost both parents through death. The client expressed deep sadness to Henry because she felt guilty about "speaking ill of the dead," particularly since these were her parents, for whom she still felt love despite what they had done to her.

Since the client had a sense of spirituality and a concept of "heaven" as being a place where people were healed and whole, Henry asked the client to imagine her parents healed and whole and now finally able to give her what she needed from them. He pointed out that, now healed themselves, they would be deeply supportive and even grateful and happy to see her efforts to heal herself through therapy. In self-hypnosis she could use this new concept of her healed parents to elicit trance experiences of the needed developmental experiences they would have provided had they been already healed while still alive. The client could pray to them for help with her current healing and rightfully expect their blessings on her therapy endeavors.

Individualized versions of the above intervention obviously have great potential for providing a healing context for adult survivors of childhood sexual abuse when the abusive parent is deceased. Versions of it (with or without the spiritual implications) can also be of value in helping victims with living parents who continue to be abusive but intersperse the victimization with loving gestures and constricted, but nevertheless apparently genuine, attempts at support. The client in these situations is faced with a painful and paradoxical double bind, as poignantly described by one of my adult clients:

> I know they victimize me, I can see it, and the people in my support group point it out to me. They still blame me for what my cousin did to me [sexual abuse], and they put me down a lot, making fun of me for trying to make something of myself. They tell me I'm stupid, and every once in a while it seems like my Dad is going to start beating me up like he did when I was in high school. And I start thinking I don't ever want to see them again.
>
> And then all of a sudden they're nice to me, or I remember something really nice they've done for me like last winter when I lost my job and they paid my rent for three months. The trouble is that I never know when they're going to flip from being real nice to me, loving me, to being real abusive again. I don't see it coming, I can't even predict it.
>
> This may sound really nuts, but they're the only parents I have and I don't want to give up the ways that they do love me, and yet I just can't reconcile the loving things they do with the abuse. I used to tell myself I was just imagining the abuse—that's pretty much what they've said these past few years. They say, "C'mon now, you had a pretty good childhood, it wasn't that bad," and they just go nuts if I point out to them that they beat me and my uncles sexually abused me. And then they start saying abusive things to me.
>
> I feel like I'm supposed to give them up, like I have to give up my relationship with them and yet it literally breaks my heart to think of never seeing them again and saying that I never had loving

parents. Because sometimes I did have loving parents and I just can't deny that. If I think of them as "all bad" I get so depressed and feel so guilty I feel suicidal. I just don't know how to deal with it. I feel like I shouldn't see them anymore and yet I wonder if that erases the times in my mind when they were good parents. I don't want to lose what little they did give me; I just can't afford to part with that because it's all I have from them.

While some clients are able to clearly identify the abusive aspects of relationship with their nonsupportive parents and have somehow developed enough inner security to simply terminate the relationship (Courtois, 1988), others struggle with wanting to believe that the parents have finally changed into the consistently loving and functional parents they needed or attempt to over-emphasize the parents' good qualities to offset their abusive behaviors. Since many victims of sexual abuse use idealization as a defense mechanism (Herman, 1981), the client may, even after extensive treatment, fall back on the familiar strategy of seeing her abusive parents as ideal. To counteract this tendency, the client needs to be given a frame from which she can view her parents' good qualities as being real without denying the truth of their abusive behavior. If she is to protect herself from further abuse without irrationally feeling guilty for abandoning the parents, "persecuting" them, or "betraying" them by telling the family secrets to the therapist, the client needs to be given an explanation for her parents' behavior that incorporates both functional and dysfunctional aspects of their behavior.

In case of ongoing abuse, where the client obviously has to terminate her relationship with her parent(s), ironically it will be easier for her eventually to end the relationship if she feels that, in assessing her parents, she has given them their due. If the therapist simply points out their abusiveness and refuses to acknowledge their "good" aspects, no matter how pitifully small, the client will eventually flip from self-righteous self-protection to irrational guilt for betraying "the only mother (father) I'll ever have." If the client feels that she has sufficiently acknowledged the parents' "good" attributes, it will be easier for her to initially recognize and protect herself from their abuse.

Here is a frame I have found useful in empowering clients to use conscious and unconscious inner resources to reconcile the "good" and "bad" qualities of abusive parents:

I know this is really painful for you, because you are telling me if you stop (or severely lessen) contact with your parents, even though it will prevent you from being further victimized, it will also prevent you from getting the love and support that your parents are at times able to provide. And since they are not always supportive, in fact sometimes are downright abusive, the instances of love you have gotten and perhaps occasionally still do receive from them are all the more precious to you, like rain falling on a desert, perhaps.

With your parents it is clear that, for whatever reasons—and we can speculate on those reasons from their background—and probably because of reasons we'll never fully know, they are unable to be consistent in being supportive and functional. I think we can look at all the good things they have done as signs that *if they weren't impaired* they would have given you all the love and support you needed.

Part of their psychological impairment is the inability to take responsibility for the times they were abusive. And that really makes sense because, if they were able to take responsibility for it, they wouldn't continue to do it. So, instead of denying the good things they have done, I would encourage you to appreciate it to whatever degree you are able, because those are the instances when they overcame their own psychological constrictions and expressed in their own way the natural love that parents, even very disturbed ones, feel for their children.

Even though they couldn't do it consistently, at times they did give you some good things, and these times are probably all the more precious to you because of the infrequency.

It may be, however, that, in order to continue to develop and grow as a healthy person, you have to set limits about the kind of contact you can have with them. You have to determine when it's safe, when their impairment doesn't result in your being further abused by them, and when it isn't safe. For some people, the phone is safe; some people can only see their parents in person; some people choose contact by mail; and others feel safe seeing their parents only in certain groups and settings, as, for instance, when another family member such as an aunt or uncle or grandparent, helps the parents to behave in a healthy, loving way just by his or her presence. And in some cases, contact just has to be stopped, so that there isn't any more victimization. The impairment may be stronger than your parents, so that it isn't safe for you to be around them. You have to protect yourself *for them*, since they are unable to do so themselves. But that doesn't mean you don't love them or they don't love you. If your parents had a contagious disease so that you might get really sick by being near them, *if they were not impaired, if they were healthy*, they'd want you to stay away. Even if they weren't capable of saying it by speaking, you'd know. And so you can use the loving experiences you have experienced at times with your parents as encouragement to protect yourself from their impairment, so that you aren't further victimized.

And you can, based on the good things that have gone on between you, imagine in your mind the experiences you would have had if they had not been impaired, fill in those good things happening between you in your dreams and your imaginings . . . doing for yourself what your parents were unable to do . . . what they, if they had not been impaired, would have done. And, when you find yourself thinking of the good things that did happen . . . you can soak up all the nourishment you can from remembering those experiences, and look for all the other areas in your life where you can also get love and support . . . because there are many different relationships in your life . . . and maybe it's in part because of the love you did get from your parents at times that you're able to have these relationships. (Mention or allude to other supportive relationships in client's life, even using pets if necessary.)

In families where incest occurs, one parent is often missing. If the parent is dead or incapacitated through no fault of his/her own, sometimes the victim can experience comfort by imagining what that parent would say to her and what he or she would say to the perpetrator. This process can be enhanced by having the client write first a letter to the dead parent and then the letter she would imagine the parent writing in response, as described in the healing letters exercise. Another version of this involves directing the client to imagine or experience in trance what the parent would say under guided imagery. During hypnosis it can be suggested that the client continue to experience healing interchanges with the missing parent in her dreams.

In some cases clients reexperience therapeutically altered versions of their childhood in dreams. These meet their developmental needs in ways that were unavailable in the actual childhood because of the parent's absence, deficits, or pathology. When

I have had a client write the three healing letters in reference to disclosure to a long dead parent, I like to simply wonder aloud what it would be like if the client somehow could "find a way to continue this healing process in your dreams." Some clients respond to this thinly veiled suggestion by indeed experiencing a continuation of the healing interchange in their dreams.

Occasionally, a client has directly or indirectly asked me for validation of the healing dream experience. I am careful to make no judgment one way or the other about the validity of what could be perceived as a "psychic" experience occurring in the client's dreams. Instead, I simply observe that "the dream is obviously a very valuable healing experience." Interestingly, a number of my clients have reported a "healing visit" from a long dead and forgotten but supportive relative in their dreams. I wonder if it is yet another extension of the unconscious process evoked by the healing letters exercise.

Dealing with Issues Related to the
Loss of the Family of Origin

If family members are clearly not willing to be supportive of the client, she will ultimately have to separate from them in order to end her victimization. This is a painful process, in which she must grieve the end of her fantasy that the family could ever function in a healthy way and her idealized vision that family members would be there for her if she needed them. It is likely that family members will try to make her feel guilty about separating, and the effects of this will have to be dealt with in therapy.

It will be a painful and demanding process, and at times the client may doubt herself. It is very important that the client be provided with adequate support in the form of therapy appointments, group support, and, when possible and appropriate, a marshalling of social support, such as friends and any supportive extended family. This will offset to some extent the client's understandable feelings of isolation from and rejection by her abusive family of origin. The risk of suicide is very real during this transition. It is crucial that the therapist provide hope for the future by reassuring the client that she will not always feel this intense pain regarding her family. It will be a difficult transition, but it will enable the client to finally be free from further abuse from her family.

When the client cannot get closure with family members in a satisfying interactional exchange because of their denial, she can nevertheless be assisted in achieving some closure through the healing letters described earlier. In addition, as she separates from her family of origin, she will be increasingly better able to connect meaningfully with her partner, friends, and/or children and to establish a second and far healthier and more nurturing family of her own.

A Spiritual Reframe

Some clients, particularly those with strong religious convictions, feel terribly guilty that they apparently do not have enough forgiveness and love within them to overcome the past and ongoing effects of the sexual abuse trauma and maintain a relationship with abusive family members. For example, Christian clients who feel trapped into maintaining relationships with psychologically or even physically abusive family members commonly ask, "How can I justify ending the relationship with my abusive relatives when Jesus always turned the other cheek?" These clients may find comfort and resolution of their conflict in the story of Jesus throwing the money lenders out because they were showing disrespect for God's temple. Since the body is often metaphorically depicted as a "temple" in the religious sense, a good spiritual person would be justified in "casting out" those who defiled her "temple" by sexually abusing her or who do so indirectly by supporting and protecting the abusers.

A New Family

The establishment of a nurturing and healthy circle of significant others with whom to celebrate traditional holidays and enjoy ongoing contact will be a significant "healing sign" for the adult survivor of incest who breaks off contact with her nonsupportive family of origin. A major turning point in the survivor's life occurs when she is able to realize that breaking ties with her family of origin doesn't have to mean being alone or unloved. In fact, given the inherent dysfunction of most incestuous families, the converse is probably true.

One survivor poignantly expressed what her self-chosen family of friends had meant to her over the past decade:

> When you lose the family you were born with, the world becomes your family. I look at some of my friends, and I realize how lucky I am to have been able to deliberately choose the people I spend holidays and free time with rather than being forced by custom to be with people who don't really care about me. I have a more supportive family than many people I know whose original birth family is still intact.

5

ENSURING SAFETY
IN THE PRESENT

THIS CHAPTER WILL offer techniques to help the adult survivor of sexual abuse overcome dissociation so that she can realistically evaluate the level of safety within her current family system and reduce the likelihood of future sexual abuse. This is particularly important because of the sexual abuse survivor's tendency to experience revictimization (Runtz, 1987). Because she may dissociate when exposed to behaviors or perceptions reminiscent of her childhood victimization, the adult survivor is at high risk for unwittingly entering into relationships where there is potential for further abuse (Briere, 1989).

Because of conditioned responses of passivity and dissociation stemming from the original sexual abuse, the adult survivor may be rendered helpless to act on her own behalf even in the face of obviously imminent victimization (McCord, 1985). Moreover, this learned helplessness can interfere with her natural parental instincts and prevent her from recognizing and intervening when her own children are being victimized.

The techniques discussed here to help the abuse survivor/ mother and her family overcome her learned dissociation and perceptual constrictions will enable her to both recognize sexual and physical abuse and protect herself. Techniques include scaling, externalization of safety, and two ways of giving the adult survivor and the potential next generation of victims a safe means of signaling the therapist and their mother for help.

Obviously, these techniques will not be necessary or even appropriate for every adult survivor of sexual abuse. As with any other approach, the therapist is expected to use good clinical judgment in assessing whether these techniques are indicated in working with specific individual survivors. They are intended for use when the therapist believes that the client and/or her children may be currently being victimized or at risk, but are helpless to acknowledge the victimization and seek protection and help. They are definitely not intended to be misused as a means to placate the perpetrator or to misplace blame or responsibility for the abuse onto the victim. Nor are they intended to be misconstrued as a message that survivors of sexual abuse are necessarily unable to protect their children.

Scaling Safety

Having the client rate the degree of problems she is experiencing on a scale from one to ten and then identify solutions through further ratings on the scale is a technique developed by the staff at the Milwaukee Brief Family Therapy Center (Berg, 1990). I have adapted it here with survivors of sexual abuse for the purpose of helping them identify the specific indicators of safety (and danger of revictimization) in their current family and social system. Being able to identify the specifics gives the client greater ability to gain control over the situation in ways that protect her and her family from further victimization. The more specific the client is in her responses, the more likely it is that she will succeed in overcoming her learned dissociation from abuse to accurately assess potential danger.

For example, a client might be asked:

> On a scale of one to ten, how safe do you feel your family is from sexual and physical abuse? Zero would mean that it is happening now, and the family is not at all safe. One would mean it has happened in the past and could happen again, five would mean that it is about as likely to happen as not, and so on, all the way up to a level of ten, where all family members feel safe and secure that sexual abuse is not happening now and will not ever happen in the future.

If the therapist suspects that the mother may be currently in a relationship with an abusive partner who may intimidate her and inhibit her responses, these questions should definitely not be asked, particularly initially, in her partner's presence. This is to protect her from possible violence from the abusive partner in retaliation for her response and to ensure that she is free to answer accurately.

Alternatively, the question could be asked to several family members and the responses could be written by individual members on secret ballots. The therapist then averages the responses to obtain the family's perceived level of current safety. This technique is not intended for use with untreated perpetrators who might use it to further their denial of the abuse and should be used with caution if the family session includes former perpetrators, even those who have received therapy, show remorse, and appear to have accepted responsibility for their crimes.

If a former perpetrator rates safety as very high while another family member rates it as low, the therapist should consider the possibility that the perpetrator is denying current abuse or the potential for abuse.

Once a mother (or family) has given a number that represents the family safety level, she can be asked to identify what specifically would have to happen for her to know that the safety level was being maintained at an acceptable level or being raised. For example, one mother said that, if she put a lock on her daughter's door and made a point of supervising her stepson (a former perpetrator) and her young daughter when they were in the basement, she would feel more secure and "that would raise the level from a five to at least a seven." With support from the therapist to "identify anything else that you think could raise the safety level," one mother said that she and her husband should not have the children seeing them in the nude or let them climb into bed with them on a regular basis, and that her husband should not be giving her eight-year-old daughter a bath. The questions related to the safety level provide a nonthreatening context for the adult survivor to identify appropriate behaviors that minimize the likelihood of sexual abuse.

Other adult survivors of sexual abuse have responded to the safety scale in ways that suggest consequences for a relationship with an abusive partner, e.g., "In order for it to be an eight, my husband would have to quit hitting me and the kids, and I guess that, for it to be a nine, I am going to have to find a way to move out or get him to move out until he gets treatment." Others have looked at safety in terms of their own self-destructiveness, saying, "I have to stay sober so that I don't put myself into situations where I am unable to say no to going home with a man I don't even know who may be really dangerous to me."

Some adult survivors of sexual abuse respond to scaling questions with an idealized version of their family: "We're at least a 15 on the safety scale." While, of course, some adult survivors have already succeeded in ensuring safety in their own family by the time they come to treatment, the therapist should be aware that the client may currently be unable to accurately assess the situation because of dissociation responses and denial. In some cases the therapist can help the client break through constrictions that are limiting her ability to perceive and respond in a healthy, protective manner by externalizing the concept of safety (Johnson, 1990).

Externalizing Safety

Over the past five years, Charlie Johnson and I have consulted on a regular basis to several intensive family treatment teams treating families with histories of sexual abuse and domestic violence. Needing a way both to assess families' level of risk for further abuse and their ability to change and to assist them in identifying and acting out alternatives to abuse, Charlie applied a concept he had used in other areas of his work for several years—externalizing the solution. Inspired by Michael White's externalization of the problem (White, 1986, 1988; White & Epston 1990), externalizing the solution in families where safety is an issue provides the therapist and the adult survivor with a powerful tool: externalizing safety.

Externalizing safety is the process of making safety an abstract entity that the client can identify as being present or not present in her home and family in specific ways. For example, "What are the signs that safety is present in your family? What are the

identifiable things that go on that would help you convince another person that your family is safe from sexual abuse?" When
these signs are identified, the client can act to make sure that they
are present. While these questions may appear rudimentary, they
are unlikely to be so to many survivors of sexual abuse, who
function in a highly dissociated manner around basic issues of
protection.

For example, some adult survivors of sexual abuse have identified that, in order for safety to be present, they would have to
believe their child any time she said that someone was hurting
her. Or, highly dissociated former victims of sexual abuse have
said that they would "probably" have to be present whenever their
child was around a former perpetrator. This may sound incredible
to the therapist reader, who in all likelihood would not even consider leaving a child in the care of a former perpetrator of sexual
or physical abuse, at least without having evidence of extensive
and effective treatment. However, it is indicative of the level of
dissociation of some adult survivors of sexual abuse, who are
nevertheless granted continuing custody of their children by the
court system. It is vital that they be assisted in formulating a
highly specific concept of the specifics of safety to counteract the
debilitating perceptual constrictions of their learned dissociation
and denial.

Using Externalization of Safety With a Hostile Mother

A young mother of three preschool children came to therapy
"to get social services off my back." She admitted to having a
great deal of hostility towards the local social service agency staff
because she felt that they were accusing her of not watching over
her children sufficiently. They had threatened to remove them
from the home if she did not participate in psychotherapy. She
said that her oldest child, a girl, had told the daycare worker that
the mother's boyfriend was touching her "down there" in ways
that "felt bad." Although the boyfriend had once been accused by
another parent and child of sexual abuse, the mother did not feel
that this suggested that her own child was at risk, because "he
had not been found guilty" at the court hearing due to insufficient
evidence.

Asking the mother what would convince her that safety was present in her home was a dead-end street, since she believed that her boyfriend could do her children no harm. However, asking her what she could truthfully say to social services to convince them that SAFETY was present in her house yielded different results. The mother said, "Well, I'd have to say, with his history, that my boyfriend was never left alone with my little girls . . . and I guess I would have to say that I confronted him with what she told me and the daycare worker and he gave me a satisfactory answer that really convinced me that he wouldn't be capable of doing anything to my kids. When I asked him about it before, he just got mad that I even asked him, that I didn't trust him." The mother was not initially invested in rocking the boat with the boyfriend and was protecting that relationship at the expense of protecting her children. However, when asked to demonstrate that things were safe in her home through the eyes of a protective agency, she began to see the situation more accurately.

She eventually did confront her boyfriend. Initially, he was able to convince her that nothing had happened, saying that he'd been watching TV and the child "made it up just like the other kid did." However, when she tried in her next therapy session to imagine how well his excuse would work in convincing a protective agency, she began herself to question the safety of her kids in his presence. At first, every time she tried to discuss this with the boyfriend, he responded with intimidation and accused her of "caring more about your kids than you do about our relationship." This made the mother feel very guilty. But when she thought about *safety* and what it would take to convince a social worker outside her family, she realized that she was not overreacting or being abusive towards her boyfriend; rather, she was being a good mother. During this period, she also had to deal with some feelings of resentment towards her young daughter for "causing" this problem by what she said. When asked how her parents had handled her own disclosure of sexual abuse, she realized that her blaming of her daughter was similar to her own parents' response and needed to be corrected. Realizing how hurt and angry she still felt towards her own parents for their discounting, blaming behavior toward her when she was little, she apologized to her little girl. At least she could make things different for her own daughter.

As the mother explored the issue further in the context of convincing social services that safety was present, she came to the conclusion that there was no way she should leave this man alone with her kids, especially since her four-year-old daughter was not known to lie, and another kid had said the same thing, even though currently there was not enough evidence to convict him. This realization came gradually, and it took several more weeks for her to realize that she didn't want to expose herself or her kids to a relationship with a man could who very well be a sexual abuse perpetrator.

The mother then spent some time grieving—for her daughter's pain, for the loss of what she had thought might be a workable relationship for herself, and also for the pain she suffered herself as a child. She required much support and encouragement from the therapist in order to acknowledge these feelings, but she said that acknowledging them resulted in relief for her. As the grief gradually began to lift, the mother said that she felt she had learned some important things from this experience, not only about keeping herself and her kids safe, but also about things that she used to ignore that she shouldn't ignore anymore—"little feelings" about people. She had overcome her dissociative tendencies regarding self-protective instincts (her "little feelings") and could now let herself pay attention to those important inner signals.

The externalization of safety works with some adult survivors of sexual abuse, but of course not with all. The following two techniques are designed for situations in which safety appears not to be present and yet more direct techniques to make things safe for the mother and children have failed. In such cases, the therapist may have the eerie feeling that sexual and/or physical abuse is going on in the family or could easily occur, yet the adult survivor mother is unable to recognize this or act appropriately to protect her children and herself. She may be unable to overcome learned passivity and dissociative mechanisms stemming from victimization, or perhaps she, as well as her children, are intimidated by an abusive partner.

An Object of Safety

The "object of safety" is a way for a family member to anonymously signal for help. It is also a symbol to remind the family—even the perpetrator—that safety needs to be present in the home.

With the help of the therapist, family members choose a special object that is somehow symbolically associated with their feelings of safety. It may be something associated with an experience they describe as a time when they all felt especially good and safe. For example, one family used a small dried branch from a tree because it reminded them of a time they had all felt very peaceful and loving on an outdoor picnic. Or the object may be something associated with calm and stability, such as the rock one therapist gave to a family to symbolize the safety members had been describing in his office. Some families have chosen statues, religious symbols, photographs, mementos of meaningful vacations, or other personally meaningful objects.

The therapist directs family members to select a place in their house where the object will be highly visible and within reach of all family members participating in therapy. The object is not to be moved unless someone suspects that safety is at risk. In this case, the object is to be moved anonymously when no one else is around. When any family member or concerned relative or friend notices that the object has been moved from its accustomed place, he or she is to contact the therapist immediately. This may result in the therapist's receiving calls from all family members in quick succession, which further enhances the protective anonymity of the person seeking help in maintaining safety. It should be emphasized to the family that it is not necessary for safety to be violated; just *feeling* that safety is at risk is a sign that the object should be moved. The therapist can then schedule a session to further identify and strengthen safety and protection in the family.

Rebecca's Family

A mother of two children, aged eight and ten, Rebecca came to a conjoint session with her husband as part of her treatment for her own sexual victimization as a child. She had said, when asked to rate safety level, that things were at a ten, "in terms of sexual abuse"; however, she was not at all sure about physical abuse.

Her husband was currently in treatment for domestic violence. Upon completion of his treatment, the family was asked to select an object of safety. They first selected an old frisbee that represented good times in the family. Although it had now been replaced, the dog had chewed on it and it was the one the kids had used in play with their parents. However, after contemplating the symbolism of the frisbee, the couple decided to choose an object more symbolic of the present, since they both believed that the husband had made some changes that made family life safer now. They selected a sea shell, and the children agreed that the sea made them all think of "calm" and that being "calm" also meant being "safe." The parents, the kids, and the two mother-in-laws were enlisted to watch the object and call for help if it was removed.

Several phone calls came a month later. Both the parents were concerned and confused because they knew for a fact that there had been no physical violence between them, and the children seemed to be doing all right both at home and at school, except for one child's recent truancy.

Since no one knew who had moved the object, the family and the therapist began to conjecture about what might have made someone think that safety might be at risk. The therapist emphasized the importance of the object's being moved rather than allowing the family to spend the session simply focusing on speculations about who might have moved it.

The parents admitted to having had several verbal fights recently and thought that perhaps someone—maybe even one of the grandmothers or perhaps the kids—had been concerned about them. The husband admitted that he had been somewhat intimidating to his wife during one of the fights, and added, "Maybe someone was afraid we were backsliding." They resolved to use some of the communication skills they had gained in therapy, and the husband set up an appointment with his individual counselor to help him "keep on track." The family agreed at the end of the session that "safety was present in the family again." When asked to rate the safety level on a scale, the family members' responses averaged out to an eight, and individual responses pointed out that, in order to reach a nine, Mom and Dad would be talking out problems with each other instead of yelling, and that would be true of the kids as well. A ten on the scale would be reached only after these behaviors had continued over time, maybe for a year or more.

The above scenario shows an ideal use of the object of safety and the healing scale. Sometimes the object of safety is a means to to cry for help for the children and the mother who is a survivor of past sexual abuse and unable to protect her children and herself more directly. In these cases, the phone call resulting from the anonymous moving of the object may ultimately result in an investigation by a local protective agency to determine if abuse is occurring and to provide protective measures for the victims.

Postcard

Postcards are used in extreme cases, when there is a history of abuse, yet the perpetrator refuses treatment, and legal measures are unavailable, ineffective, or insufficient to lower the high risk of future abuse.

The therapist may have reason to fear that the children are at high risk for sexual and physical abuse and unable to signal for help by moving the object of safety because of direct or implicit threats of violence. Moreover, the therapist may have evidence that the parents would not reliably cooperate with the use of the object.

When the therapist feels that the children are desperately at risk, stamped postcards may be privately given to the children by the therapist with the understanding that any postcard sent to the therapist will be interpreted as a message that the child needs the therapist's help *regardless* of its actual content. This is to be used as a last ditch effort when the therapist has good reason to believe that the child is seriously at risk and there are no alternatives for offering the child help and protection.

The techniques discussed in this chapter are intended primarily for use with the adult survivor of sexual abuse and her children. They are probably not going to be sufficient in themselves to overcome the denial system of an unmotivated abuse perpetrator, although in some situations they may result in the family's recognition that the perpetrator's behavior is abusive and that he needs treatment. These techniques are useful in empowering the adult survivor to recognize when safety is not present and to act to protect herself and her children if necessary. In some cases, the scaling and externalization of safety may result in empowering the otherwise dissociated adult survivor to escape from an abusive relationship with a perpetrator who is unwilling to seek treatment and change. In other cases, the object of safety and postcards may allow a child to get help and protection before the abuse extends throughout the next generation. None of these techniques is "foolproof," but they may succeed when more traditional alternatives are unavailable.

6

HEALING THE SPLIT

SURVIVORS OF sexual abuse tend to spontaneously dissociate from resources and inner strengths at the times when, ironically, they most need them. Experienced therapists attending my workshops seem to know immediately what I mean when I refer to the gap or "split" between the client's awareness of psychological resources and healthy coping mechanisms while in the therapeutic session and her regressed state when under stress that unconsciously symbolizes or otherwise reminds the client of the original trauma.

A variety of practical techniques can be used to lessen this dissociative "split," including imagining and answering the solution-focused questions, self-induced pattern interruption, notes to the self, and nondominant hand-writing. Associational cues for comfort and security are provided to empower the client to reliably reaccess a state of comfort and security even in the midst of severe post-traumatic stress reactions. Also included are a specific four-step technique for mitigating and overcoming the unconscious response to negative associational cues, which can powerfully eclipse present resources and result in flashbacks, and a simple but effective method for "consulting with the unconscious" to determine what needs to happen in therapy based on the client's unconscious understanding of the problem.

Imagine What the Therapist Would Ask ✓

Many clients have told me that sometimes "just hearing your voice" on the telephone can help re-elicit a state of security when they are feeling overwhelmed. It is my belief that the therapist's voice in and of itself does not elicit security; rather, it elicits the client's ability to evoke that state in herself. As one of my clients said, "It's your attitude, the kind of questions you ask me that then gets me in touch with these things I already know, except I had temporarily forgotten that I knew them."

Some clients, when given the suggestion that they can "feel free to do so whenever needed," are able to "imagine what the therapist would ask" when they are upset in everyday life situations. As a result, they are able to reclaim their awareness of inner and behavioral resources. Eventually, they learn to ask themselves solution-eliciting questions such as those initially accessed by imagining the therapist's responses.

For example, a client was given a reprimand at work and began to access childhood memories of being brutally blamed for her victimization. She asked herself how she would know that she was dealing with this painful memory in a healthy way and then imagined saying reassuring words to herself. She immediately felt better.

Pattern Interruption — Doing Something Different

Some clients are helped by being taught to view repetitive post-traumatic responses, such as urges to overeat, abuse drugs and alcohol, self-mutilate, and engage in sexually compulsive behaviors, as learned responses that respond well to "pattern interruption." Sometimes reasoning with oneself when experiencing a self-destructive urge is just too passive a task to overcome the urge. However, stopping and *doing something different* (Berg, 1990; de Shazer, 1985) may enable the client to break the self-destructive cycle and shift to a state where other resources can be accessed.

It would appear that post-traumatic stress reactions have some of the features of state-dependent memory (Rossi, 1986), in that, when the client is generally in that state, she is able to access all the other traumatic experiences that she has ever had. However, she may have great difficulty accessing recently identified solutions to her difficulties.

"Something different" can be the same thing each time. The behavior needn't be novel; it just needs to be something that elicits an inner state different from the current trauma-focused one. For example, some clients seem to get consistent relief from such things as "stopping everything and playing the piano for an hour, and then thinking about what was bothering me so much," or taking a walk, calling a friend, exercising, or drinking a cup of tea. The content of the activity appears to be not as important as the fact that it is not trauma-based but, rather, something benign that she would characteristically do "when everything is all right." This allows her to have access to problem-solving resources rather than being overwhelmed by feelings of panic.

How does the therapist empower the client to remember to do something to interrupt the post-traumatic stress symptoms once they have started? Especially early in therapy, some clients instinctively call the therapist on the telephone and in so doing re-elicit a state in which they can do something different to defend themselves from the intrusive symptoms. However, this is unsatisfactory as a permanent solution, not only because of the vulnerability and dependency it creates in the client, but also because therapists cannot always be available.

Notes to the Self

An alternative is to have the client write down, while in the therapist's office, instructions for healthy pattern interruption behaviors and messages to say to herself when she begins to feel overwhelmed by symptoms of stress. The client should be directed to make several copies of these instructions, carrying one in her purse or pocket, and putting others in spots of the house or workplace where she might be prone to a PTSD attack.

For example, one client who felt extremely upset and vulnerable to self-destructive behavior after phone calls from her relatives placed an instruction sheet next to all three of her phones. The message to herself said, "Keep breathing. Remember, you can hang up if you want to. You are not the cause of their abusing you." Looking at the written message helped her progressively learn to remain emotionally distanced during family members' attempts to induce guilt and essentially revictimize her. After several calls in which she responded in an apparently disengaged manner, they stopped calling and harassing her. She said, "I didn't have to hang up—that's what I knew in the back of my mind I could do if they started abusing me on the phone again—I guess just knowing I could do that was enough to keep me centered and not regressing back into that really frightening state I used to experience so often as a kid, like I was paralyzed, looking at a cobra and somehow couldn't act to protect myself."

Another client who had a history of cutting herself on her arms and wrists posted a note to herself inside the drawer where she kept the kitchen knife that she used. The note said, "Before you do this do one of these other things: Call someone for support, go for a walk, play the flute for half-hour, write your feelings in your diary, clean out a drawer, paint a picture—at least START a painting, knit a dozen rows on a sweater." The client said that sometimes she did one of the things on the list and sometimes she read the list and didn't do anything on it but then didn't cut on herself either. In the latter case, she felt this was because she had reminded herself just by looking at the list that she had other ways to cope. "Besides," she said wryly, "looking at the list somehow makes it a lot more effort and work to cut on myself. It's easier not to."

Nondominant Hand Writing

Further pattern interruption can be introduced by having the client write messages to the self with her less dominant hand (Capacchione, 1988). This is likely to be a more laborious and therefore more compelling experience than writing it in her usual way. Whatever healthy and healing message she writes can the later be utilized, either by carrying it with her and subsequently reading it again and again or by reaccessing it through writing it again with the nondominant hand. This can be useful to strengthen the client's ability to focus on associational cues or on useful symbols or messages. Several clients have told me that writing the message with their nondominant hand in subsequent times of stress is very powerful and has a stronger effect than writing it with their dominant hand.

Associational Cues for Comfort and Security

In times of stress, sexual abuse survivors tend to have difficulty connecting to inner resources of comfort and security. The purpose of developing an associational cue (Dolan, 1985; Erickson & Rossi, 1979, 1980; Erickson, Rossi, & Rossi, 1976) for comfort and security is to make it easier for the client reliably to reconnect to much-needed experiences, as well as associated feelings, of comfort and security.

The sexual abuse survivor is likely to be all too familiar with the naturalistic phenomenon of associational cues. An associational cue is a signal that elicits an unconscious response (Dolan, 1985). For example, a favorite song may bring back feelings associated with other times one has heard that song. In some cases, a person may consciously remember experiences associated with the associational cue, as Marcel Proust (1928) did and delightfully described: As he ate a lemon-flavored "madeleine" cookie with a cup of fragrant jasmine tea, he felt transported back to the comfort and peace of his aunt's kitchen, where he had enjoyed the same treat as a child. Sex abuse survivors seldom associate to such pleasant memories.

Associational responses can be both useful and problematic for the client, depending on what is elicited. For example, a sight, sound, sensation, or other event that vividly reminds the client of her experience of victimization is likely to elicit a flashback of the original trauma. Movies depicting sexual violence are common examples, as are contacts with individuals resembling the perpetrator in appearance or behavior, or environments resembling the settings in which the abuse originally took place. On the other hand, an experience that vividly recalls a time of comfort and well-being is likely to re-elicit the feelings of security associated with that calm, pleasant state. This experience can be used to develop an associational cue for comfort and security.

Associational cues for comfort and security can provide survivors of sexual abuse with a healthy way to reconnect to inner resources in times of stress. The associational cue, once developed and strengthened, can provide an alternative to other less healthy ways of dealing with symptoms of pain and anxiety associated with a history of sexual abuse, such as wrist cutting, drug and alcohol abuse, and other self-destructive symptoms.

If introduced in the early stages of therapy, the associational cue can function as an ongoing resource to help the client move in a more secure and comfortable manner through the various stages of dealing with the sexual abuse trauma. For example, the associational cue can be used to strengthen the client during the therapy session when facing difficult facts about her victimization, as a resource during difficult interactions with nonsupportive or overtly abusive family members, such as confrontations and legal hearings, and to reorient from frightening flashbacks or nightmares.

The easiest way to elicit an associational cue for comfort and security is to ask the client to think of an experience in which she felt "relatively calm and secure." (By "relatively," I mean that, while perhaps she did not feel "perfectly" calm, she felt calm in relation to other times when she was more anxious.) In general, I would not suggest asking clients sexually abused as children to think of the time when they felt "the most" comfortable and secure or even a time when they felt "great." Extreme positive words seem to carry more risk of eliciting the polarity.

Even when the therapist asks the client merely to identify an experience of "relative" comfort and security, some clients will be unable to think of any time in their past, present, or future life that was or could be in any way comfortable and secure. In fact, they may angrily chastise the therapist for asking such an insensitive and presumably covertly cruel question! This is just the sort of response that probably helps such clients acquire the "borderline" diagnosis. Rather than simply discarding the associational cue for comfort and security as a technique with the many sexual abuse survivors who truly cannot consciously remember a time of even relative comfort and security, it is helpful to ask the question in a less direct but still quite pragmatic way: "What do you like to do when you are not thinking about the concerns that brought you to therapy? What are your favorite pastimes or hobbies?"

The "first session formula task" list (see Chapter 2) can function as an excellent source of potential associational cues for comfort and security, since it identifies experiences and activities the client wants to have continue. The client can select an item from her list and that can be used to develop the associational cue.

Yet another way to elicit the necessary information to develop an associational cue with clients who have particular difficulties responding to questions that are framed in too positive a manner is to ask them to think of a time when they were "bored." Most experiences of boredom are not anxiety-provoking and are relatively safe in content. One more way of framing this question, which I have found successful with clients who have been unable to respond to other attempts at identifying experiences of relative comfort and security, is "What do you *least dislike* doing?"

Once the client has identified an experience of comfort and security, the associational cue can be developed. The process can be divided into the following steps:

1. Ask the client to "think of an [already identified] experience of comfort and security." This step can be done with eyes open or closed.
2. Direct her to "notice and describe all the details of that experience with special reference to sights, sounds, and sensations."
3. Invite the client to "take some time to enjoy the experience."
4. Then, after a moment or two, invite her to "feel free to make any adjustments, additions, or subtractions of details that would further enhance the comfort and security of the experience."
5. Ask her to let you know when the experience is "just right" for her by giving her head a little nod.
6. Invite her to "enjoy the experience one more time . . . and while you are doing this, you can select a little symbol that can serve to remind you of this pleasant experience in the future . . . a sort of 'souvenir.' The symbol may be any sight, sound, or sensation that evokes the experiences for the client. I then suggest to the client that she might like to "take a little rest and let your unconscious choose

for you, and see what meaningful symbol comes to mind."

7. Ask the client to refocus for a moment on the external reality of the present, and then ask her to "think of the symbol for a moment and notice how that feels for you" to reaccess the state of comfort and security.

8. Suggest to the client that she can "feel free to use this symbol whenever you need to reconnect to a state of (relative) comfort and security." In some cases the client may benefit from writing the word for the symbol down on a piece of paper that she can then carry with her. Or she may access the experience by writing it down again. Another option is for the therapist to give the client a symbolic and appropriate object to remind her of her symbol for the associational cue or to assign the client to find and acquire such an object.

Once identified, the associational cue can then be strengthened by repetition. The associational cue for comfort and security will probably alter in content over time, as the client's needs and perception shift and change.

Mary

The following case example illustrates the specifics of developing an associational cue for comfort and security with a survivor of sexual abuse.

A successful 30-year-old bank secretary, the client had a history of sexual, physical, and emotional abuse by her natural parents. She had been removed from their home in her early teens and placed in a series of foster homes and group treatment facilities. Early in therapy, she requested a way to "feel calm" so she could function at work and cope with feelings of fearfulness that seemed to "come out of nowhere and make me so anxious I can't think straight."

To help her identify an experience of comfort and security, I asked, "What do you like to do when you are not occupied with dealing with the problem that brings you here?"

She responded, "I like to go for walks in the mountains, and I like to walk my dog. I like to read mystery novels, not really scary ones but interesting ones, especially sitting by the fire at night with popcorn and music on. I also like to swim at the YMCA."

I asked her, "Would you be willing to pick one of those for us to focus on as a way for you to connect to the good, calm feelings you were talking about earlier?"

She agreed and selected the experience of reading by the fire.

I asked her to identify the sights that went with that experience: "I would like you to think about and describe aloud to me all the sights that go with that experience, the light in room, the colors, the shapes, shadows etc."

She gave the following description: "It is my living room, and I have a bright green couch. I can see the street light outside the window reflected very slightly in the glass on the picture frame hanging over the fireplace mantel which I face when I am sitting on the couch. It is early evening, and it is dark outside and I can see the streetlight because it is winter and already dark. There is a nice fire going in the fireplace, and the flames are red, and gold, and yellow. My dog is curled up at my feet on the floor in front of the couch. She is a black lab, with a little bit of white on her muzzle because she is getting old. She is looking at me with her big brown eyes. I also see the rug on the floor. It is a little bit dirty from the dog and all my friends' boots tracking inside, but I don't mind. It is kind of a dirty beige color. There is a wood coffee table in front of the couch and I have a cup of hot tea sitting on it. There is steam rising from it and it is a blue flowered mug. I am wearing blue denim pants that I can see when I look down at my book which is resting on my lap under the chrome reading lamp. The cover of the book is black with red and white letters. I can't think of anything else I can see."

I then asked her, "What sounds are you aware of in this experience?"

She replied, "There aren't that many sounds, just a few: my dog sighing every once in a while and shifting her position on the floor, and the sounds of the fire. Occasionally I turn a page, or there is the sound of my picking up the mug of tea and taking a sip and putting it down again. Sometimes there is the sound of a car passing outside or people walking by. I thought there was music, but I'm not aware of any music. Mostly just the breathing sounds of me and my dog, pages turning, and the fire crackling now and then."

Next, I asked her to describe in as much detail as possible the physical sensations associated with the experience.

She said, "I am aware of the warmth of the fire radiating out from the old bricks and warming my feet. I am wearing soft socks and no shoes, and I can feel the texture of the rug under my feet just slightly. I feel my body leaning against the cushions on the back of the couch, and every once in a while I feel my dog leaning against my leg as she cuddles up to me. My body feels very relaxed, not aware of much other than the texture of the couch and rug and the nice warmth from the fire. I also have the sensation of smelling wood burning in the fireplace."

I then directed her to "take a moment to enjoy this nice experience, and when you have done that for a moment or two, feel free to make any adjustments, if you want, that would enhance the comfort and security of the experience. Let me know when it is just right by giving your head a little nod."

After a moment or two, she gave a little nod. I then invited her to "feel free to let your unconscious select a pleasant little symbol, a sort of souvenir that you can use in the future to remind you of this experience of calm. It might be a sight, a sound, or even a sensation that reminds you of this nice experience. . . . When you know what it is, come back to focus on the here and now of the room and please tell me about it."

After another few moments, the client focused her eyes on the area around my chair and told me, "I selected the little flowered mug as a symbol. It is really neat because I still have it, and I can touch it, and see it, and even smell it if I fill it with tea."

I then respectfully distracted her from the symbol so she could have the experience of reaccessing it to experience comfort and security. I accomplished this by asking her, "Would you mind identifying what you see in the room here right now? And I wonder what your plans are for this weekend, since I need to distract you for a moment."

She identified several plants, a painting, and my container of business cards, and told me that she had plans to go to a movie on Saturday with friends and attend a church function on Sunday.

I then invited her to "take a moment to think of your little blue flowered mug, really focusing on it and all it represents, and notice how you feel."

After another moment or two she looked up with a relaxed expression, and said, "I feel peaceful . . . calm."

I invited her to "take a moment to enjoy this, and know that you can use this mug symbol anytime you wish to reconnect to those calm feelings you identified today."

Mary continued to use her imagining of this visual symbol throughout treatment and in various daily work situations to help her remain calm enough to function. She also benefited from carrying the mug with her when she had to leave town.

Flashbacks: Overcoming the Effects of Traumatic Associational Cues

Flashbacks cause sexual abuse survivors to temporarily associate powerfully to the reexperiencing of emotions and sensations associated with the sexual abuse trauma, while simultaneously dissociating from the comfort and security of the present.

Flashbacks that occur in the therapy session can be depotentiated by reminding the client of her associational cue for comfort and security, or her symbol for the present (Chapter 2), and can also be therapeutically utilized (see Chapter 7) to connect corrective messages of safety, comfort, and validation to the past memory of victimization. However, the client also needs a way to experience a sense of control over the seemingly "random" flashbacks that can occur in social situations and when she is alone.

A Four-Step Approach

Although flashbacks may appear to be random, they are usually triggered by a "traumatic associational cue" in the form of a sensory experience (sight, sound, taste, smell, touch) or an event that literally or symbolically resembles some aspect of the sexual abuse trauma. Once it has been mastered with the therapist's help, the four-step approach described here can be used by the client to depotentiate the effect of flashbacks both as they occur and when trying to make sense of them afterwards. In reference to this technique, one sexual abuse survivor said it enabled her to feel more control because "if you can name it you can tame it."

These following four steps will help the client experience more understanding and resulting control of her flashback experiences both in and outside of the therapy setting:

1. When have you felt this way before? What situation were you in the last time you felt this way?*
2. In what ways are this current situation and your past situation similar? For example, is the setting, time of year, or the sights, sounds, sensations in any way similar to the past situation when you felt this way? If there is another person involved, how is she or he similar to a person from the past who elicited similar feelings?
3. How is your current situation different from the situation in the past in which you felt similar feelings? What is different about you, your sensory experience, your current life circumstances and personal resources? What is different about the setting? If another person or persons are involved, how are they different from the person(s) in the past situation?
4. What action, if any, do you want to take to feel better in the present? For example, a flashback may indicate that a person is once again in a situation that is in some way unsafe. If this is the case, self-protective actions should be taken to alter the current situation. On the other hand, a flashback may simply mean that an old memory has been triggered by an inconsequential resemblance to the past, such as a certain color or smell. In such cases, corrective messages of reassurance and comfort need to be given to the self to counteract the old traumatic memories. Associational cues for comfort and security are useful for this purpose.

*If the client is unable to identify when she has felt that way before, unconscious resources can be elicited to help her gain the understanding necessary for resolution. The original situation can be elicited by inducing a trance either with the externally focused self-hypnosis technique or by connecting an ideomotoric signal (Chapter 9) to hypnotic readiness. Then the therapist can suggest that the client "go to the source of these feelings in whatever way is helpful for understanding and healing."

Utilizing Unconscious Understandings to Create Solutions

The split between conscious and unconscious awareness is common in all individuals but often more dramatic in survivors of sexual abuse. The dissociated learnings inherent in the unconscious can, in some cases, constitute a valuable resource for the therapist seeking to assist clients for whom more traditional solutions have been unsuccessful or unavailable.

Recently, in a workshop setting, a student asked me, when I referred to the unconscious as a resource, "How can you imply that the unconscious is so benign when people have all these horrifying symptoms of frightening psychotic experiences, terrifying recurrent nightmares, and flashbacks of past trauma?" I answered that the intrusive unconscious reaction may be understood as an originally protective unconscious response that has outlasted its usefulness and instead become a symptom.

An example of the above is the flow of adrenaline that occurs when someone is badly frightened. It is a response that is very valuable in that the increased energy available may allow the person to escape the danger. However, the same response may later be translated into pervasive and constricting symptoms, such as anxiety attacks and panic disorders. Another example is the psychological numbing that originally occurred as the much-needed and only available escape from the victimization experience. If it continues past the experience of victimization and becomes chronic, ironically, it can prevent the client from recognizing and escaping from current danger.

Similarly, a constricting inability to tolerate touch and strong impulse to flee from intimacy can originate as healthy self-protective instincts; however, later, far removed from the original context of abuse, they become limiting and troublesome. Recurrent flashbacks can be viewed as originating as unconscious attempts at desensitization. However, flashbacks are likely to be insufficient in cases of severe trauma; having outlasted any usefulness, they constitute further traumatic experiences for the client.

In situations where originally protective unconscious responses have outlasted their usefulness only to become pervasive and problematic symptoms, the unconscious can be used a resource for understanding how to resolve the problem. The most straightforward and reliable way to accomplish this is through a "consultation" with the unconscious. This can take the guesswork out of interventions; sometimes it is the only way the client and therapist can arrive at a solution that relieves the client's post-traumatic stress symptoms.

One way to elicit this unconscious resource of understanding is to gently ask the client to "go inside and ask your unconscious what needs to happen in order for these symptoms (and any other effects of the abuse) to no longer be a problem. What needs to happen in therapy to provide relief for you?" I ask the question in this rather direct way and then suggest that she "go inside and see what comes to mind." The effectiveness of this rather direct approach to the unconscious probably derives in part from the highly developed natural hypnotic abilities characteristic of most survivors of sexual abuse.

Getting Help From the Unconscious: A Case Study

This case illustrates how the above question and its answer can be utilized for resolution of symptoms that have not responded to other forms of treatment.

The client, an adult in her mid-twenties, was in the process of spontaneously recovering previously dissociated memories of being sexually abused by her grandfather. She began to experience intrusive flashbacks of more and more memories of the abuse, which then progressed to a semi-psychotic state in which she would go for several moments without being able to tell the difference between the flashback she was experiencing at the moment and the present world around her. She began to experience intense feelings of rage and terror and impulses to physically destroy things around her. She also began to hallucinate images and voices of long departed family members and even of her mother begging her to keep the fact that she had been sexually abused a secret.

Antipsychotic and antidepressant medications were prescribed but had little effect on her increasingly intrusive and psychotic experiences. She came to her session with me after experiencing several days of this condition. Focusing on her associational cue for comfort and security offered temporary relief, but the comfort stopped as soon as she attempted to think or do anything apart from the cue. Suggestions that she could "keep it in the corner of her mind" while she did whatever things she needed to do slightly mitigated but did not completely relieve her from the intrusive and uncomfortable sensations and hallucinations.

At the beginning of a session, I asked her what seemed to make the sensations she was experiencing even a *little* better. She could identify nothing. I then asked her what others would say appeared to make things even a little better, and what she would be doing differently when these sensations were less of a problem.

She was unable to respond, except to say, "I cannot even concentrate enough to figure that out right now — I don't know the answer." I then suggested that we get some help from her unconscious. I did this somewhat in desperation, because she appeared to be decompensating further and further. Medication and more consciously oriented therapy hadn't relieved her symptoms, and it was obvious that the restraints that she would inevitably be put in if hospitalized because of her rage and escalating threats of violence to herself would ensure nothing but further regression for her.

She indicated that she was certainly willing to get some help from her unconscious because, as she said, "Why not? Nothing else is helping."

I then asked her to: "Find a comfortable position for your body, and then go inside and ask your unconscious to tell you what would need to happen here today for you to experience some relief. Your unconscious can give you a nice little signal when it is ready to work on this, it may be that a finger or a hand lifts, or it may be simply a very pervasive feeling of deep comfort and relaxation, or maybe some other little sign that you will recognize. When you know what you need to tell me about what needs to happen for you to experience relief, you'll have a pleasant urge to refocus on this room. Then, when you are ready, you can reorient and help us understand whatever wise and helpful ideas your unconscious gave you."

The client took a deep breath and comfortably closed her eyes, an apparent signal of readiness to work. Several minutes later, she slowly opened her eyes and gazed at me. I looked at her expectantly and asked, "What did you learn?"

She said, "This is really weird. My unconscious said that I have to find a way to have all these memories put away like on little orderly shelves and cubbyholes, so that I don't have to look at any of them until I have the whole picture and can get some understanding of them. So it would be like the information would keep coming, but I wouldn't look at it until all the memories were in place and organized in such a way that I could look at them all at once and both get an understanding and reach a decision about how I am going to deal with this information. It is really important that I don't have to go through these feelings over and over again every time I have a memory, but instead to just put each memory in its place until I can look at all of the memories and see them in a pattern from which I can make one meaning and sense. I would be retrieving and sorting them without realizing I was doing so until one day all of a sudden I could look at them and they would all be in place and I would have it all sorted out, each in its place. You need to find a way to help me do this, and I don't know how specifically."

To say the least, this unconscious solution initially struck me as a rather tall order. In trying to help the client elicit this sort of unconsciously defined, but not yet developed, response, I wanted to metaphorically communicate a naturalistic example of the desired response. Using a metaphor allows the unconscious more latitude, access to more ways to translate the request into a useful therapeutic change. Because it is less direct and creatively constricting than simply suggesting to the client that "you can now unconsciously do what you just said you need to do," it has more potential for success.

In developing a metaphor likely to elicit the unconscious response dictated by the above "consultation" with the unconscious, I thought of analogous naturalistic examples that might be easily communicated to the client. As I searched my mind for associations to her description, I remembered a recent conversation with a college professor regarding his adventures writing a book using a new computer program. After a brief pause, I told the client the following story:

> In thinking about what you just said, I decided that I should tell you about an experience I had several months ago. I had cooked dinner for some friends and we were all sitting together around a big table outdoors enjoying the warmth of the summer night and the stars. I had been working on an article I was writing that

day, and after cooking a large meal, I was feeling quite tired, but pleasantly so, looking up at all the stars, under the little Russian olive trees in the backyard making their lacy patterns in the shadows and light. One of my friends began to tell me about a book he is working on using this new computer program that has built right into it criteria to automatically organize whatever information it receives in into chapters based on similarity and relatedness of the material. And then the program automatically does an index, cross-referencing everything, doing automatically all those things that used to be a long, drawn-out nightmare for the poor editors, who would have to look at and organize material that they didn't even create. He has written before, and he said that this really made a difference. I just sat there marveling at what human beings can create, and a computer is very limited compared to the incredible capacity of the human mind.

I looked at her expectantly and then changed the subject, telling her a long and pleasant but apparently irrelevant story about a vacation journey. This was intended to prevent her from beginning to consciously analyze and possibly depotentiate the effectiveness of the previous story. I then distracted her by asking her if she was physically comfortable, and as she made the resulting shift in focus away from the story and towards her physical sensations, I asked how she was feeling right now. She said, "Very, very calm."

The remainder of the session focused on practical ways that she could nurture herself that evening and the next day, involving arrangements with supportive others, daily logistics, such as visiting the grocery store, etc. She did not mention and gave no indication that she was still hallucinating as she had been prior to her "unconscious consultation" and my metaphorical communication of her suggested solution. Several months later, she continued to be free of the hallucinated images, voices, and other related symptoms.

Of course, with a metaphor it is hard to pinpoint the precise aspects that cause an intervention to be a success. Based on this and similar but less dramatic cases, I believe that the analogical resemblance of the metaphor to the unconsciously elicited definition of the solution is essential to its effectiveness.

Although I did not think of it at the time, I might have told a story about people resting safely inside a building in the eye of a storm while the hurricane blows everything around, rearranging it into a new terrain that is noticed when the townsfolks emerge from the hall in which they found shelter. They lost some things; however, they were actually able to feel relieved and even somewhat pleased when they realized what they had survived. The rearrangement of the beaches and even the waterways offered new possibilities now that the storm had stopped and they could assess the changes.

The metaphorical response outlined above is very indirect compared to the associational cues, pattern interruption, notes to the self, nondominant handwriting, imagining of solution-focused question, and four-step approach to flashbacks outlined earlier in this chapter; however, all these techniques share the characteristic of utilizing the client's available resources to best healing advantage. While they are effective alone, they can be used to best advantage when combined.

7

THERAPEUTIC DISSOCIATION: TURNING A SYMPTOM INTO A RESOURCE

DISSOCIATION IS the mental process of splitting off information or "systems of ideas" (Gilligan, 1987) from the normal personality in such a way that this information or system of ideas can exist and exert influence independently of the person's conscious awareness (Hilgard, 1977). The adult survivor of sexual abuse is likely to be highly skilled at dissociation. Oftentimes, she is not even consciously aware that she is dissociating, much less that she is good at doing it. She is most likely to dissociate when feeling stressed or when encountering any experiences that remind her symbolically or literally of her abuse.

Generally, dissociation originates as an attempt to survive intense psychological or physical stress. However, with sexual abuse survivors it can sometimes become a pervasive symptom that limits the client's ability to function in everyday life. Rather than trying to eliminate the dissociative response, I have found it more effective to teach the client new and more effective dissociative techniques to use when she is under stress, so that the old, more pervasive natural ones are no longer necessary. This both serves to make the client more aware of when she is dissociating and when she is not and also allows her to chose how and when to do so.

This chapter teaches the therapist how to recognize and utilize naturally occurring dissociation and presents several effective dissociative strategies to assist the client in using her existing dissociative abilities for therapeutic purposes. These include an externally oriented self-hypnosis technique, dissociative containment of post-traumatic stress symptoms such as nightmares and flash-backs, a state-dependent memory retrieval technique to improve information retrieval in test-taking situations, and a naturalistic partial age regression/age progression (Dolan, 1989) technique for the purpose of resolving traumatic memories.

Signs of a Dissociated State

There are various signs that a client is experiencing a naturally occurring dissociated state. One is a lapse in verbal response time, as if a client is "off somewhere else." Another is a stillness in her body or an economy of movement. Still another is a flattening of affect or an apparent numbing of feeling responses. For example, the client may speak about a highly emotionally charged experience with no feeling, as if she is "reporting" it or as if it happened to someone else in whom she has no emotional investment. Pupils may be dilated.

More extreme versions of dissociation include "spacing out," in which the client does not remember the question that was just asked or perhaps stops mid-sentence, forgetting what she was talking about. This more pervasive degree of dissociation can result in concentration difficulties that interfere with academic and work performance.

Of course, the most extreme example of dissociation is multiple personality disorder. Signs of the possible presence of a multiple personality disorder include: dissociative disorders (especially those dating back to early childhood), a history of blackouts, hypnogogic visions, auditory hallucinations experienced as if they are coming from inside the person's head, time distortions, memory lapses, severe headaches, depersonalization and derealization, hysterical conversion symptoms, and phobias (Courtois, 1988). In some cases the client with a multiple personality disorder refers to herself as "we" rather than "I." She may be self-diagnosed, or relatives or friends may have witnessed her "switching" personalities. Switching is often preceded by a severe headache. The personalities may evidence distinctly different mannerisms, styles of dress, speech patterns, and values.

With multiple personality clients, the usefulness of the therapeutic dissociative techniques presented here will depend on the degree of rapport the therapist has managed to achieve with the various personalities. Given the extent of the multiple personality client's already existing dissociation, the more consciously oriented solution-focused techniques described elsewhere in this book may be less threatening and more immediately practical than unconsciously oriented hypnotic approaches, particularly in the earlier stages of therapy. The hypnotic exception may be the externally oriented self-hypnosis technique, which may empower the multiple personality client to elicit a relaxing self-hypnotic state while staying oriented in the present and without changing personalities.

Externally Oriented Self-Hypnosis Technique

The externally oriented self-hypnosis technique is a useful and reliable way for the client to experience the relieving therapeutic dissociation and access to unconscious resources characteristic of hypnosis. It can be used as a relaxation technique, to overcome sleep disorders, as means to connect more thoroughly to the present while in a hypnotic state, to overcome flashbacks, as a deepening technique used in conjunction with associational cues, and to overcome panic attacks.

In teaching the externally oriented self-hypnosis technique in my workshops, I often refer it as "safe self-hypnosis" for survivors of sexual abuse. In inducing self-hypnosis, sexual abuse survivors sometimes inadvertently move immediately into an anxiety attack—or worse, into a hypnotic reliving of their sexual victimization. This is particularly traumatic when they are alone and there is no one around to offer support and to intervene, because it tends to replicate the circumstances of their original experiences of victimization.

Survivors of sexual abuse who learn self-hypnosis can sometimes inadvertently elicit a highly traumatic flashback. This does not result in integration or resolution but becomes merely one more unfortunate experience of victimization. The externally oriented self-hypnosis technique makes this unlikely to happen by virtue of the external content and the fact that it can be used by the client with eyes open, thereby strengthening the connection to the safety of the present. A particular advantage of this technique is that the client can set the context and maintain as needed the security of an outward rather than internal focus, while reaping the benefits of relaxation, comfort, and unconscious resources potentially available in a hypnotic trance state.

I first learned of this technique in a workshop taught by Paul Carter and Stephen Gilligan (1983), who referred to it as the "Betty Erickson technique," respectfully named after Dr. Milton Erickson's wife. I have adjusted it slightly for the sexual abuse survivor by primarily emphasizing the external orientation and the client's option of keeping her eyes open throughout the experience or until she experiences a sense of comfort and security accompanied by a "pleasant" little urge to close her eyes.

The technique itself is very simple and permissive and so is likely to be very nonthreatening to the client. It can be made even safer in feeling by having the therapist first demonstrate it on herself before inviting the client to try it in front of her during the session. I highly recommend that the therapist do this little demonstration of autohypnosis in front of the client, since it will reassure her and inspire confidence. Many clients go into a pleasant trance just from watching and listening to the therapist demonstrate the technique.

Instructions for Teaching Clients Externally Oriented
Self-Hypnosis

The therapist first describes the general procedure and models it for the client, answering any questions. Then the client is guided through the following instructions.

1. The client is invited to "find a comfortable position for your body and a pleasant place to focus your eyes, knowing that throughout the experience you can feel free to make any physical adjustments necessary to maintain your sense of comfort and ease."
2. The suggestion is made that "you can keep your eyes open throughout this experience, or perhaps you will choose to close them, but do not do so until you feel a pleasant little urge to close them."

3. A suggestion is then offered to enable the client to reorient at any time she wishes to do so. "If you want to reorient at any time, of course you can do so very easily just by moving around a bit, or another nice way would be to count to yourself to five, telling yourself that you will be progressively awake, alert, and refreshed with each number, e.g., one . . . more and more awake, two . . . a little more alert, three . . . beginning to feel refreshed and alert. . . . four . . . even more awake, and five . . . all the way awake." The reorientation counting can be repeated if the client feels a need for more time to reorient.

4. The client then names aloud five sights, five sounds, five physical sensations, then proceeds to four sights, four sounds, four physical sensations, and so on, until progressing downward to one of each category. At this point the client can either choose to start again and repeat to further deepen the level of the pleasant, relaxed trance or stop there and enjoy the peace and comfort she has created for herself with her externally focused self-hypnosis.

5. "Losing track of the number or category is actually a very good sign that you are doing well." Often, by virtue of going into a trance state with this technique, the client eventually becomes confused about what "number" or sensory category (sights, sounds, sensations) she is currently focusing on. In this event she should congratulate herself, since the confusion indicates that she has succeeded in entering a nice trance state. She can then either stop and enjoy the sensation of a nice relaxed trance for a while or "guess" where she is and continue with the technique to further deepen her trance state.

6. Further considerations: This technique can be used aloud or silently. The advantages of doing it aloud include the comforting quality of hearing one's own voice and the fact that it allows the therapist to know where the client is on the instruction diagram and estimate what level of trance she is achieving. If it is done aloud, the therapist can use the client's eventual silence as a signal to remind the client of her associational cue for comfort and security. The already existing trance state will generally make the asso-

ciational cue for comfort and security more powerful and effective for the client. Advantages of doing this technique silently include affording the client more privacy and meeting the needs of the client who prefers not to do the technique aloud in front of another person.

Many of my clients successfully use this technique to get to sleep, to relax in stressful situations, and to reconnect to the present when they are feeling symptoms of post-traumatic stress.

Dissociated Containment of Post-Traumatic Stress Symptoms

Inherent in dissociation is the ability of the client to respond unconsciously in an intelligent and autonomous manner (Gilligan, 1987). This ability can be a useful therapeutic resource for the sexual abuse survivor, as the following intervention illustrates.

Sexual abuse survivors commonly complain of intrusive, recurrent nightmares and flashbacks that literally or symbolically replicate the original abuse. They can be chronically pervasive and can, as a client put it, "make life a living hell," in which the abuse is reexperienced over and over again.

Therapeutic interventions focusing on retrieval and resolution of the traumatic source from which the nightmares or flashbacks stem do not always immediately or reliably halt the symptom. Some clients may become psychotic in an apparent primitive attempt to defend from these excruciatingly frightening and intrusive symptoms. In these and related cases of chronic flashbacks and nightmares, the client's dissociative abilities can be used to alter the degree of intrusiveness and the manner in which the symptoms are experienced, providing a safe dissociated "container" for the symptom.

Since flashbacks and nightmares are essentially unconscious phenomena, it is not surprising that an unconscious intervention can be effective. In some cases, the following technique has provided relief even when antipsychotic and other psychotropic medications have failed to ameliorate the symptom.

The therapist begins:

> This is a funny-sounding question, but I'm asking it very sin-
> cerely and asking it to your unconscious mind especially, since that
> is a part of you that has been experiencing these symptoms, and so
> it is the part of you we turn to for help with them. . . . Would you
> be willing to have that nightmare in your right arm while you are
> asleep here instead of in your dreams? You really wouldn't have to
> be aware of it at all, just your arm feeling it, and your arm can be
> nicely asleep, having its own dreams while the rest of you relaxes.
> And when you're ready, please give me a little signal that your
> unconscious is ready and willing to do this for you; it could be an
> effortless little lifting of one of your fingers, a little head nod that
> feels like it is happening all by itself, whatever sign that you and I
> would be able to recognize. And in the meantime you can just relax
> and leave it up to your unconscious.

The above may initially appear to be a ridiculous question or
suggestion. However, it is a practical, achievable option for some
survivors of sexual abuse, who may be excellent hypnotic subjects
by virtue of their coping and survival skills. The client can be
asked to signal an unconscious response to the above question
using an ideomotoric finger lifting. In cases I have observed, if
she is indeed willing, the client's arm then will show the only
evidence of an apparent flashback or nightmare, usually slight
ideomotoric tremors or rigidity, but without any accompanying
images or emotions.

In some cases, a client may deliberately choose to have her arm
"have the nightmare" before she goes to sleep, so that she will not
be traumatized or awakened in her sleep by the intrusive symptom. Other clients have used this to contain and reduce the recurrent flashbacks that previously have chronically troubled them in
their waking state. Yet other clients are able to apparently "let
their arm do it" with little awareness of when or how this occurs;
nevertheless, they achieve symptomatic relief. I do not have statistics to prove the percentage of effectiveness of this technique; I
simply offer it as one more option for empowering the client to
achieve relief from symptoms that defy more direct and conscious
techniques.

State-Dependent Memory Retrieval

Sexual abuse survivors are prone to memory problems (Briere, 1989; Gelinas, 1983; Herman, 1985) that can impair academic performance and, as a result, severely limit job acquisition. The scaling technique described in this section is a simple but effective way for clients to overcome this dissociative response.

Conceptually derived from a study technique originally developed by Freda Morris (1979), this approach helps sexual abuse survivors overcome the dissociative difficulties that tend to make it difficult for them to retrieve information learned in one setting in another setting. Empowering the abuse survivor to overcome these memory problems is crucial in order for her to succeed in such practical and necessary endeavors as completing high school, training in a chosen profession, and passing initial or periodic exams required by employers in various fields.

The client is asked first to imagine that there is a scale of alertness from one to ten, ten being so anxious that she could have an anxiety attack and have difficulty both studying and performing on an exam, and one being so relaxed that she is on the verge of sleep, so drowsy that her studying and test-taking ability would be similarly impaired. She is asked to imagine the optimal level in between these two polarities. Generally, the client's response is somewhere between four and six. She is then asked to imagine the highest level of alertness that would be tolerable for her in the test-taking situation. Most often my clients select seven.

She is then asked to "imagine that you are about to take the exam. What level is your alertness right now as you vividly imagine being in that situation, your pencil in your hand, at the exam table?" Most clients respond with a nine or ten. I then ask them if there is anything that could make it worse. Classical responses include, "if I couldn't get a parking space and I was late," "coming to a question I don't know the answer to," "if I got lost on the way," and most often, "if I didn't study." Many of these, according to my clients, would raise their anxiety to the top of the scale or over the scale, to eleven or twelve!

I then ask the client, "What could you say to yourself or remind yourself of that would lower it back down to where it was?" I write down whatever response she identifies. Generally, it is a response along the lines of, "It's going to be all right," "I already know this stuff because I studied," "It's not the end of the world if I fail the test." I then ask the client what would lower her level just the smallest bit more. That may include a deep breath, an image of other things in her life that are important, or even her symbol for the present (Chapter 2) or her associational cue (Chapter 6).

Surprisingly, most clients seem to skip down more than a half point in response to my asking what would lower the level "just a little bit more." The associational cue often allows them to lower it two or three points at once. When the client reaches her "tolerable" level, often a seven, I ask her to "just take a break and rest for a moment." I then ask her what she could imagine or say to herself that would lower it just a little more. When she has reached her optimal level, I ask her to again imagine the exam and become as anxious as possible, thinking of anything that would scare her about it, and then we repeat the above steps, using any helpful key words she has identified, until she again reaches her optimal level. After several repetitions, the client is generally able to go from a state of anxiety in imagining the exam room to a state of reasonable comfort in just a few seconds.

I then ask the client to imagine herself in the study situation and to identify her level of alertness there. Generally, it is somewhat lower than the optimal state she identified for the exam situation. I ask her to imagine or think of something that would raise her anxiety just a little higher so that her level of alertness was the same as the level for the exam situation. Generally, the act of imagining the exam situation works quite well for clients in raising their alertness level! We repeat the steps used for the exam situation if needed until she reaches the optimal alertness level when imagining studying.

It should be noted that sometimes a client has difficulty in retrieving information in exam situations because she was a little too relaxed in studying. The exam then evokes a greater disparity in emotional states and this locks out some of the information. This is particularly true with sexual abuse survivors, who tend to become numb and dissociated in anxious states and have trouble at those times reconnecting to resources or information available in calmer states. Just as it is important for the client to be able to gauge and then lower her "alertness" to a more comfortable level in the exam situation, she needs to raise her alertness to a reasonably high "optimal" level for the study session.

I tell my clients that, if they cannot remember something, they can sometimes benefit from simply raising or lowering their alertness to see how that affects their information retrieval. They also may benefit from imagining the setting in which they learned it. Generally, by the end of a one-hour session learning this technique, clients are able to lower and raise their alertness at will in just a few seconds by imagining the things they have identified as helpful.

The session ends with the client's receiving an assignment to begin each study session by imagining herself in the exam setting, identifying her *current* level of alertness and then adjusting it, as needed, to her identified optimal level. I suggest that she end each study session with the image of herself finding out that she passed the test.

This technique can be easily mastered in one session; however, one or two additional sessions of repetition often prove useful in increasing the client's level of confidence and comfort. The dissociative tendencies which cause difficulties in test-taking situations are harnessed with this self scaling technique into an ability to dissociate from anxiety or "spaciness" to reach a helpful level of alertness. I have used it successfully with wide variety of clients from clinical and nonclinical populations; however it has proven particularly effective with my clients who are former victims of childhood sexual, physical, and emotional abuse.

Naturalistic Age Regression/Age Progression Technique for Resolution and Integration of Traumatic Experiences

Age regression is an example of dissociation away from the present and association to the past. Regression back to the trauma does not always occur as the result of therapeutically induced age regression, such as "going to the source of the symptom" or "asking the client to remember what is necessary in order to heal" (see Chapter 9).

Clients may spontaneously regress (Beahrs, 1982), as evidenced by flashbacks and intrusive, vivid memories that appear to occur spontaneously when the client begins recalling already conscious material about the abuse or when memories are triggered by stressors symbolically or literally resembling aspects of the original trauma. The following technique is useful when such situations occur during a therapy session.

If the client appears to be vividly reexperiencing the trauma during a session, the therapist can work with her experience therapeutically while allowing her to access the needed comfort and security that were not available in the original experience.

In some cases, this occurs spontaneously, and there is little time to prepare for the experience. In such cases I suggest the following:

1. If the client has an associational cue for comfort and security (Chapter 6) and a symbol for the safety of the present (Chapter 2), take a moment to remind her of them. Suggest that she can keep these two resources "in the corner of her mind," while she works on the issues currently at hand.

2. As she continues to reexperience the trauma while also being aware of safety and security, ask the client to describe what she is experiencing. As she does this, ask her to go ahead and "tell that more grown-up part of you everything you need to know to heal and what you need right now." (This should be done with care, if at all, with a multiple personality client, so as to ensure that a nonsupportive personality part is not inadvertently elicited.) This request implicitly introduces a mixed state of awareness, allowing the client to shift between thinking of herself as the young child experiencing the trauma and as the older adult person who survived it and presumably has more resources available. The client can express what happened to her in the first person and then shift to the nurturing adult part of herself to express much-needed acceptance, understanding, and meaningful corrective messages.

3. Help the client make the shift, when ready, to the nurturing adult part of her personality, e.g., "What does that younger self need to hear right now? What can you say to comfort her?" Common responses are "I need to feel safe,"

or "I need to know it will never happen again," or "I need to know it wasn't my fault."

4. When the client identifies a healing message, such as "you're safe now," or "it wasn't your fault," she can be directed to "tell that younger self that message now, and notice what difference that makes . . . and imagine as the years go by . . . the difference this now makes in future . . . all the different ways that healing message affects you . . . and your unconscious mind can repeat this healing message anytime it is needed or useful."

The above technique can be used to empower the client to insert the healing messages she needs into the traumatic experience and integrate the effects into the future.

Suzy

A 25-year-old divorced mother of two, Suzy came to therapy requesting help resolving symptomatology associated with her known history of sexual abuse by her stepfather. The session described here occurred in the seventh week of her treatment.

During a psychotherapy session, Suzy had been discussing the possibility of confronting her stepfather regarding his sexual abuse of her. In the midst of discussing how she could best protect herself while doing so, she began to vividly reexperience memories of her victimization. Although the information was not new, the emotions attached to the memory were more vivid than ever before. She began to cry and said, "I'm really scared. I'm remembering it like it's happening again, and I can't make it stop. I feel like I'm going crazy, or that I could really hurt myself just to try to escape from this. I can't make it go away." She began to tremble.

I asked her to take a deep breath, to open her eyes and take a look at the room, and remember the symbol that reminds her of the safety of the present (her wristwatch). I then asked her to think of her associational cue for comfort and security (an image of herself in a favorite "safe chair" at home in a certain body position). She looked around the room, touched her watch, and assumed the body position she associated with her associational cue for comfort and security. I reminded her that "You can keep these two things in the corner of your mind all through our session today, while you work with these feelings and memories."

I then asked her to describe what she was experiencing. "I feel like he is touching me again 'down there' (indicating thighs and genitals) just like it's happening again—when I was nine years old."

I asked her, "Is there anything else you're experiencing?"

She answered, "Well, every once in a while I kind of remember to feel my watch and I think of the chair and it's a lot easier to breathe then, but all through this I keep coming back to feeling so scared. I'm just so scared. I want to run away but I can't."

I wanted to identify what she was needing, so I gently asked, "What does that little girl need right now? Tell the older part of yourself what you're needing, and anything else you need to say, too."

She answered. "I need to feel safe. I'm just so scared."

I asked, "Anything else you need right now from that nurturing, older, part of you?"

She said, "No, just to feel safe."

Wanting to elicit the adult part of her personality, I asked, "What comes to mind that would be a nice way to comfort that younger self who is feeling so scared right now?"

She replied, thoughtfully, "I need to tell her it won't happen anymore, that it's safe now. And I'll protect her."

I repeated slowly, "You'll protect her," and added, "Tell her those things you just said, and [with expectant emphasis] then notice what difference that makes."

She said, "I feel better, but I'm still scared."

I said, "Ask the little girl what else she needs."

She said, "I don't want to confront him alone. It's too scary. I want someone else there with me."

I asked, "How does that loving adult self respond to that fear?"

She said, "I'm not going to do it alone. And I am *never* going to let anyone hurt me or touch me when I don't want them to ever again."

At the end of the last sentence, she began to sound angry. I said, "You sound really angry and I wonder what that means for the little girl part of you—and the adult part, too."

She said, "When I'm mad, I'm strong. I don't have to think

about doing it alone so I don't embarrass him. I'm going to have someone with me—you or maybe my aunt or maybe both. I don't have to take care of him anymore."

I asked, "What difference does knowing that mean for that little girl part of you, now and in the future?"

She said, "It's going to be a lot different. More free, I guess."

Her face had regained some of its normal color and she was again breathing in a regular rhythmic fashion. I asked, "Is there anything else you need right now—either as the little girl or as the grown-up you?"

She said, "No—I feel okay. I just need to do some planning. But I'm not feeling those feelings anymore like I was before. That was very scary."

I wanted to validate the healing messages she had given herself, so I said, "You did some important work today. I wonder what it will be like in the coming years as a result of those important messages you gave that little girl part of you today."

She said, "It will be a lot better. I just know."

The above session was not the first or the last time in the course of her two-year therapy that Suzy had to deal with intrusive feelings or memories that "spontaneously" occurred as she struggled to restructure her current life and relationships into a meaningful and nurturing pattern. However, the utilization of the "little girl" and nurturing adult "older, wiser self" concept served her well through the various feeling memories that tended to intensify just prior to addressing core issues like confronting the perpetrator, attempting to resolve nonsupportive relationships and ending those that did not subsequently become nurturing, and moving toward healthy life goals such as starting college, applying for a job, and looking for a good, safe daycare program for her kids. Ultimately, what was good for the "little girl" held wisdom for the adult self as well, who also needed to protect herself and choose situations that were in her best interest.

I believe that Suzy's practice in nurturing the "little child" part of herself also positively affected her ability to be a nurturing and loving mother to her own two young children. She could later remember addressing her own "little girl" while also experiencing herself as a nurturing adult and draw on these experiences to achieve the same kind of nurturing responsiveness to her own children. This relationship between her inner adult and child self images provided her with a model of how a nurturing adult responds appropriately to a child, in contrast to the damaged, narcissistic adult mother who focuses on the child's fulfilling the mother's needs.

Originating as healthy and adaptive response to survive childhood abuse, dissociation becomes a constricting and often frightening symptom after outlasting its usefulness. The therapist needs to empower the client to redirect the learned dissociative tendencies in useful and integrative ways, so that they become resources rather than bewildering afflictions. The various techniques offered in this chapter provide ways to accomplish this, so that, rather than "unlearning" the dissociation, the client merely refocuses it in a healing direction—a far easier and more therapeutically rewarding endeavor.

8

THERAPEUTIC TASKS

THIS CHAPTER describes various therapeutic tasks that I have found to be helpful in working with adult and teenage survivors of sexual abuse in individual and group treatment settings. Included are tasks to facilitate integration of recently retrieved memories, exercises to strengthen the client's ability to connect consistently to her inner resources and to contain her symptoms, and rituals to facilitate feelings of completion and letting go. I offer these tasks in the hope that the therapist will not only use them to assist clients in the healing process but also be inspired to co-create new therapeutic assignments with their clients. For further resources, I recommend *Symbol, Story and Ceremony* (Combs & Freedman, 1990) and *Rituals in Families and Family Therapy* (Imber-Black, Roberts, & Whiting, 1988).

A major advantage of therapeutic tasks is that they can function both during therapy sessions and apart from the therapy hour, enabling the client to integrate therapeutic learnings and changes in uniquely meaningful ways. When the client is allowed to individualize them, appropriate tasks can accelerate her healing process. Tasks should only be assigned to clients who are willing to do them. Trying to get a client to do a task she doesn't want to do risks symbolically replicating the abuse situation. If a client refuses to do a task, the task is probably not sufficiently meaningful for her, or perhaps the timing of an assignment is too early or too late in the therapy process.

With the exception of those learned from other therapists and teachers, all of the tasks described in this chapter came from the ideas of clients in response to my asking them what they felt they needed to do to heal. The best assignments are often those that a client gives herself!

Time Line

Derived from a technique developed by Lucia Capacchione (1979), the "time line" is a way to record the information the client remembers in chronological order. A line is drawn horizontally across the middle of the longest side of a sheet of paper. The client's birthdate is recorded vertically near the far left edge of the line. Any important events affecting the client before her birth (such as the loss of a family member) can be recorded in the space just to the left of the birthdate. All other significant events can then be recorded vertically across the time line in their order of occurrence, until all of the client's significant memories have been recorded. Often, we need several pages, which are taped together to give the client a visual record of life events. When not in use, the record can be rolled up as a scroll.

The time line is a good way for the client to record traumatic memories; however, to be most helpful, it should include memories involving other significant life events, such as starting and completing school, moving to a new house, meeting and knowing a childhood friend, a first date, etc. These provide perspective, as well as a more accurate portrayal of the context of the client's life. Clients have told me that the time line provides the relief of "having it all written down once and for all." It can be used in individual therapy and is also useful in group settings.

Future Time Line

The time line can be extended into the future to allow the client to record goals she would like to achieve in a chronological and concrete manner. For example, one client recorded projected dates for completing college, getting a job, moving, etc. In combination with the actual life time line, the future time line can be particularly evocative. Like the time line, it can be used in group and individual settings.

Rainy Day Letter

Like the healing letters described in Chapter 4, the following assignment is designed to provide comfort and resolution for the client in times of future stress. The "rainy day letter" (Schaub, 1989) is a letter the client writes to herself when she is feeling strong and hopeful. The purpose of the letter is to remind herself of her strengths, so that the letter can be read as needed during subsequent periods of pain and doubt. Included in the letter should be reminders of all the things that she feels are reasons to keep living, as well as the progress she has made, her strengths and accomplishments, and her hopes for the future.

Rainy Day Tape

This is simply a tape-recorded version of the rainy day letter for clients who prefer to speak rather than write their messages.

The Medicine Bundle

A meaningful task for adult and adolescent survivors of sexual abuse is to make and use an Indian "medicine bundle," derived from the medicine rituals of the American Indians. The bundle is composed of symbolic articles and perhaps written words evocative of the client's healing resources. The bundle can be wrapped in leather or cloth or other material, and can be tied up and carried around with the client.

If small, it can be worn in a pouch near her heart; if larger, it can perhaps be carried in a purse or knapsack. The contents are highly individualized; however, they should evoke feelings of strength, healthy inner convictions, and self-nurturance. For example, a bundle might contain pictures of supportive loved ones, dried flowers or herbs from a favorite woods or field associated with peace and safety, a piece of jewelry or scrap of clothing from strongly supportive others, and something symbolic of strength such as an eagle feather.

The medicine bundle can be used in individual therapy as an assignment and later as a resource the client can draw upon during times of stress. It can also be used in a group setting. Each member can show and describe the contents of her medicine bundle in a group ceremony.

Letter from the Future

The purpose of the letter from the future (Capacchione, 1979) is to help the client create hopeful associations about her future self. My clients have found this assignment to be particularly powerful and often repeat it at times when they need to acquire self-confidence before attempting various goals, such as enrolling in school or succeeding in a job. The letter is written by the client as if several years have passed and she is writing to a friend or perhaps to the therapist. She describes her life as if the events she wishes to have happen have already happened. For example, a client who wishes to enroll in college might write a letter from the future to a friend, describing her life now that she has finished college and mentioning how she is now spending her time as a result of completing the degree. The letter, of course, is not mailed, but is kept by the client to read as needed to reconnect to feelings of hope and positive future expectations.

An Imaginary Funeral for Lost Family of Origin

A client said to me, "Even though I lost my family, my mother and father, and one of my sisters because of the incest, I never got the same kind of resolution of my grief that I would have if they had actually died. At least if they had died, I would have been able to go to a funeral and know that my relationship with them was really over. I'd really grieve it and finally be done with it."

In the assignment that evolved from this client's grief, the client is asked to hold an imaginary funeral for the family members she lost as a result of the incest. In preparation, she may want to collect and discard any pictures or objects that symbolize her past connection to them. Burning the pictures will have a special and relieving significance for some clients. The client can invite understanding and supportive others and hold a wake in which she speaks about her feelings toward each of the people she is "laying to rest." She may want to hold the funeral alone, with supportive others, in the presence of the therapist, or in a support group.

At the conclusion, she is to bury something that symbolizes the person(s) for whom she held the funeral. She is to prepare by telling the other participants their role in advance: that after the burial she will receive expressions of comfort from them, just as a bereaved family member would at a real funeral. If others are not invited, she might prepare words of comfort that she can read to herself, plan comforting recordings of music to play, and send herself flowers. Sexual abuse survivors who have devised their own versions of this ritual have described powerful feelings of relief and closure.

Divorce Ceremony

Other clients have said similar versions of, "I don't feel like [unsupportive family members or perpetrator] are dead; it might even be less painful if they were. But I feel that I need to separate from them in a clear and permanent way, like a divorce."

In the resulting task, the client creates a meaningful divorce ritual to symbolize a complete and final parting from the family member(s). The divorce ceremony can be prepared for in a manner similar to the above funeral ritual. The client might choose to write a divorce decree and read it aloud or play a tape of it or have someone read it aloud to her. If this is done in the presence of others, they should be aware that their role includes expressing comfort as they would to someone who has just been divorced. Like the funeral ceremony, this ritual allows some clients to experience closure that is otherwise unattainable.

Bodywork

A client said, "I have all these bad feelings stored in my body, I need to find a way to release them." The resulting therapy task of finding a positive manner of releasing the "bad feelings that had been stored" there led her to seek bodywork. For many clients, massage, Feldenkrais bodywork, or other kinds of body therapy done by a respectful and sensitive bodyworker can be very meaningful therapeutic experiences. Such bodywork may accelerate the healing process and provide the client with integration that psychotherapy alone could not achieve.

Artistic Self-Expression

"I have so many feelings bottled up inside me. I need to get them out. Words alone just don't do it for me." This was the complaint of a client who later produced a series of wonderful personal watercolors depicting her feelings about the childhood trauma, her feelings as an adult, and the eventual feelings associated with resolution.

Several sexual abuse survivors whom I have seen in therapy have already been very accomplished in artistic self-expression. However, even those without previously identified artistic ability have found meaning in the assigned task of expressing their different feelings about their sexual abuse, their healing, and their integration. Creating art that reflects such feelings can result in a series of meaningful works or in one large project. Responses to this assignment include collages, a series of face masks, dance, a tape of music, sculpture, painting, videotape, photographs, and an Amish "sunshine and shadow" quilt.

Consultation with a trained art therapist can provide both therapist and client with fruitful ideas. Dance therapy can also provide a meaningful direction for clients who "speak" their feelings more fully with movement.

The Healing Symbol

One way to empower a client to individualize a task is to ask her to find a metaphor or symbol that speaks to her (Combs & Freedman, 1990). The client is asked to find something that reminds her of her healing self and then watch as her image of this symbol evolves. One sexual abuse survivor purchased a fragile plant, saying that it symbolized her present and future healing self, because she knew that she could nurture it into a large healthy plant with love and tenderness. The image of the large healthy plant then grew in her mind into a tree that sheltered her and eventually evolved into the symbol of a house that was solid and safe. It is probably still evolving.

Self-Nurturing Rituals

Sexual abuse survivors are likely to be all too familiar with self-destructive rituals, such as internally criticizing and blaming themselves following social and work interactions, bingeing and purging, drug and alcohol abuse, cutting on self, and other painful behaviors. In addition, as a consequence of learning to put their needs aside, they may be very good at taking care of others. What is needed, as one of my clients said, is "a way to develop habits of being good to myself."

The self-nurturing ritual task requires the client to discover and act out a self-nurturing ritual that is new and enjoyable. I ask clients to repeat the ritual daily for at least two weeks, since the repetition within the therapy context allows it to become familiar enough so that the client is more likely to continue it when it is no longer assigned. It may seem odd that clients who recognize that they need to become more self-nurturing need an assignment to help them accomplish this. However, as one client explained, "Having to tell someone else whether you did it or not gives you permission to do it. I seem to need it to be homework in order to feel that I have the right to do it in the first place."

Nurturing rituals that clients have started and continued include buying themselves fresh flowers every week, taking a special herb-scented bubble bath every night; going to a botanical garden, park, zoo, or other nurturing place every week; writing regularly in a journal or diary; cooking a special meal for themselves one day a week; having weekly afternoon tea and cookies with a loving friend; reading for an hour a day; laying their clothes out the night before and preparing in advance to make mornings serene; and regularly doing artwork or some other form of creative self-expression, dance classes, etc. To help clients identify useful components of self-nurturing rituals, I ask them to make a list of nurturing activities, places, and people (Capacchione, 1979). If they later have difficulty figuring out ways to nurture themselves, the list can be used as a resource.

This assignment can be used in group or individual settings. Just as making an agreement with the therapist to be nurturing with the self strengthens the client's ability to allow herself to do so, the group responses to the task assignment and completion can function as a powerful permission for members to become self-nurturing.

A Present-Focused Activity

A client said, "I need to get more in the present. I'm thinking about the past all the time, and I'm spacing out in the present. I feel like I'm more involved with living in the past with all these terrible memories than I am with living in the present. They're always in the back of my mind, and sometimes in the front, too." This called for a task that would empower her to do what she asked: "get more in the present."

In the resulting task, the client is asked to choose to learn something new that will require her full attention in the present in a rewarding way. Learning a new language, dance lessons, stained glass lessons, a nature class, learning a new sport, Zen meditation, and taking an acting class are examples of the kind of present-centered activities that some clients have selected.

Write and Burn

Commonly, a sexual abuse survivor complains, "Now that I'm in touch with my anger, I don't know what to do with it. I've tried to express it with physical activities like working out, but I have so much rage that I am afraid I'll really overdo it and hurt myself." The task of writing the feelings out, reading them, and then burning them (de Shazer, 1985, pp.120–122) can be very satisfying for some clients, and the metaphor of the letter going up in flames can provide some relief and closure. This can also be applied to feelings of hurt and sadness. In a group setting, clients may want to put all their writings together and watch the flames burn them, knowing they will no longer have to carry these feelings inside them.

Anger or Hurt Tape

"I know I need to get my anger out, but I don't like to write, and writing doesn't access those feelings for me. How can I let it out?" The task of expressing anger verbally on a tape recorder has been a very powerful release for some clients. I suggest that they add to the tape, listening to it over time, until they feel that they have truly expressed the feeling completely. Sometimes this has taken hours and, in other cases, days, weeks and months. The client can then play the tape for the therapist or other supportive people, who can validate the feelings expressed and congratulate her on letting the feelings out. After this the client can decide what would be most meaningful to do with the tape. One client, clearly recognizing the hard-won value of her anger, chose to put it in a safe place so "it would be there for protection" in case she ever needed to remember those feelings again. Other clients have buried, stored, or destroyed their tapes; one client carried the tape around for a while to "become more comfortable with anger." Feelings of hurt and loss can be expressed and validated in the same way.

A Message to the Child from the Past

A client said to me that she had "left a part of myself back on that land in North Dakota. I need to reconnect with that little girl I left behind." The task of finding a way to speak to the little child within can be highly individualized and highly rewarding for the client.

The client who had lived in North Dakota made a tape of loving things she needed to say to that little girl who had been abused. She then took a journey across several states, ending up in the field where she had played as a child. She buried the tape there and felt satisfied that she had reconnected to that younger self and repaired some of the damage that had been done to her. Clients have written letters, poetry, and children's stories; others have expressed their "message" in music and artwork. Choosing where to put the message is also very important. For example, a musician might choose to listen to the recorded music message for the inner child just before she goes to sleep, like a bedtime story, to feel nurtured. Another person might like to bury it in a significant place, as the woman from North Dakota did. Others have chosen to place the resulting message in a drawer where it is safe, and still others have put the message somewhere prominent where they will see it every day.

Nurturing the Inner Child

A client who had been badly abused told me, "I never got nurtured as a child. I missed out on all those normal things that a little kid should get." The task of experiencing some "little kid" activities can be very rewarding and nurturing as well as bringing a lightness into the client's life. The client is asked to identify appealing and meaningful activities that would be appropriate for a child and arrange to experience them. Some clients have chosen to have actual children they know join them in their versions of this task, such as doing things like going to the zoo, having ice cream, going to a toy store, playing frisbee, and getting a new puppy. Other clients have bought themselves wonderful transitional objects missed in their actual childhood—like cuddly teddy bears, rag dolls, and other meaningful symbols. In many cases, they report experiencing comfort from these things.

This task can be very significant for some very deprived clients, who without it may feel unable to give themselves permission to create and enjoy these much desired childhood activities. I have found this to be particularly true with male clients, who as children may have received powerful messages that they were not supposed to need these things. Sexual abuse survivors who are parents may take special delight in enjoying these experiences with their children, knowing that they are not only nurturing their daughter or son, but also symbolically nurturing the child within themselves.

By necessity, this list is far from exhaustive. My hope is that it will encourage therapists and clients to explore and develop the unique and highly personalized therapy homework tasks that can evolve from the special needs of sexual abuse survivors.

9

SAFE REMEMBERING OF
DISSOCIATED EXPERIENCES

HOW DOES ONE go about making the process of remembering dissociated sexual abuse experiences a safe one for the client? By "safe" I mean that the process should be conducted in a manner that maximizes the client's sense of comfort, security, and control while retrieving and resolving memories of the abuse.

A common phenomenon of sexual abuse is the victim's tendency to dissociate from the traumatic experience for the purpose of self-protection and survival. Since dissociation is unreliable as a long-term defense, the memories are likely eventually to emerge. And even clients who maintain partial memories of the abuse from its onset are likely to remember more in the process of therapy.

Dissociation is most accurately viewed on a continuum, from mild dissociation such as daydreaming to lapses in attention, spacing out, and, in the more extreme forms, traumatic amnesia and multiple personality (Braun, 1986). While this chapter deals with some degree of dissociation and traumatic amnesia, a thorough discussion of the extreme dissociation seen in clients with multiple personality disorder is beyond the scope of this book. However, the techniques offered can generally be used with multiple personality clients once rapport and trust have been secured with the various personalities associated with the original trauma.

Techniques to assist the client in safe remembering include the use of ideomotor signals to assess the extent of the material that needs to be recalled, retrieval of basic information through yes and no signals, and various options for remembering material while protecting the dissociated state. These options include orientation to the source of symptoms, reviewing memories separate from emotions, and retrieval of information through automatic writing. Last will be included a pseudo-orientation in time technique for the purpose of integration and resolution of the retrieved memories.

Traumatic Amnesia

Traumatic amnesia in its extreme form refers to the complete repression of memories associated with a traumatic event. It is an extreme defense reaction to inescapable trauma. Survivors of sexual abuse may suffer from extreme forms of traumatic amnesia, sometimes having no memories for extended periods of childhood (Courtois, 1988). Some clients have no memories of years. This extreme and very thorough form of dissociation needs to be approached with care. The main reason to help a client break through such an amnesia is that it is unsuccessful in completely protecting the her from the debilitating symptomatic effects of the sexual abuse trauma and is actively interfering with the resolution of those symptoms.

There are two specific situations in which it is therapeutically indicated to assist a client in recalling and then working through the repressed traumatic material: (1) when the client is already beginning to remember the previously repressed material; and (2) when both the client and therapist strongly suspect sexual abuse, the client is suffering from symptoms known to be indicative of sexual abuse, and these symptoms have not responded to less intrusive forms of treatment, such as solution-focused therapy. Often in these cases there is a known family history of sexual abuse, and the client may be aware of a sibling's abuse but have no memory of her own.

The client is assisted in overcoming the amnesia not just for the sake of remembering but specifically in order to resolve her symptoms. These symptoms might include repetitive nightmares symbolically representing the abuse, such as dreams of being endlessly pursued or mutilated; sleep disturbance; eating disorders; substance abuse; compulsive sexuality; sexual dysfunction; chronic anxiety attacks; and other symptoms outlined in Chapter 1. The therapeutic goal is to assist the client in accomplishing the memory retrieval and therapeutic resolution of the trauma and associated symptoms as efficiently and comfortably as possible.

Doubting the Reality of the Information Remembered

Commonly clients who have very recently reclaimed previously dissociated memories of sexual abuse subsequently doubt that the memory is real. I believe that clients actually need that bit of doubt at first in order to ease into the realization that the abuse did occur. Rather than trying to dissuade them, I encourage them to hang onto the doubt as long as it seems necessary for them to develop their own sense of truth about the experience. Eventually, they come to terms with the reality of the memory.

Doubting clients should be cautioned, however, also to respect the individual truths of other family members who do consistently remember being sexually victimized. There is an unfortunate tendency during the "doubting" and denial phase for some victims to aggressively verbally attack other victims who are farther along in the remembering process. This needs to be monitored by the therapist, so that clients in the process of beginning to recall dissociated memories of their abuse do not discount and thereby psychologically victimize their siblings or peers in group treatment settings.

Preparation for Safe Remembering

In cases of unconscious dissociation and traumatic amnesia in the context of physical and sexual abuse, it is important to retrieve *only what is necessary for healing* and to frame all hypnotic work with this goal in mind. "Only what is necessary for healing" should be kept in a corner of the therapist's mind at all times when working with clients suffering from dissociated traumatic memories. Never should traumatic memories be elicited merely to satisfy the therapist's curiosity, clinical experimentation, or, as I have seen in some cases, apparent voyeuristic tendencies of colleagues witnessing the hypnotic work.

The client's unconscious protective mechanisms must be respected and worked with cooperatively. To do otherwise by having the client summon all her traumatic memories without discriminating which are crucial to her healing is much worse than sloppy clinical work. It is tantamount to a "rape of the unconscious" (Erickson & Rossi, 1989) and constitutes revictimization.

When a client tells me that she is beginning to recall long dissociated memories of sexual victimization, she often sees her unconscious as an enemy that has betrayed her either by repressing the memories in the first place or by failing to keep them from coming up now. I respond with empathy about the difficulty of having the memories come up for her unexpectedly like this. At the same time, I respectfully point out the benefits of her dissociative abilities, which protected her in the past at a time when she really needed that and when, presumably, nothing else was available for her. I point out that healthy children dissociate when possible to protect themselves and survive experiences that they cannot otherwise control or escape. I express appreciation that she had this healthy ability to help herself unconsciously. And I express my sincere belief that, even though coming to terms with these intrusive memories may seem very difficult or even impossible at the moment, she has resources that can be utilized to help her eventually achieve greater resolution, relief, and peace than she has ever known before. Sometimes the client asks if we can use hypnosis to "shut the memories off." I tell her that we can use hypnosis to make the memories less intrusive, but that she will probably have to remember whatever she needs to remember in order to heal and feel relief.

In *The Courage to Heal*, there is a poignant exchange between the two authors, Ellen Bass and Laura Davis, describing the time period when Laura was coming to terms with her own previously dissociated memories of sexual abuse. Laura asks Ellen, "Isn't there any way out?" and Ellen replies, "The only way out is through . . . " (p.15). I like to tell my clients this story because it contains the therapeutic presupposition that they *can* get through this experience.

It is also important to reassure the client that she does not have to get through this experience alone, that the therapist will see her through it. While the therapist may assume clients know this because of the therapy setting, clients with long dissociated memories of sexual abuse are likely to feel extremely fragile and vulnerable as the memories begin to emerge and greatly fear abandonment despite the therapist's past support and availability.

In order to be prepared to safely remember whatever emerges in response to these techniques, the client should have in place a symbol for the present (Chapter 2) and an associational cue for comfort and security (Chaper 6). These symbols, which may in some cases be one and the same, function as a sort of unconscious "safety net" if the traumatic memories become extremely vivid and overwhelming or if the client experiences difficulty reorienting. In some cases these devices may avert a psychotic episode for clients accessing extremely intrusive traumatic experiences. The therapist is cautioned *not* to proceed with deliberate retrieval of traumatic memories with any client without first developing these basic devices for reorienting the client to the safety of the present and connecting to the comfort and security of the associational cue. Not only does this way of proceeding ensure a comfortable and safe hypnotic experience for the client, but it also encourages unconscious cooperation from the client.

Ideomotor Signals

An ideomotor signal is an unconscious response that often feels effortless to the client, as it were occurring "all by itself." Eye closure and arm levitation are examples of ideomotor responses that commonly occur in response to hypnotic requests. I like to use finger signals with clients who are in the process of remembering previously dissociated material because they allow both therapist and client to monitor the unconscious process. One way to use ideomotor signaling is to induce a trance and then develop the signals. While the therapist's request for an ideomotor response can function as a trance induction in itself, I like to begin by having the client first identify something that reminds her of the safety of the present and then take a moment to recall and enjoy her associational cue for comfort and security.

If trance deepening is needed, the externally oriented self-hypnosis technique (see Chapter 7) can be used. When a comfortable state of trance has developed, I ask the client to sit back and enjoy the state and, when she is ready, to "notice which finger lifts first, knowing that finger will be a 'yes' finger, signaling readiness to do unconscious work, and also a way to signal 'yes' in response to questions. The next finger to lift can be the 'no' finger, and the third finger to lift can be the 'I'm not yet ready to know consciously finger.'"

Perhaps because they had to develop naturalistic hypnotic abilities to survive childhood trauma, my clients tend to be very adept at developing these signals. Usually all three fingers lift sequentially within a few minutes. However, sometimes it has taken a half or three-quarters of an hour, and in some cases it certainly may take much longer. During that time, the client can be told a relaxing story or invited to just let her mind drift while her unconscious does the work. I give the client the suggestion that her "unconscious can make whatever inner adjustments are appropriate and meaningful while the fingers are in the process of lifting."

Client's Personal Styles of Signaling

It should be noted that some ideomotor signals are so small that the therapist must watch very closely to notice the little flicker of movement in the finger. Often the client will report that it "feels" like a much bigger movement than it is. Conversely, sometimes the finger will lift quite dramatically, and the client will have no sensation that it is lifting; in fact, she may not be aware of the movement until she happens to look down at her hand.

Occasionally, a client decides, apparently unconsciously, to make the signals so subtle that only she can identify what they are, and the therapist can only learn by having the client report the response. One client experienced the ideomotoric response only later, when she tried to elicit it herself, away from my office. Perhaps these departures from the exact hypnotic request reflect a need for self-protection and privacy. At any rate, in such cases I express appreciation for the client's ability to choose her own special way of signaling herself, and simply rely on her telling me what her ideomotor experience is and what it means in terms of "yes, no, and I'm not yet ready to know consciously."

Some individualized signals can be very idiosyncratic; for instance, one woman chose these signals: "Yes" was a "funny feeling in her forehead," "no" was "tingling in her right knee," and "I'm not yet ready to know consciously" was a spontaneous deep sigh!

Another chose arm levitation for both "yes" and "no" signals, using alternate arms; her "It's not useful to know consciously" response was a slight stiffening of one arm and a lack of levitation.

Others "do it their own way," while making things fairly easy for me to observe. For example, some clients have used very tiny head nods and shakes for yes and no signals and chosen a finger lifting to be the "I'm not ready to know consciously" signal. With a signal as basic as a head nod, how does one differentiate unconscious signaling from conscious signaling? In such cases I rely on the client's sensation that her head is moving "all by itself" and my observation of small, jerky movements typical of ideomotor responses and not characteristic of the client's more conscious head movements. When the client wants me to see her signaling and other observable signals appear to be unavailable, I sometimes suggest the unconscious head shakes and nods as an alternative or as a way for her to "translate" her ideomotoric response into something I can discern.

While the client's occasionally idiosyncratic departure from the standard approach to these signals can make things a little more complicated for the therapist, the resulting signals can be used in the usual way for the purpose of empowering the client to obtain answers to yes and no questions without re-eliciting the actual experience of trauma.

Testing the Ideomotor Signals

Once the ideomotor "yes," "no," and "I'm not ready to know consciously" signals have been set up, they should be tested using neutral questions to elicit the appropriate response and to provide the client with comfort of increased familiarity with ideomotor signaling. For example, to elicit a "yes" response, the therapist could ask a client named Mary, "Is your name Mary?" Similarly, the "no" response could be elicited by reversing the first question, asking her if today is Tuesday (when in fact it is not), or posing other innocuous questions that require a negative response. The "I'm not yet ready to know consciously" can be tested even without knowing what specific material could elicit this response. The therapist says to the client, "Let's ask your 'I'm not yet ready to know consciously' finger to lift one more time just so you can be confident that signal is nicely in place."

Once the client has developed the ideomotor signals for "yes," "no," and "I'm not yet ready to know consciously," she can ask herself various questions regarding her dissociated memories without re-eliciting the actual experience of victimization. The most common question sexual abuse survivors ask themselves is "Was I in fact abused?"

Ideomotor Signals to Gauge the Extent of Dissociated Memories

The ideomotor arm or finger lifting can afford the therapist and client with a helpful unconscious "map" of the extent of the work that lays ahead in retrieving the necessary dissociated information. This can be accomplished in a rather straightforward manner, by asking the client to let her unconscious finger response show how much of the material that must be recalled in order to heal has already been remembered. The finger (or arm or hand) raised to the fullest extent possible can serve to indicate that all the material that needs to be recalled in order for the client to heal has been recalled.

This assures that sufficient work has been done on recalling the past and that the remainder of therapy can focus on supporting the client in sorting her feelings into a manageable order and making the life changes necessary for her to know that she is truly healed. Slightly or halfway raised will show the client and therapist that progress has been made but that there is still some retrieval work to be done. These signals can be confirmed by using the "yes" and "no" signals to answer such questions as, "Have you now remembered everything you need to learn at this point in order to heal?"

As mentioned earlier, it is important to emphasize recall of material "necessary in order to heal" or "necessary to live a satisfying life" rather than the general category of all repressed traumatic memories. When the finger signals that the remembering has become complete for healing purposes, the client is afforded a sense of resolution—she knows then that she has accomplished remembering what she needs to know about the past in order to go on in the most productive, healing way possible. The client may always have some repressed memories; however, ideomotor signaling enables the client and therapist to to accurately judge the point at which sufficient work has been done on the resolution of the past. This ideomotor "gauge" can be used throughout the therapy process as a way for the client and therapist to assess and monitor progress made with various other complementary hypnotic techniques for safe remembering.

Finally, the client can experience further self-validation by experiencing her own ideomotor "yes" response to the question, "Have you learned everything you need to know in order to heal?"

Ideomotoric Signals as a Resolution Technique

For a few clients, when, through ideomotor signaling with their unconscious, they have obtained verification that something did in fact happen to them and identified that the person they suspected of the abuse did abuse them, this has resulted in an apparent resolution of the problems stemming from the past dissociated memories. Apparently, this simple verification of the abuse, accompanied by the suggestion that the unconscious will make appropriate adjustments, allows the client to sort out and restructure associated feelings and family relationships and work successfully to resolve symptoms that are occurring in the present. Sometimes, it happens that the abuse was relatively limited in its degree of trauma and the client has apparently already succeeded in making some healing inner adjustments, although she has not been consciously aware of doing so.

This response of "letting go" of the dissociated memories and experiencing symptom resolution relatively quickly after obtaining answers using the ideomotor signaling is not, however, common. Nevertheless, the exceptions are intriguing. Along with the gentle, nonintrusive quality of this approach, the exceptions argue for using this ideomotor technique as one of the first approaches to addressing the client's request for retrieval of dissociated traumatic material.

Remembering a Dissociated Resource from Childhood: Regression to a Pleasant Memory

Sexual abuse survivors often complain that, as part of forgetting traumatic experiences, they have also presumably forgotten some pleasant and very meaningful experiences from childhood. A delightful way to build comfort and familiarity with the process of retrieving dissociated memories helpful for healing is to suggest that the client "let your unconscious choose a long forgotten pleasant memory that will be a healing resource for you now and in the future." This suggestion can be preceded by having the client do the externally oriented self-hypnosis technique (Chapter 6) or correlated with an ideomotor signal. For example, "When your unconscious is ready to give you a long forgotten memory of a pleasant time in the past that will be helpful in your healing . . . your finger will lift comfortably all by itself. When you have remembered what is appropriate about that resource, your finger will effortlessly drift back down to rest on your lap."

In response to the above suggestion, one adult sexual abuse survivor remembered a poignant and rare (in her life) experience of being held tenderly by an old Catholic nun while riding in a crowded car. She fell asleep and when she woke up the nun had gently placed a little medal in the child's open hand with the suggestion that God would watch over her. There was much comfort attached to the memory, and it became a valuable present resource for eliciting feelings of peace. Other survivors have remembered loving encounters with pets, nature, instances of appropriate behavior from otherwise abusive parents, simple but precious moments of carefree play with childhood friends, and other meaningful experiences.

When Memories That Bring Comfort Also Bring Pain

Occasionally the resource from the past will also elicit some feelings of loss, particularly if the memory is associated with a loved one who has died. The client's feelings of loss need to be respectfully and compassionately acknowledged. However, emphasis should also be placed on identifying what good things the positive memory she retrieved symbolizes to her and what valuable aspects of the experience she wants to continue to remember and make use of in the future out of respect and loyalty to the loved one.

For example, in my own life, memories of my deceased grandmother still carry the pain of loss; however, intertwined with that pain is the much more important experience of knowing her and the resulting conviction that healthy relationships that existed in the past can make powerful and healing differences when recalled later in life.

Going to the Source of the Symptom

Clients sometimes come to therapy wanting to "remember what happened so I can quit having these problems" with compulsive eating, panic attacks, kinesthetic flashbacks, and other symptoms of sexual abuse that have defied more traditional forms of treatment. In such cases, a useful technique is to induce a trance and to ask the client to return to the source of her symptom (e.g., sleep disorder, nightmares, sexual compulsions), remembering only what is necessary for her to know in order to accurately understand and resolve the presenting symptoms and any other symptoms that have brought her to therapy. Once the client identifies her symbol for the present, trance can be induced with the use of the associational cue to provide a context of safety and comfort.

A nice adjunct to the above induction is to tell the client that her finger or arm will lift while she is doing the remembering and rest back on her lap when she has done as much work as is needed or is appropriate at this time (Rossi, 1986), and she will feel an ongoing sense of comfort in that part of her body. This ideomotor signal will allow both the therapist and the client to gauge the process of the remembering, while providing the client with a constant kinesthetic sense of comfort in her fingers, hand, and/or arm.

This hypnotic procedure can be guided by three simple successive requests from the therapist. For example:

1. "Let's ask your unconscious mind to let us know when you are ready to begin working on this, by signaling with your finger lifting, as you go comfortably back to the source of those symptoms, remembering only what is necessary and helpful for you to remember in order to heal. . . . "
2. "And while you are working on this, doing the remembering, your finger will stay lifted up so we both know that work is being done. And all the while you can be aware

at the same time of that nice comfortable feeling in you finger, and it can extend into your arm and hand and wherever else it is needed. . . . "

3. "And when you have done whatever remembering and helpful inner adjustments are necessary and appropriate right now for you to heal, your unconscious will let us both know by having that finger come back to comfortably rest in your lap."

Automatic Writing

Some clients present writing as a powerful resource for them. While writing, they have experienced expressing and sorting out important feelings and in some cases learning of repressed memories through seeing the words form on the paper as they pen them. Here, automatic handwriting can be a valuable naturalistic technique to assist the client in learning whatever additional information she needs to know in order to heal. This can also be used with the directive that the client go to the source of a specific symptom in order to learn what is necessary in order to heal.

The technique I like to use is as follows: I have the client put a pen in her hand and a large tablet of paper on her lap. I begin by having her write a word that reminds her of her associational cue for comfort and security at the corner of the page, where she can see it easily throughout the experience. I also have her identify something that reminds her of the safety of the present; if it is different from her associational cue for comfort and security, I have her write that in another corner of the paper where she can see it and remember what it symbolizes.

After having the client focus on her associational cue for comfort and security, and optionally, also employ the externally oriented self-hypnosis technique, I gently invite her to:

1. "Feel free to take some time to really enjoy all the things your symbol for comfort and security brings to mind, while your hand and fingers get ready to write whatever is appropriate for you to know today in order to heal."

2. "When your hand is ready to start doing that helpful and

valuable work for you, you'll feel a nice urge for your hand to move and it will do so all by itself, while you continue those comfortable and meaningful thoughts about that symbol."

3. "And you can read along as it writes, or not, as you like, always knowing you can look at the word on the corner of the page whenever you need extra comfort, because that is true also, and you can experience what those corner words mean, even as you're remembering the other information with your hand and fingers."

Upon completing this technique, some clients do not look at the new words they have written, preferring to have me keep them in their file so that they can look at them later, when they are ready. I respect these requests, because clients are in the best position to know what they need and when they need it. Some have later spontaneously remembered what they wrote, and others have told me that knowing they left the information with me meant that it was "no longer locked inside." If the client has given permission, I usually read what she has written. If for some reason she has requested that I not read it, I of course honor her request.

Generally, my clients have subsequently expressed readiness to look at the material they have written. This is fortunate, since I sometimes greatly need their help in deciphering the handwriting! Apparently, the unconscious is not necessarily concerned with good penmanship. In some cases, however, the hand writing has been quite legible, which suggests that perhaps the client has become well practiced at writing in trance states in her journal and in other naturalistic contexts.

Most frequently, the client chooses to read what she is writing while she is writing it or just afterwards. An interesting unconscious phenomenon for the client is the sensation of not knowing what word will come next until she writes it.

The Movie Screen

Some highly visual clients prefer to retrieve dissociated information in a more exclusively visual manner. A nice technique is to suggest that the client "view the information appropriate to learn today in order to heal from a comfortable distance as if it were a movie or video, with the sound off, the color altered or changed to black and white, as needed, to ensure that you can watch it without feeling the feelings of the characters on the screen but . . . merely viewing it from the compassionate vantage of the adult you are, watching a movie from the past."

The client can be asked to report what she is learning as the "movie" progresses and, if she begins to feel overwhelmed, coached to change the color, size, or distance from the picture, or even temporarily stop the movie while she accesses her associational cue for comfort and security or symbol for the present. Some clients have watched the whole movie in one session, while other clients have watched a little at a time over several sessions, based on their preferences and instincts about what they need. Telling the therapist what she is experiencing during the movie may help the client to avoid becoming the person in the movie. However, some clients prefer to "watch" the movie silently and then describe it, and succeed in maintaining their observer position.

The above techniques are certainly not all-encompassing, and are meant to provide ideas and examples of how safe remembering can be adjusted to meet client's various individual needs.

The Advantages of Connecting the Intervention to the Trauma State

Despite the various techniques presented above for maintaining the client's level of dissociation from the full impact of the trauma, when a memory comes up the resulting state is likely to be one of emotional intensity. This emotional intensity may or may not occur while the memory is being retrieved, but it will certainly occur afterwards, as the client begins to integrate the new information and resolve the traumatic memories. This heightened state is sometimes necessary (Erickson & Rossi, 1989) and can actually be ideal for effective therapeutic intervention to lessen the impact and constrictions caused by the original trauma.

Simply having the client consciously visualize the addition of a significant experience to the trauma memory does not appear to have the same therapeutic effect as introducing these interventions when the client is already in the highly emotional state that results from remembering or having just remembered the trauma. It appears that the lingering symptoms associated with a past trauma may be most effectively mitigated when the client is in a state that to some degree elicits the actual feelings associated with the original event.

The above should not be distorted to imply that the strategies outlined to make remembering safe for the client should not be used! While those dissociative strategies offer the advantage of providing some control over the degree and duration of the traumatic feelings elicited as part of remembering, they do not block out the associations to the trauma that are necessary in order for the therapist to intervene effectively. They simply give the client more control of the remembering process and, in so doing, make mitigating it more manageable for the therapist.

Techniques for Resolution and Integration of Memories

Mitigating or removing the impact of the trauma from the client's life does not mean "erasing" it. That is really not possible, except in the sense of repression, which is what the client has already been doing without many therapeutic advantages. A better way to view the task of resolution is as the therapist's addition of something else to the original experience. That significant "something else" does not knock out or erase the trauma; instead, it greatly reduces its impact or effects. There are, of course, many ways to accomplish this, and I will provide several examples of techniques that can be adjusted by the therapist to meet specific client needs.

Adding New Content to the Memory

Simply reminding the client of her associational cue for comfort and security will to some degree change and mitigate her experience of the memory of the trauma, because, as one of my clients said in retrospect, "When it happened back then, I didn't have any resources except to go inside and hide. Just remembering the park and my dog made it feel much different—it was still scary to look at, but it couldn't consume me to the same degree it did when it happened the first time."

However, the associational cue for comfort and security is unlikely to be sufficient to significantly alter the impact of the trauma. To truly restructure the experience of the trauma and thereby alter the effects on the client, a more personalized and significant piece of information needs to be added and that information is best elicited from the client. There are two reliable ways to do this: (1) adding what she needs and noticing the difference, and (2) attaching a different understanding and meaning to the trauma.

The first involves asking the client as she reports the trauma she is remembering, "What are you experiencing right now, and what are you needing there that you're not getting?"

When the client identifies what she is needing, ask her to "go inside and notice in detail what difference it would make to get that." (The use of the word "would" here is essential, because it functions both as an accurate and respectful conditional term and also contains the implicit unconscious suggestion that it "would" work for the client to do this.)

The therapist can then tell her, "You can continue to be aware of that difference, and you can continue to experience it in whatever way meets your needs. . . . "

Alternatively, if the client is dissociated and experiencing the remembering as an observer, the therapist can request that she "notice what you are needing, and then notice what difference it would make to get that."

In response to the above suggestion, one client imagined going to a hospital and having a large invisible bandage placed over her genitals to heal them and to prevent anything else from intruding into that area. She immediately experienced relief and an absence of the unpleasant tingling sensations in her genitals that had been troubling her. Another client imagined screaming out and having a "security guard" (interesting choice of words!) come to her rescue. Another client imagined white light surrounding her and protecting her so that the perpetrator could not get near her.

The second way to resolve traumatic memories is to arrange for the client to experience a new and mitigating understanding that alters the meaning and resulting impact of the experience. The client is given the suggestion while remembering a traumatic experience that she will notice something *different* in the experience that she never noticed before, something *important and helpful*. Frequently, this directive allows the client to come up with her own unique adjustment.

One specific way to elicit this is to give the client the following directive while she is remembering or otherwise reviewing the memory of the trauma: "As you review that memory this time, you will learn something very valuable and important that you have needed to understand all along in order to begin to integrate and move beyond this."

In response to the above directive one client "really realized" that she could not have escaped and appreciating that she was nevertheless strong enough to survive the experience of victimization. She was subsequently proud of her strength, whereas previously she had been very ashamed that she had not somehow found a way to escape. Another observed that "He thought he could, but he could never touch the 'real me.' I had left my body and was observing at a distance. It was horrible, but I did escape in that way. He could never touch the real person within, my soul." One client said that her "guardian angel was watching and whispering" to her that it was not her that was being abused, just the shell of her body, and it was not her fault. Another "got away" as a result of noticing something different and subsequently remembered the abuse as something she had eventually escaped from.

The Conscious/Unconscious Split

Sometimes, after remembering a previously dissociated traumatic memory and adding a mitigating detail, clients look at me searchingly and say very seriously, "Now I need to forget this again." These requests should be respected. Generally, I respond with the following suggestion: "Your unconscious knows how to forget it again, but knows also that you can bring it up here with me anytime that you need to add anything to it as we did today or to look at it again." In these cases the client appears to be communicating on an unconscious level and protecting her conscious mind from the impact of the trauma by asking my permission and help in "forgetting it again."

One client, in what appeared to be a quite deep trance state, looked at me and said, "I want you to forget it too, so that it's really gone." Perhaps she was afraid that I might bring it up and interfere with the adjustments that she had just made. I did not bring it up again, although she did a few weeks later, at which time she again revisited the memory and added a few more mitigating details. The "security guard" mentioned above was replaced by a shield of transparent spiritual light that protected her, and she began to notice how sweet and lovable she had looked as a little girl and to experience a very loving feeling about herself for the first time she could remember. Afterwards, she again asked to forget what she had just remembered and just to keep the feelings. I realized how correct I had been to honor her request. It was not escape or denial but a request for the necessary space and time to let the therapeutic additions of mitigating hypnotic details have their effects.

A request to forget the trauma after revisiting it may, in some cases, be a dysfunctional form of denial that does not lead to eventual mitigation of its effects. However, that has not been my experience in working with the clients who have made this request. I would urge the therapist to be very careful in assuming that an apparently unconscious request to forget recently retrieved memories should be ignored even partially. Maintaining rapport with the unconscious is essential in assisting the client to overcome the effects of dissociated trauma. To override the unconscious is, essentially, to take control over the client and to overpower her instinctive defense mechanisms by assuming that the therapist knows better than the client what the client needs. This overriding of unconscious defense mechanisms resembles the process of victimization all too well and is apt to be experienced as such by the client, despite the therapist's good intentions.

Nora: The Color of Panic

This case provides an idea of how some of the above techniques as well as techniques, presented in previous chapters, can be integrated in the process of assisting a client in remembering, resolving, and integrating previously dissociated memories of sexual abuse trauma.

Nora sought therapy because she was experiencing panic attacks and physical sensations at work and on the bus that were very intrusive, characterized by choking feelings and intense fear. She had a "funny feeling" about an old family friend that no one would talk about, and anxious, frightening feelings about her father. Recently, her panic attacks had worsened, and she had been repeatedly waking up in the middle of the night, trembling and terrified by dreams of being endlessly pursued and mutilated. Traditional therapy (not focusing on the suspected sexual abuse) over the previous two years had not been helpful in resolving these symptoms; in fact, they had worsened. While voicing some apprehension about what she might learn, she specifically requested hypnosis to "get to the bottom of whatever is causing this so my symptoms will go away."

Preparations were made for the session in which Nora would remember previously dissociated traumatic material in the following ways: A symbol for the present (Chapter 2) and an associational cue for comfort and security (Chapter 6) were developed. She had been given the "first session formula task" list assignment (Chapter 2) and I asked her to bring it with her for the "remembering" session as a reminder of some of her present resources and "all the good things you can count on to keep doing for yourself now and later."

In response to solution-focused questions about her treatment goals, Nora had said that she would know that her problems were better when she was thinking more about her daily life, her husband and kids, and what she wanted to do to enjoy herself, instead of feeling panicky and wondering about the past. She had already identified some things that she had done and could continue to do that helped her feel better, e.g., exercising and treating herself kindly by not overworking or overeating.

She was trained in ideomotor finger signaling and was able to identify and elicit finger signals to communicate "yes," "no," and "I'm not yet ready to know consciously." Prior to the remembering session, we had a session in which Nora accessed a "pleasant experience from the past." In her case it was a memory of rocking her baby sister when she was little. After the above preparations, the client's fear of what she would encounter in her remembering of the dissociated past had been to a large degree replaced by curiosity and a gradually growing impatience to "get on with it."

The retrieval of the dissociated traumatic material then occurred as follows:

Therapist: I would like you to take a moment to get comfortable, knowing that you can make any physical adjustments at any time you need to do so to make sure that your body remains in a comfortable position throughout your hypnotic experience today. I would like to start by having you take a moment to notice your symbol for the present.

Client: Well, I really have two symbols—I have this list on my lap here, and I also have my wedding ring, and of course that symbolizes my marriage, and my husband and my kids, and the life I have now with them.

Therapist: Take a moment to focus on those symbols and know that the feelings and awarenesses associated with what they mean can stay with you all in a corner of your mind all the while you are doing the other remembering work today.

Client: (Nods)

Therapist: And your associational cue for comfort and security— your ocean image?

Client: I can feel it.

Therapist: And that, too, can be a resource in the corner of your mind even as part of you works on the memories.

Client: (Nods again. Her pupils are beginning to dilate, and it is apparent that her thoughts of the associational cue for comfort and security have resulted in the beginning of a light trance state.)

Therapist: And now, is it all right to get some help from your unconscious with this?

Client: (Again nods)

Therapist: I'm going to talk directly to your unconscious, and you can consciously listen . . . or not . . . maybe your conscious mind wants to listen along or maybe you want to visit the ocean for a little rest . . . your unconscious knows what to do to best take good care of you while we get this work done. . . .

What I am going to ask right now is . . . when your unconscious is ready to give you some help with this . . . help in remembering only what is necessary for healing . . . what is necessary in order to understand . . . whatever you need to understand to be able to clear things away . . . and experience comfort in the daytime, and comfort in the nights and in your dreams (*an allusion to the panic attacks and nightmares*). . . . There are so many interesting and comfortable ways to learn things . . . like watching a movie or even watching oneself watch a movie about something very meaningful on a videotape . . . so you have the controls right there in the room to adjust the picture and the volume and sound quality so that it is most comfortable for you as the viewer. . . . And some people prefer to learn from reading about things in a book and still others like to write things down, making a list in your mind of what you understand . . . and many other ways to comfortably learn what you need to learn . . . (*suggestions for protective hypnotic dissociation so that she can "learn" the needed information without reexperiencing the trauma as if it is happening to her now*).

When your unconscious is ready to do this, your "yes" finger will comfortably lift up and let us know that your unconscious is ready to work on this . . . (*suggestion for ideomotor signaling*).

And you can feel free to tell me anything you wish about what you are learning . . . (*suggestion that she will be able to talk during hypnosis if she desired*) or you can save it for later if you like . . . and all the while the ring is on your finger and there's the ocean, too, and of course the list on your lap. And if you need to reorient or need my help for any reason, you can just tell me, or you can have one of your other fingers lift, effortlessly (*suggestion for ideomotor signaling to monitor hypnotic work*), knowing all along that I am here for you with my support, and even when my voice falls silent you can be aware of my friendly and supportive presence here with you in this room (*reassurance*).

Client: (Her eyes have closed, and her "yes" finger has lifted.)

Therapist: And your yes finger can comfortably stay up there while you do whatever work is needed and appropriate for today, and when you have done whatever is appropriate in this session, your unconscious can give you a signal by letting that finger gently lower down until you feel your own reassuring touch on your lap, knowing that you are finished with the work today (*suggestion for ideomotor monitoring of hypnotic work*). I will now fall silent for a little while as your unconscious takes care of the work at hand . . . and you can know that my support and friendly presence are available to you even while I am silent . . . and your unconscious knows how to make the time we have available, 15 minutes of clock time, stretch to feel like and really be just as much time as you need to accomplish this useful understanding. And when your work is done, your finger will give you that pleasant touch and you will have a pleasant little urge to open your eyes.

The client takes a deep breath and her breathing progressively alters to a rhythmic rate; facial coloration alters slightly and her face takes on a slightly asymmetrical form, as her eyes close. These signs are indicative of a gradually deepening level of trance.

As the trance progresses, she apparently chooses not to talk. Her other finger (signal of a need for my help) does not lift, and there are no overt signs of distress. After several minutes, her "yes" finger begins slowly to drift down. Eventually, her eyelids flutter and then open. Her pupils are still quite dilated and she looks at the therapist expectantly.

Therapist: I wonder if it would be a nice idea to pause first, just for a moment, for you to feel that ring and notice that list, and maybe even remember the ocean . . . as you begin to tell me what you learned.

Client: (Her body seems to relax a little more as she begins.) I found out what I thought I would. My dad did things to me. . . . He put his penis in my mouth . . . that's why I feel kind of gaggy and sick to my stomach sometimes and I feel so panicky . . . He, I mean his penis, looked kind of pinkish orange . . . almost the color of this one kind of funny manila envelopes we have at work. It makes me so sick (suddenly holding throat and looking panicky).

Therapist: (Gently) Take a deep breath and look at your ring and your list for a moment. Then go back to what you were saying.

Client: I know now why I get so panicky for no reason at all at work sometimes—it's that color. And in other places, too, now that I think about it. There's that color, sort of, on the ceilings of one of the busses I ride.

Therapist: Anywhere else?

Client: I don't think so.

Therapist: Anything else you learned that you need to remember?

Client: Just that—I know he's dead now, and if he wasn't I think I'd feel really scared . . . maybe that's why I couldn't remember this before.

Therapist: What do you need to tell yourself from now on if you see that color? What do you need to remind yourself?

Client: Well, mostly—that it isn't happening now. It's safe now . . . that it's only an envelope.

Therapist: What will help you remember that?

Client: All the things that remind me of my life now. I guess my wedding ring and all that symbolized, maybe the picture of my kids in my wallet.

Obviously, there was more work to do after this session, as Nora worked through her feelings about her father. However, her panic attacks immediately improved and after a few weeks stopped occurring on a regular basis, despite her sadness about the loss of her tenuously held yet treasured image of her "good" father. No feelings surfaced about the family friend, and I wondered if perhaps his image had originally functioned as a sort of unconscious "screen memory" to protect her from memories of her father she was not ready to face.

Eventually other memories surfaced in her dreams and in the waking state; however, her nightmares were no longer as intense, frequent, or frightening. After approximately 18 months, she began to experience relief from symptoms of nightmares and reported no further panic attacks even in times of high stress. She continued to rely on her associational cue and symbol for the present to ward off anxiety when she was aware of a stimulus that evoked the "pinkish orange response."

In understanding the success of hypnotic memory retrieval and resolution of related anxiety symptoms, it is important to remember that the hypnotic technique was used in combination with the techniques described as preparations and were followed up with the use of the healing scale and regular use of solution-focused questions. The solution-focused techniques described helped this client keep a strong connection to her current resources and maintain her stability while she acquired a positive future orientation and restructured her understanding about the self, gradually replacing guilt and negative beliefs about herself with a belief in her ability to achieve various practical goals identified as healing signs.

As a general rule, when doing any regressive hypnotic work with a sexual abuse survivor, I am careful to begin and end the session with solution-oriented questions. I do this to make sure that the client's connection to current resources and growing "solutions" continues to be maintained and strengthened. This is necessary in order for the client to maintain her sense of stability while resolving issues from the past that are related to her victimization.

10
RECLAIMING THE BODY

ONE OF THE challenges that faces the therapist working with a survivor of sexual abuse is finding an effective way to enable the client to establish — or, in less severe cases, reestablish — a positive identification with her body. This is a particularly powerful therapeutic achievement, which reverberates through many areas of the client's life, most notably affecting her self-esteem, self-awareness, and her ability to be sensuous and sexual in functional, healthy, and personally meaningful ways. In addition, a positive identification with her body will increase the client's ability to monitor "gut level" feelings that are useful messages about her reactions in daily life and decrease nontherapeutic dissociation. Consequently, for example, it will be more difficult for clients with eating disorders to continue to fast and/or purge because they will not have the numbness that earlier pervaded their body sense. As one client said wryly, "It's very hard to vomit now that I'm so aware of how my body feels. I know you're probably not going to be surprised by this, but gagging and vomiting is not a very good feeling thing to do! (laughter) It was a lot easier when I wasn't so aware of how it felt."

Similarly, reestablishing this connection may also help self-abusive clients to stop cutting or otherwise mutilating themselves. One client who periodically slashed her arms, told me, in retrospect, "When I used to do that back then, it was like I wasn't doing it to me. It was just a thing I was doing, an action separate from my body, and either I didn't feel anything or, if I did feel anything, it felt good because it hurt less than the memories and it made the memories go away for a while because I could think about having the power to kill myself. Now when I think about it, and I still do think about it sometimes, I get this tight reaction inside like, ARE YOU NUTS? THAT'S MY ARM!" Other clients have told me that they cut in the past because it made them feel "real" and that reassociating to their body made them feel real in a different way.

Probably the most poignant result of empowering a sexual abuse survivor to reestablish positive feelings about her body is the subtle joy of everyday sensuality. One day a client told me with a visible sense of wonder, "This may sound silly, but I had completely forgotten the feeling from when I was a little kid and I could feel the sun warm on my face and arms. Yesterday, walking through the park it happened, and for the first time in so long I can't remember, I FELT it." She had tears of joy in her eyes.

In talking frankly about sensuality and sexuality, the therapist must model an obvious sense of healthy comfort, so that the client can openly discuss any difficulties she is experiencing and identify possible solutions. Empowering a formerly sexually abused client to reclaim her sexuality may be a delicate step for the therapist. It is imperative that the client not feel intruded on, lest the invasive aspects of the original trauma be symbolically reenacted. In most cases, this is easier to accomplish if the therapist is the same gender as the client. In terms of actual physical intimacy, it is important that the therapist communicate that the client has the right to say no to her partner or spouse about sex, so as to avoid giving a message of obligation.

In many cases I have observed both as a therapist and consultant, techniques traditionally used in sex therapy, such as sensate focusing, not only appear to offer little help for the sexual abuse survivor but may even exacerbate symptoms of anxiety and flashbacks. Consequently, we have developed solution-focused interventions to enable the client to reclaim her ability to experience her sensuality and sexuality positively. These were originally tailored to the expressed needs of various individual clients but have subsequently proven useful to other clients who were sexually abused as children. Most important, these ideas have passed the ultimate criterion as described succinctly by a sexual abuse survivor: "I've been to a lot of therapists to try to deal with my bad feelings about my body, and they've talked a lot about developmental steps I need to go through and weird exercises I have to do in order to have healthy feelings about my body and sex, and I never know exactly how to do them—they make me so uncomfortable. What's different about the things you and I have been coming up with in here is that they're *doable*."

What follows is my list of "doable" approaches for working with sexual abuse survivors who want to reclaim their good feelings about their body.

Following the Client's Easiest Path

An effective way to follow the sexual abuse survivor's path of least difficulty in reference to body awareness is to ask her to identify any times when she does experience positive feelings in her body. For example, many clients have identified warm bubble baths, hot tubs, and exercise as times when they notice a good feeling.

Along the lines of the Milwaukee Brief Family Therapy Center's use of exceptions to the problem (de Shazer et al., 1986), clients can be empowered to reclaim more good feelings through an assignment to notice any other times the good body feelings occur. Once the client has identified activities or rituals that allow her to enjoy her sensuality, she can continue to do more of these things. For example, one client realized that angora and other soft fabrics against her skin made her feel safe and protected while she enjoyed the pleasure of the texture. She noticed that skiing and aerobics made her feel a healthy, vibrant sense of her limbs moving freely and her heart beating vigorously. Having initially noticed these aspects of her sensuality as part of a homework assignment, she could then experience them with conscious awareness as she continued to enjoy and identify similar experiences.

While this noticing task usually works well with survivors of sexual and physical abuse, some clients seem initially too dissociated to identify positive body awareness. I suspect this comes from a very legitimate need to protect oneself from painful associations originating with the abuse. In such cases the following exercises can be helpful in enabling the client to reassociate to the body in a gradual, controlled manner that also addresses the pain that may be stored there.

Hypnotic Accessing of Good Body Feelings

For clients who are so dissociated that they have difficulty identifying any time they consciously notice good body feelings, I may use hypnosis, asking clients to recall a time in past when they felt safe and felt pleasant sensuous body feelings. The process is similar to the associational cue technique, except the client is directed to let the unconscious identify a moment of good body awareness from the past. Specifically, the client is first asked to use the externally oriented self-hypnosis technique (see Chapter 7) to induce a trance. The therapist then suggests, "Let's ask your unconscious to come up with a time in which you experienced wholesome, safe, and very comfortable body sensations." The client is directed to "Let the unconscious do the work for you, and you can feel free to just enjoy the surprise or unexpected familiarity of a nice experience. When you have the experience, take a moment to enjoy it and then come back and tell me what it was like for you."

For example, one of my clients identified the long forgotten feeling of meadow grasses brushing against her bare legs while she picked a bouquet of soft buttercups and bluebells and smelled their delicate fragrance. Another client identified the cool feeling of an ice cream cone on her tongue on a hot day as she sat on a cool plastic chair in an air-conditioned restaurant.

Once an experience has been identified, the client can be invited to add or subtract any details that would improve the experience in any way. She can then be directed to focus on all the good feelings that are associated with the experience and have her unconscious select a symbol of the experience that she can use to reaccess those good feelings as needed in the future.

Healing Drawing Exercise

Many clients who were abused still carry associations of the abuse in specific parts of the body. There may be physical scars, or there may simply be very negative associations to touching areas that were involved in the trauma. For example, an abuse survivor who had been forced to perform fellatio as part of her victimization subsequently felt very vulnerable in the area of her throat. Another client responded with great alarm whenever anyone came from behind her and touched her shoulders as the perpetrator had once done. Other examples include trauma associated with the genitals, breasts, and virtually all parts of the body.

Some of my clients have responded very well to a simple drawing exercise (Capacchione, 1979), which may be used both individually and in group settings. The client is asked to draw a simple outline of her body with one line. She is then asked to mark with one color all the places in her body where she feels okay or good. She then is asked to mark with another color any places where she feels she is carrying pain. She then draws the outline of her body on another piece of paper and picks out a color that she associates with healing. She then draws little hearts of healing into all the areas of pain identified in the previous drawing. The client is then asked to identify ways she can be particularly loving to all the parts of the body that she has identified as carrying pain, so she can heal further.

Clients have come up with a variety of symbolic ways to heal their bodies, including wearing soft fabrics in meaningful colors against the affected area, gentle bathing rituals with special scented soaps, herbs, etc. One client drew in a clear shield around her genital area and visualized its presence to feel safe. Many clients have told me that just envisioning a healing color or light in their areas of trauma has proven very meaningful and comforting and has become a meditative practice for them.

Dialogue With Individual Body Parts

Another exercise, which may be adapted for use within the therapy session, as a homework journal assignment, or in a group, involves the client's engaging various body parts in dialogue. The client imagines that each body part has a voice of its own. She is asked to imagine what story the body part has to tell about her life, what gifts the body part has to offer her, and what the body part needs from her. She converses with the body part, offering whatever messages of comfort and healing are needed and receiving whatever information comes forth from the body part's imagined voice. This exercise is not suitable for a client with poor reality testing due to a psychotic or near psychotic state; however, I have found it to be helpful and meaningful for clients who are simply very dissociated from their body due to sexual and physical abuse.

Professional Bodywork

Massage or other kinds of bodywork such as Feldenkrais (Feldenkrais, 1972) have proven very positive for some clients; however, for others bodywork is at least initially too threatening to be helpful. Before treatment, survivors of sexual abuse may sexualize nonsexual touch and find it threatening. Feldenkrais group lessons, in which the participants are led through a variety of subtle movement exercises—on their own but guided by the leader—may provide the right combination of guided self-awareness, privacy, and availability of professional expertise. The group lessons, if led by a sensitive Feldenkrais teacher, are probably the most soothing and nonintrusive bodywork option.

The choice of a bodywork practitioner is very important, since it is vital that this person communicate safety and security to the client and be able to respond appropriately if memories are triggered by touch. I would suggest that the therapist experience a session with the bodyworker before referring clients.

Dance and Exercise as a Way of Reconnecting to the Body

Before a client can feel comfortable with her sexuality, she needs to become comfortable with her body in general. Exercise may be an appealing and nonthreatening way for a formerly abused client to establish a positive sense of body awareness. Several of my clients have found dance to be particularly appealing in that it not only reestablishes awareness in the body but also provides a vehicle for self-expression. When using exercise to reestablish a positive context for body awareness, care should be taken that the client does not overdo to the point of self-abuse, as is sometimes the case with clients with a tendency toward anorexia nervosa.

Self-Massage

Some clients have found it helpful to begin by simply touching their own body parts, starting with a foot or a hand and working gradually over their body, moving from the least difficult to the next least difficult. If the client is interested, she may be given names of books on sexual self-pleasuring. Self-massage may be done as a homework assignment; it certainly should be done privately by the client and not in the presence of the therapist.

The reader may think I am stating the obvious. However, tragically, over the past dozen years I have encountered a number of sexual abuse clients who have been retraumatized by their therapist's inappropriate behaviors, such as a male therapist holding a female client against his bare chest for the purpose of "reparenting" while working alone in a closed office. The client felt understandably frightened and uncomfortable, but felt more uncomfortable protesting this to the therapist, so she endured physical touch that she found intrusive. Perhaps this therapist had good intentions, but these were not enough to spare the client unnecessary additional trauma. She was victimized again in the context of treatment.

Dieting and Treatment of Eating Disorders

Since survivors of sexual abuse are at high risk for eating disorders, this should not be overlooked in diagnosis and treatment planning. It is common to see clients who were sexually abused carrying some extra weight. Conversely, these clients may be painfully thin, suffering from anorexia, or they may be bulimic. What possibly started out as an unconscious attempt at self-protection may be eroding the client's self-esteem in the present.

The specific treatment of eating disorders is beyond the scope of this book; however, it should be noted that often survivors of sexual abuse suffering from these disorders do not overcome the eating disorder until the underlying cause, the sexual abuse, is treated (Courtois, 1988). If an eating disorder is present or suspected, it should be treated concomitantly with the sexual abuse issues.

If the client is obese, she may well gain self-esteem by successfully participating in a nutritionally balanced diet program conducted in a group settings. As excess weight is lost through a healthy regimen and the client hears compliments from others and notices improvement in her reflection in the mirror, she may establish a more positive identification with her body. Some clients have described the loss of their excess weight as a powerful healing sign and constant reminder of "how far (they) have come." Even clients who suffer from anorexia or bulimia may benefit from a nutritionally balanced supervised regimen, as long as care is taken to ensure that they are not starving themselves or bingeing and purging.

The therapist should be aware that the weight may have functioned to help the client feel safe, and issues of protection may well have to be addressed if the weight is to stay off. For example, a 30-year-old attorney who had been 30 pounds overweight since adolescence discovered that as the weight dropped she began to feel very vulnerable around the men in her office and her male clients. It was necessary to identify alternative ways to feel safe. She identified that wearing suit jackets made her feel safer, and she also felt safer if she was sitting behind a table or desk. If there was no table or desk available, she found it helpful to place a large folder on her lap. Other clients have found it helpful while losing weight to take self-defense or martial arts classes to strengthen their sense of personal safety. In addition, martial arts classes may provide yet another context for body awareness. Some clients have found such classes to be very helpful, and others have found them meaningless or even disturbing.

From Sensuality to Sexuality

This simple noticing task can be very powerful, as evidenced by a case seen by Charlie Johnson, in which traditional sensate focusing techniques had been tried and failed. A formerly sexually abused client came to him and requested help in overcoming inhibited sexual desire. He asked her if she had ever experienced any good feelings in her body, and she said she wasn't sure but probably not because the abuse had started very early.

Charlie respectfully but clearly labeled the good body feelings he was talking about as sensuous rather than necessarily sexual and pointed out that it was possible to not feel one's sensuality, as sex abuse survivors had learned to do for good reason. "However," he said, "it's impossible to not *have* sensuality, because we're all born with it. It's just that some people for various reasons learn to separate from it. Sensuality is a very natural part of being alive." His assignment was for her initially to simply "notice" positive sensations that were pleasantly sensuous, such as the texture of her cat's fur, or the feeling of her feet in her skis on the snow, or the sensation of a cool refreshing drink of water in her mouth, etc.

As she noticed more and more pleasantly sensuous experiences in her daily life, he told her that her sexuality was simply one more aspect on the continuum of sensuality she had already been doing a good job of noticing. So he asked her to notice any subtle sensations she experienced that seemed sensual in ways that were even remotely sexual, and to note where and when these occurred, and what difference this made for her.

Sensitive to the fragile boundaries it is so important to maintain (particularly when male therapists are discussing sexual issues with female abuse survivors), Charlie did not ask the client for intimate details; in fact, he encouraged her not to share anything she preferred to keep private. He did ask her to imagine what her life would be like if this sensuous noticing continued, and what effect she thought it would have on her potential enjoyment of sex with her husband. The client decided that it was time to share her noticing with her husband, who was very supportive.

Gradually, the client's noticing what difference her awareness of sensuality made for her enabled her to experience sexual desire for the first time in her life. The couple could then use the client's noticing reports to identify positive ways to be sexual together. This case illustrates how a simple noticing of the exception to the problem, no matter how small (de Shazer, 1985), can lead to a powerful yet nonintrusive solution for the sexual abuse survivor.

Rebellious Behavior

This "path of least resistance" intervention is similar in nature to Charlie's noticing task, except that it allows the client to utilize positive sexual experiences even when they have been very rare and seemingly insignificant. Again, in this case, the couple had previously tried treatment with a traditional therapist without any positive results. In fact, the sex therapy had appeared to exacerbate the problem. I saw this case with Charlie Johnson.

The client, a former incest victim, came to therapy requesting assistance in learning to enjoy sex. When questioned, she disclosed that early in the courtship there had in fact been times, albeit sporadic, when she had found sex enjoyable. However, since the birth of her second child several years ago, she had not experienced any enjoyment and had felt unable to engage in sex with her husband.

Her husband was very supportive and attended the session with her. The spouses were asked to identify what they thought had been different about the times she had found sex less aversive or more pleasant. We pointed out that there is a lot more to sex than just the physical part, and asked them to focus on the details associated with the more positive sexual experiences, for example, the setting, their activities, their moods, style of clothing, etc.

The client and her husband both recalled a memorable experience of positive sex during their courtship, when they had both been relaxing and reading after playing tennis. They had been living in a beautiful setting, and the outdoors had been all around them. We told the couple: "We think you may have been onto something useful back then. Therefore, we suggest that you schedule a weekend or two to go off alone in the next month, and do whatever you can to replicate that kind of very relaxed, beautiful setting, pleasant outdoor activities, and see how you feel in response to that. But most of all, make sure you both have a good time apart from this problem, because you really do deserve a break from the stresses of your work and parenting young children."

Not surprisingly, the couple came back and reported that sex had occurred and had been mutually satisfactory. However, the wife complained that she shouldn't have to rent a room at a resort and schedule a babysitter and a weekend away in order to enjoy sex with her husband. She needed a less demanding way to replicate this experience.

We responded by asking them to think again about the original experience she associated with good feelings about sex with her husband, and to try to think about any other details of the experience that might be significant. They then identified a similar experience during their courtship that had occurred at a resort, when they chose to have sex outdoors and had to be very quiet lest they be discovered.

Asked how she had felt about choosing this setting, the wife smiled and said she had felt "rebellious." So we asked her to imagine other ways that she might express that rebelliousness in her life here and now, ways that would be appealing and allow her to feel that rebellious feeling. She thought of several whimsical ideas, including wearing unmatched socks, serving breakfast at dinner time and vice versa, taking creative but unexpected routes to and from work, refusing to cook at all some days, dressing rather outrageously, and exceeding the speed limit just a little bit now and then. Her husband was amused and intrigued about what effect this might have on their sex life.

Two weeks later the couple returned to therapy and disclosed that the wife had been wearing highly creative and outrageous outfits, had gotten a parking ticket, and had both refused to cook one day and fixed a salad for breakfast and bacon and eggs for dinner on another day. We asked them what effect this seemed to have had on their love life. They began to laugh and told us that they had engaged in satisfactory sex several times since the previous session, but NEVER in the bedroom. Rather they had sex in the dining room, the closet, and other odd places in the house when the children were asleep.

We asked them both what seemed to be different and what seemed to be working for them. They mentioned that, on all of the recent occasions of mutually enjoyable sex, the experience had been preceded by treating each other in very thoughtful and considerate ways apart from sex. The rebelliousness, they felt, had also made a big difference, in that they had become playful together in the context of their sexuality. They pointed out that in the past, because of her history of sexual abuse, discussions of sex and sex itself had taken on a very somber tone. They said, "We lightened up about it."

Wholesome Outdoor Clothing

A variation of the above intervention was used with another client, who was part of a couple but seen alone rather than with her husband. Her recently surfacing memories of being molested as a young child had resulted in painful intrusive flashbacks, and she had not engaged in sex with her husband for several months. She requested help in being able to enjoy sex again and wanted to achieve an orgasm, something she had never experienced. I asked her if there had been any times in the past when sex had felt more the way she wanted it to now. After thinking about it, she disclosed that sex made her feel dirty about her body and said that sex felt safer and more pleasant when she was already feeling wholesome.

I explored what helped her feel more wholesome. In particular, this included outdoor clothes, such as those sold in sporting goods catalogs, and being at places where she had in the past felt more comfortable and somewhat sexual with her husband. Since associations were pleasant, she did not mind trying them and noticing what difference it made. Gradually, she noticed and began to feel more pleasure in any form of physical interaction with her husband. As she began to be aware of sexual desire, she initially felt guilt but then noticed the "wholesome aspect." This was enhanced by her identifying more reminders of wholesomeness, such as flannel nightgowns, cookies and milk, and being really physically fit. Her first orgasms came in dreams about sex with her husband,

and currently she is convinced that it is only a matter of time before the wholesomeness results in orgasmicity within the context of actual sexual relations.

Eliminating Flashbacks During Sex

Flashbacks during sex are a common difficulty for people who have been sexually abused. The flashbacks may be sporadic or they may happen so intrusively and so frequently when sexual relations are attempted as to make sexual intimacy impossible. The client should be given a strong injunction to feel free to say no to sex if she wishes and to engage in sexual activities only when she truly wants to do so. The following are suggestions my clients have found immediately helpful in overcoming or minimizing the impact of flashbacks when they occur during sex:

1. As soon as you are aware that a flashback is beginning or occurring, open your eyes (if they are closed) and notice where you are now. Notice the differences between your partner and the perpetrator, between your current physical surroundings and those recalled in the flashback.
2. Focus on your symbol for comfort and security and use that to defeat the flashback.
3. Stop attempting to respond sexually until the flashback is over and let your partner know what is going on so that it is mutual.
4. Have your partner say some reassuring words that you have identified previously as being useful in this situation. For example, one client taught her husband to tell her, "I'm your husband. You're safe now."
5. Tell the "little girl inside" that it's safe now and you'll never let her be hurt again.
6. Ask for whatever you need to feel safe again. Do not resume sex unless you feel comfortable doing so.

The purpose of these strategies is to assist the client in having more control over the flashback's duration and degree of intrusiveness, if not to stop it altogether. As one client explained, "Now that I have something to *do* in response to the flashback, it isn't quite so scary, because I know it can't go on forever and ever. It sounds silly, but I used to get scared it would never go away. At least now I can make it go away a little faster."

Fortunately, many clients find that using the above techniques halts the flashback very quickly. For example, in some cases, clients report that eventually just opening their eyes stops the flashback so quickly that it is over before they even have a chance to tell their partner that it is occurring. Others have reported that they are very comfortable resuming sexual contact even just a few moments after overcoming the flashback. With time, once a client learns what is effective for her, she may reach the point where any nuance of the flashback can trigger an automatic corrective response. One client who has practiced opening her eyes and reassuring herself to control flashbacks during sex told me, "Now the way I know I had a flashback is my eyes are open for a few seconds. I don't seem to experience much of the flashback anymore that I can tell." In presenting this ray of hope to a client, the therapist should be careful that it is not seen as a "should," since these abilities vary, just as the level of trauma varies.

Some clients report that, once a flashback has started during sex, it is so intrusive that they cannot resume sexual relations for hours or days. In sharing the above suggestions, it is very important that the therapist reassure the client that her need to abstain from sex is understandable and more than acceptable. Too often, survivors of sexual abuse are so adept at putting others' needs before their own that they choose to engage in sexual relations even when the experience is highly traumatic for them, thereby continuing the victimization.

Partners may need support in fully understanding the sexual abuse survivor's legitimate need to abstain from sex to protect herself from trauma. As discussed in Chapter 3, it is valuable to arrange for the supportive partner to come in for a conjoint therapy session with the sexual abuse survivor. The conjoint session gives the therapist the opportunity to ensure that the partner understands the survivor's healing needs in reference to sexual activities. It is very important that the partner not misinterpret the sexual abuse survivor's abstinence from sex as a personal rejection. Some partners are better able to accept the recovery process if it is likened to a surgical procedure, which requires abstinence from sexual relations for an indeterminate period of time to allow healing.

Reclaiming body awareness can be a highly rewarding, although challenging, experience for the survivor of sexual abuse. Many of my clients have said that they had once doubted that they would ever be able to feel anything but loathing toward their bodies. The good feelings they experienced as a result of therapy and positive experiences outside of therapy were unexpected and therefore even more precious than some of the other aspects of their healing from the abuse. The ability to enjoy physical sensations that were once the vehicle of pain, fear, confusion and humiliation illustrates the incredible resiliency of the human spirit and the ability some clients demonstrate to triumph over the past.

11

OVERCOMING THE
RELAPSE DANGER

BECAUSE OF THE nature of post-traumatic stress, survivors of sexual abuse may, despite treatment, occasionally reexperience aspects of their original symptoms as a result of exposure to events that are either literally or symbolically reminiscent of the original abuse trauma. If adequately prepared for this phenomenon, they are less likely to find the temporary recurrence of post-traumatic stress severely debilitating or frightening or so overwhelming as to cause suicidal impulses. Some clients are able to view their current level of "adjusted reaction" to post traumatic stress phenomena as a mastery experience, because as time goes by they are progressively able to limit and therefore control the symptom.

This chapter offers a technique to deal with relapses, with particular focus on preparing the client for the possible event of a temporary PTS relapse, recognizing situations likely to trigger PTS, and predicting and limiting the extent and effects of any PTS relapses that do occur.

Having an Imaginary Relapse

In some cases relapses can be prevented by having the client learn the necessary coping mechanisms from an imaginary version. Developed by Lynn Johnson (1989), the "imaginary relapse" technique can be used to help clients identify possible triggers for relapses and subsequently mitigate or even prevent the occurrence of a real relapse. The client is asked to imagine a relapse in full detail, predict what caused it, and then imagine what she would learn from the relapse. This provides the client with a symbolic, though in effect much less traumatic, substitute for having a relapse. Even if the client later does have a relapse in response to highly evocative and unavoidable stimulus, the approach of "learning from the relapse" will enable her to make some meaning of it.

For example, a client imagined having a relapse in which she reverted to old familiar symptoms of binge eating, panic attacks, and sleeplessness. She said that, after imagining this relapse, she learned that overeating probably would not be a good way to calm herself down from a panic attack, because she would feel so terrible afterwards, and that it would be an equally unsatisfactory way to deal with her sleeplessness.

She decided that, if she did have a relapse, she would need to do something different from overeating, since it did not help mitigate the other symptoms. She identified several things she could do to distract herself from anxiety and the urge to overeat. These included going to a movie, phoning a friend, cleaning her house, writing, completing tasks she would not enjoy doing when feeling good such as sorting out correspondence, cleaning her drawers, sewing, and drinking soothing chamomile tea.

All of these would also be productive—or at least not hurtful—ways to spend time if she had insomnia. She had accurately predicted that contact with her nonsupportive sister could cause a relapse, and when symptoms of anxiety, insomnia, and an urge to overeat did in fact occur immediately following a holiday telephone call from the sister, she was able to recognize the beginning of the flashback. She substituted many of the coping behaviors she had identified in imagination and as a result the "relapse" occurred in a very reduced version.

When I subsequently congratulated her on predicting so accurately and utilizing her learnings so effectively, she said, "Next time maybe I'll catch it before it even starts out of the gate." I said, "You just might. You certainly have the attitude that will help you do that."

In the above situation, I resisted the temptation to say to the client, "Of course you will." I believe that our environment is fraught with stressors that cannot always be controlled. The adult survivor of sexual abuse may, as a result of effective treatment and hard work, be successful in overcoming the effects of stressors as they occur or, rarely, eliminating all stress that could result in a relapse to old painful feelings or self-destructive urges. However, given the nature of post-traumatic stress, this degree of relief may not be permanently attainable, or at least not immediately.

Overcoming the Self-Blaming Tendency

It is very important that the client be helped to not blame herself for relapses, but instead to work to mitigate them when they do occur. One frame that will help her avoid the further damage of self-blaming in response to relapses is the explanation of relapses as conditioned responses to stimuli. Understood in this sense, a relapse can actually help the client prevent future relapses because it comprises information about likely stimuli. Identifying what sorts of situations and experiences cause relapses can in some cases empower the client to predict and mitigate the relapse before it happens.

Often most difficult for the client are relapses to flashbacks of painful sensations and self-destructive urges that appear to come "out of the blue." They can be explained to the client in terms of conditioned responses that may occur as a result of exposure to highly evocative but nevertheless subtle unconscious stimuli. I suspect that sensations involving taste, smell, sound, sight, and texture may all function at times out of the perceiver's awareness. In such cases, even apparently "benign" experiences may contain stimuli that can produce post-traumatic stressors. For example, one sexual abuse survivor experienced intrusive post-traumatic sensations when a piece of chewing gum with a liquid center inadvertently produced sensations similar to those associated with being forced to perform fellatio as part of her victimization (Bass & Davis, 1988).

Sometimes, in addition to experiencing post-traumatic stress symptoms such as intrusive sensations, painful feelings, and self-destructive urges, the client may "revert" to needing to again revisit and sort out her feelings about the abuse. Rather than viewing this as a relapse, it is more useful to understand this as evidence of further integration. Some clients are prone to "beat themselves up" because of their periodic need to revisit the old memories, feelings, and resulting understanding of their abuse experience. Often in such cases they tell themselves personalized versions of the following message: "If I had really dealt with it thoroughly enough, I wouldn't feel this need to deal with it again and again. I must have been resistant in therapy or conning myself."

More rarely, the abuse survivor blames and chastises the therapist for the relapse, with the implication that if therapy had been effective she would never have a relapse. In both cases I have found the following metaphorical story to be helpful in fostering feelings of comfort, self-compassion, and self-acceptance.

"Glass in the Knee"

When I was a little kid, I liked to ride my bicycle up and down the street where I lived. The road was gravel, and I liked to ride my bike very fast. This resulted in my falling off the bike a lot when it skidded on the gravel. Since I wore heavy denim pants, the occasional spills usually resulted in nothing more than mild bruises.

But one day, I had some bad luck. I happened to fall off the bike right on top of a broken Coke bottle. The glass from the bottle went right through my pants and into my knee. I went home and my Grandma and I very carefully and thoroughly cleaned all the glass out of my knee and put some disinfectant on the wound. I didn't enjoy the process, but even then I knew it was necessary, so I endured it. A few weeks later it had completely healed.

Then summer came and I went swimming a lot in the nearby lake. One very warm afternoon, after spending hours and hours in the water, I noticed a funny little bump on my knee as I was drying off. It felt really odd, and it hurt some as I rubbed it. As I continued to rub it, a piece of glass gradually worked its way out. I thought for sure that must be the last piece of it. But then that winter, after skiing and taking a long hot bath, I had a similar experience. Another piece of glass worked its way to the surface.

This continued on and off for several more months, and I have always wondered if even as an adult someday I may feel a funny little bump on that same knee, only to release yet another little piece of that glass. My Grandma and I did a good job of cleaning out that wound; we took care of every piece that we could reach at the time, but sometimes pieces get buried so deeply that it takes a long time for them to finally reach the surface where they can be released.

Clients usually respond to this story by saying that in retrospect they feel that they really did do everything they could do at the time to deal with abuse issues.

Likely Triggers for PTS Relapses

It is a good idea to have the client identify all potential relapse triggers, identify useful existing strengths and coping mechanisms, and then mentally rehearse how she would take care of herself should some of these stressors occur. It may also be helpful when identifying the stressors to describe some of the stressors that have tended to affect other sexual abuse survivors. This section will describe some of these common stressors.

Sometimes events that trigger PTS relapses seem on the surface only remotely related to the content of the sexual abuse trauma, but are highly evocative on the unconscious level because they reproduce the victimization experience in terms of loss of control. Common triggers may include any situation that requires increased trust and vulnerability with another person.

If the client is warned that these experiences may put her at risk for reexperiencing PTS symptoms, she will be more likely to seek support and to take precautions to mitigate or perhaps even prevent the recurrence of these symptoms. What follows is a partial and, since every client is different, necessarily incomplete list of relapse triggering stressors. Flashbacks, which can certainly occur as part of PTS relapse, are not included, since they are discussed in detail in Chapters 6 and 7.

Contact With the Perpetrator or Other Nonsupportive Family Members

A chance or planned contact with the perpetrator or nonsupportive family members can trigger a relapse to old symptomatology. Chance encounters may hold more of a risk because the client does not have the chance to prepare herself for feelings that may occur. These individuals may attempt to psychologically revictimize the client, or their mere presence may evoke powerful and vivid memories of past victimization.

Intrusive Medical Procedures

Any kind of medical procedure that makes the client feel out of control of her body and vulnerable to the actions of someone else is a potential stressor. Surgery or childbirth, which may evoke some anxiety in anyone, can be particularly difficult for survivors of sexual abuse.

The more the client can be provided with ways to experience her own sense of control in the anxiety-provoking medical situation, the more likely she is to be able to avoid or limit the effects of a relapse to old post-traumatic stress symptoms. In situations where the client feels out of control of her body, if interventions are not made, the client's anxiety may produce a relapse to a cluster of old symptomatic behaviors.

For example, a sexual abuse survivor facing an operation may, in response to the anticipated feelings of being very vulnerable and out of control of her body, feel very anxious and regress to past dysfunctional behaviors, such as binge eating and sexual compulsions. She may then experience insomnia as her anxiety increases, and this will of course escalate the other symptoms. One client explained to me why she had regressed to cutting on her arm after almost three years of abstaining from that behavior:

I went to the doctor and he told me the results of the tests. When he told me I was going to have to have surgery, I didn't really think much about it at the time. That night I went out for dinner with a friend. For some reason, I drank more than usual—I just had this urge to have an extra glass of wine. And when I got home, without even thinking about it I went directly to the kitchen drawer where I keep the knives and I started cutting on myself right away. I hadn't done this for years, and after I had done it and I was finally washing the knife off, I had this thought, "I am hurting so bad." Not so much physically, but emotionally. Then I realized how scared I was about their putting me to sleep when they did the surgery. I had heard all these stories about the subliminal things that they can say to you, even accidentally, when you are under anesthesia, and it can have this whole effect on you that you don't even realize, and then I thought, too, what if they make a mistake? I started shaking and crying. I cried all night, and then I called you. I was even thinking about taking all my pills [suicide], because at least then I knew I wouldn't have to go through the surgery.

Now, sitting here, I can't believe I was feeling like that. But it was real. It was like being back three, four years ago when I was first dealing with my victimization. It wasn't a flashback; it was in some ways harder because I've learned to deal with flashbacks and nightmares. This was more like experiencing old feelings in a different situation that didn't seem related.

The therapist should be prepared for the fact that the client may not immediately be aware of the impact of an event, even a major event such as learning that she must have surgery. The dissociative response that helped her survive the original victimization may still be activated by powerful stressors and can prevent her from recognizing her own distress at its inception. In such cases she may not know she is upset until in retrospect she recognizes that she has regressed to past symptomatic behaviors.

Intimacy

As a client heals from the abuse, it is likely that she will be capable of greater intimacy and potentially more and more rewarding relationships. Ironically, this very positive experience may also trigger transitory relapse, because of the loss of control implied in loving and therefore needing someone. The following description by a sexual abuse survivor illustrates the dangers of intimacy for these women:

I met this person and the relationship felt good. We dated for about a year, and it just felt right to both of us, and then he asked me to marry him. After thinking it over carefully, I realized I really loved him and I said yes. I should have felt really good then, but I got really scared instead. I worried that he would try to control me, and I worried that he might betray me, desert me, or abuse me, even though he had never shown any sign of these behaviors. I started to withdraw from him almost immediately. I begin to have panic attacks, and I started thinking about other guys, even though

I didn't have any real feelings for them. And I could not say no to other guys. I had sex with another guy, even though it was really likely that he would find out. But before he did, I broke off the relationship. Then I got really depressed.

It was months later before I realized, in therapy, that I had projected a lot of beliefs about my father [the sexual abuse perpetrator] onto him, and that I had gotten so scared that I regressed right back into my old dysfunctional behaviors. By then it was too late to try to explain things to him; he wouldn't even talk to me. I think he must have found out about my being unfaithful, or maybe he was just so hurt by the way I left. But when I met my husband, I had already had this experience, so I was prepared for these feelings to come up when we started getting really close, and so I had a lot more control. I was able to tell him I was scared, and I was able to realize that he really was different from my father. We got through it.

Becoming Sexual

Of course, becoming sexual for the first time in a new relationship can also trigger feelings of loss of control or, in some cases, flashbacks. Flashbacks can also occur in response to any of the stressors discussed in this chapter. (Specific suggestions for dealing with flashbacks are provided in Chapters 6 and 7 and suggestions for mitigating flashbacks during wanted sexual experiences are provided in Chapter 10.)

Betrayal

Because of the betrayal of trust implicit in sexual abuse, the sexual abuse survivor can be particularly vulnerable to regression to PTS symptoms if she has the misfortune of experiencing real or even perceived betrayal of trust. This can occur if the sexual abuse survivor is treated unfairly in the work setting, if a superior or colleague does not demonstrate loyalty in social or work politics, or if someone she has trusted fails to protect her from verbal abuse.

The most traumatic betrayal for an adult survivor of sexual abuse may well be sexual infidelity by a partner in a committed relationship, since it combines two areas of vulnerability that were cruelly violated in the past: her capacity for emotional intimacy and her sexuality. Sexual betrayal can also evoke feelings of low self-worth associated with her original victimization. When betrayal leads to loss, as it often does, it may evoke suicidal impulses, since it replicates the triangle of betrayal, sexual victimization, and loss that may have occurred when she confronted the perpetrator.

Loss

A sexual abuse survivor came to see me in therapy with the following request: "I need to find some way to make it less traumatic when I have fights with the person I'm dating. I'm so afraid he's going to leave that I force it to happen. I tell him to get out of my life, and then, when he leaves, I literally want to die. I feel like I'm going crazy. It's just like when I was first dealing with all the abuse issues, only it happens every time we have a fight." Even the perceived threat of potential loss can sometimes evoke a terror of abandonment similar to that felt at the loss of adult protection from the childhood victimization. In such cases, the client and her partner need to be aware of this pattern and create ways to interrupt it, usually including a strict agreement to refrain from making statements about the relationship ending in the heat of anger.

Potentially even more traumatic is real loss through abandonment or death. The loss may evoke old feelings associated with the profound losses inherent in sexual abuse. In such cases, it is very important that the client be helped to remain connected to her existing resources and strengths. This can prevent PTS relapses that end in suicide. As with other potential relapse triggers, the client's response to loss can be mitigated by learning from the past and identifying what helps. A sexual abuse survivor compared her two divorces:

> The first time, I got profoundly depressed. It was almost as bad as the sexual abuse. The hardest time was just after we separated. I had to make contracts with my therapist at the time to not kill myself, and I even spent one night in the hospital when I couldn't guarantee that I wouldn't hurt myself. I felt worthless and completely alone, very much as I had a few years earlier when the memories [of the sexual abuse] came up. I really don't know how I made it through that period. But I did make it through, and the feelings did go away after a while.

When my second marriage ended, I felt really bad, but I didn't feel suicidal. Sure, I thought of it, but I remembered how I had felt with the first divorce and that way I knew that these feelings wouldn't last forever—they'd eventually go away. It was very, very hard, but it wasn't like the time before. I knew that I would make it, and I think that is what kept my depression from getting out of hand. I knew what had helped before—work and focusing on the other people I cared about who loved me. I kept right on working and taking care of my kids, and one day, after some time had passed, I felt better. You really do learn from experience.

Loss that occurs through death can have similar dynamics as loss through divorce or rejection, particularly in cases of suicide. Natural deaths may be a little easier for some sexual abuse survivors to deal with, since the parting is involuntary on the part of the loved one; however, in all cases, the feelings of loss of control may be evoked.

Dealing With a PTS Relapse Once It Starts

Generally, the more in control the client feels, the less the extent of the relapse. For example, with intrusive medical procedures, having thorough knowledge about the procedure may enable her to respond to reassurances from her medical care providers.

Taking action to nurture herself may counteract the effects of current stressors. If the client is in therapy or returns to therapy or a support group, she can be reminded of her symbol for the present and her associational cue for comfort and security. Solution-focused questions are another empowering way for the therapist to assist the client in controlling the effects and extent of a current PTS relapse and identifying behaviors and perceptions that can mitigate or prevent future PTS relapse.

As described in Chapter 6, the client may be able to stop or at least reduce the intensity of a relapse by identifying the stressor that triggered it and sorting out how it resembles and how it differs from her original victimization. Identifying how *she* is different now from how she was in the past will also strengthen her ability to separate past feelings and responses from current ones.

In extreme relapse situations, in which the client's life is at risk, hospitalization may be necessary. However, in most cases, if given prompt and extensive support, the client can be empowered to reconnect to the coping mechanisms she has developed. If hospitalization is used in place of such support, it may be for the convenience of the therapist rather than in the best interest of the client.

Erica

This case excerpt illustrates how a therapist can use solution-focused questions to help a client overcome PTS relapse symptoms, so that the experience ultimately becomes one of mastery as opposed to demoralization.

Erica, a 50-year-old professional woman, telephoned early on a Friday morning. She had received treatment for the effects of childhood sexual abuse and had terminated therapy two years earlier. She disclosed that she had had a serious fight with her partner the night before and was feeling extremely anxious and depressed. The partner had left and had not returned home. Erica was afraid of the thought that she might hurt herself; last night and this morning, she had thoughts about taking a bottle of aspirins from her medicine cabinet. Erica requested a "telephone session," and since I had the hour free, I was able to comply. The following conversation ensued:

Therapist: Are you safe now?
Client: Well, for now, I mean technically, yes, but I'm really scared to be having these suicidal feelings at all. It's been a long time since I felt this way.
Therapist: How did you get past those feelings the last time you had them?
Client: I just sort of told myself that I had to hang in there because the feelings would pass—I shouldn't hurt myself because I wouldn't always feel like this.
Therapist: So that was a helpful thing to say to yourself?
Client: Yeah . . . well, I don't know what else I can say.
Therapist: Do you know what triggered these feelings?
Client: I'm not sure, but I think a letter from my sister talking about how she had seen my father. She didn't really say

anything about him, except that she was worried because he was pretty sick, but something about her being worried about him made me feel like she was defending him to me . . . that felt pretty crazy, and I guess I sort of flashed back. I'm just realizing this as I say this, I think I sort of flashed back on Mom and Grandma not standing up for me as a kid when I was abused by him.

Therapist: What difference does it make when you make that connection like you did just now?

Client: Well, it makes sense that I would react more intensely, and I think that is maybe why things got so out of hand with Stephanie [her partner] and I yesterday afternoon. She felt I was overreacting to something my boss had said at work and when she said that I really got furious—enraged is a better word. Then she said she needed to go out for a while just to calm down and think and that made me even angrier, abandoned I guess, but at the time I just felt so angry at her. So she stayed out until about 9:30 and when she came home I was really mad. She called me and told me she was going to stop at our friend's house, so I wouldn't be worried, but that didn't make me any less angry. When she came home I accused her of wanting to leave me, and when she said that wasn't true I just kept arguing. If she hadn't finally left and stayed somewhere else last night, I think it truly could of gotten physical. Now I feel terrible. I think she actually knew that I was reacting to something besides her, because she just kept looking at me kind of strangely.

Therapist: It sounds like a truly terrible evening you had right up until now. What do you feel like you need right now?

Client: I'd like to try to find Stephanie and at least try to explain and apologize, but first I need to calm down.

Therapist: What would be the first small sign to you that you were calming down?

Client: Well, the fact that I called you, I guess, is a sign...

Therapist: What do you think the next sign might be, or has it already happened?

Client: Well, breathing a little bit more slowly, and I feel myself doing that some right now.

Therapist: So what else has to happen for you to know that you have reached the calm state?

Client: I know I'll feel a lot better after I talk to Stephanie. God, I hope she'll forgive me. . . . But, I guess one more thing I could do is to think about my symbol. I didn't think about it at all until now.

Therapist: What happens right now when you think of that purple flower (*her symbol for associational cue for comfort and security*)?

Client: I feel calmer. I think I could probably call Stephanie, now; I think I know where she is.

Therapist: Are you feeling safe now?

Client: Well, I'm not going to hurt myself if that's what you mean.

Therapist: And you know what you need to do to feel better?

Client: Yes—it's not going to be that easy, but it's harder not to call her. Even if she stays mad for a while, I can cope. It was like I lost my center. And I definitely need to have a talk with my sister and find out just where her loyalties are. That feels better, just saying it.

Therapist: How do you think that will be helpful, and what difference will that make?

Client: Well, calling Stephanie will make me feel like at least I've started the ball rolling to reopen communication and try to patch things up. . . . But with my sister, it's more like I need to make sure she's not giving me double messages about my victimization. I don't need that and I won't put up with it if that's what's going on. I really need to talk with her. I just wish it hadn't gotten so out of hand with Stephanie and me last night.

Therapist: What did you learn from what you went through that would help you if you ever felt like that again?

Client: Well, I suppose just to ask myself what, if there is anything, it reminds me of to be feeling like this, feeling strong feelings really out of proportion to what is going on between us. I mean, sometimes feelings like this are justified, and sometimes, to this extreme of intensity like I felt last night, they're not—Steph was paying for what happened to me a lot of years ago.

Therapist: So were you.

Client: So was I.

Therapist: So how would you know that you were doing what

you needed to do if feelings like this somehow get triggered again?

Client: Well, identify what caused them if I can, figure out what they might be reminding me of, if anything, or maybe just acknowledge that I am really mad if, ultimately, it does feel to me that I have reason to be feeling this way.

Therapist: So you would give yourself a chance to figure it out, sort out what you were feeling—how would you do that for yourself?

Client: Well, the main thing is to remember to stop, slow down for a minute, and think, what is this about?

Therapist: Are there times when you have been able to do this in other situations?

Client: Well, I definitely do this at work, with my boss and co-workers, because I don't want get fired.

Therapist: And you've been successful doing it there?

Client: Yeah—I really have.

Therapist: I wonder how you can translate that into other places since you obviously have that in place at work. . . . Would you be willing to notice when you do it, so that you can get more information about how you do that, because it seems obviously valuable?

Client: I will do that. I feel better. I'm going to call her, and I'll call later and schedule a time with you to meet.

Erica later came in for a follow-up session, in which she identified what expectations she needed to communicate to her sister. She has subsequently noticed that there are many occasions when she routinely overcomes extreme feelings of anger that appear to stem from situations that resemble her victimization. However, she notes, "As I identify them, they get less intense. I'm directing more of the feelings back into the people in the past, where the feelings are deserved."

I suggested that she do the healing letters exercise (Chapter 3), and in the next session she described relief after writing letters to the perpetrator (not mailed) and various family members who were not supportive (also not mailed). After a total of three sessions, she has not required further sessions for the past 18 months and appears to be quite successfully integrating her self-identified solution for dealing with intense anger. She believes that she will not have any further relapses, and she is certainly doing everything she can think of to prevent one.

Solution-focused questions, as used above, may allow a client who has already adequately dealt with core issues of her sexual abuse to manage and prevent further relapses. Even clients who are still "in process" about the abuse, as many understandably are, at different stages of treatment are able to respond to questions about what they need in order to heal in ways that are uniquely appropriate to them. When used skillfully, these questions can, at times, prevent symptomatic relapses from occurring during the early or middle stages of therapy.

12
MEANINGFUL COMPLETIONS

THE THERAPIST is challenged to ensure that the client, upon leaving therapy, is able to move beyond her victimization into a satisfying and positive life. Here I present techniques from Ericksonian hypnosis for helping the client more productively utilize role models and reclaim her birthright of becoming the full person whose potential she carries, as well as solution-focused questions for identifying positive and adaptive future goals, perceptions, and behaviors. Suggestions for termination will also be provided.

Identification With Empowering Role Models

Children naturally learn by imitating the adults around them.

One problem that faces some sexual abuse survivors who grew up in dysfunctional families is the lack of appropriate role models for healthy and satisfying patterns of living in the past and present. While the therapist can function as one role model of healthy functioning for the client, this important function should not be limited to the therapist.

I like to encourage clients to identify people who embody healthy abilities or qualities they wish to acquire in the future and to "borrow" from them. Clients with good reality testing may benefit and enjoy the experience of pretending to be someone they admire for a few hours and noticing how this feels. This is not suggested for clients with multiple personality disorder, since it is presumably something they are already doing to an extreme and often dysfunctional degree.

This can be done in a group setting, or the client can choose to do it on her own. The client might choose to dress in a way that evokes for her the personality of the person who possesses skills or qualities she feels she could benefit from imitating. The client can practice engaging in activities and exhibiting the mannerisms and "style" that would be characteristic of the designated person. Of course, if her imitating the selected person is likely to be a very dramatic and potentially disturbing change for those around her, the client may need either to arrange for privacy or to let them know what she is doing, lest they fear that she is a multiple personality or has suddenly become psychotic.

Sexual abuse survivors who have used the "pretending" technique generally pick individuals who embody strength and courage of conviction as well as other desirable qualities and abilities.

They have subsequently told me that the experience of intentional "pretending" was the turning point in their own resulting integration of these abilities. Being given permission to "pretend" for a few hours may accelerate the integration of new behaviors, skills, abilities, and perceptions.

The client does not always discover, as a result of pretending, what she or the therapist thought she was going to learn. For example, one client told me, "I found myself thinking a lot more positively as Mark Twain." Given Mark Twain's wonderfully cynical humor, I was surprised by the pure childlike whimsy and joy the client accessed as a result of her "pretending." This was nevertheless valuable to her as she subsequently showed the ability to ask herself "What would old Mark say?" before approaching daunting tasks. The accessed response was always playful, and her resulting lightheartedness allowed her more easily to do many necessary things, such as applying for a job, setting limits for her children, and making decisions about the future.

If the individual selected to be imitated is highly meaningful, the effects of learning from the "pretending" can be long lasting and fruitful. For example, years ago, while participating in a similar exercise in a workshop setting (Carter & Gilligan, 1983), I chose to "pretend" to be Anais Nin because she was a writer.

There had been no writers in my family of origin. Eight years later, I continue to keep a regular journal, have published several articles, have one book published, am nearing completion on the current one as I write this sentence, and have already started a third!

Solution-Focused Questions to Build a Healthy Map for the Future

As one delightful sexual abuse survivor told me in the final stages her treatment, "I don't want to just overcome the effects of having been sexually abused—I want to be much, much more. I want to be really alive all the way." A former bulimic, this client then described what she wanted in order to "be alive all the way," which formed the outline for her resulting map of a healthy, satisfying future. The solution-focused, future-oriented questions illustrated in the following dialogue can be used to ensure that the client has developed a specific map of what she needs to do to have a future that is satisfying and worth living.

"Alive All the Way"

Therapist: How would you know that you were, as you say, really alive all the way?

Client: For one thing, I wouldn't be deadening myself with drugs or alcohol, and I wouldn't spend all my time sitting eating in front of the TV like I used to.

Therapist: What would you be doing instead?

Client: I would be out of the house, doing things.

Therapist: Are you doing some of that now?

Client: Sure.

Therapist: What kinds of things are you doing these days that would fit that "out of the house, really alive" criteria?

Client: Well, I'm in school. I'm working for my G.E.D. (a high school equivalency degree) and I am working for the future. And my bills are getting paid because I'm working fulltime. And I've been going roller skating.

Therapist: And those things are part of the really alive, out of the house feelings?

Client: Yes.

Therapist: And what difference is it making that you're doing these things now?

Client: Well, I feel a lot better.

Therapist: And you feel a lot better. And I wonder, what difference will your feeling a lot better now, and continuing to do the G.E.D., and working and going roller skating—what difference will those things, *continuing over time*, make in the future?

Client: Well, I'll have a degree and I'll get a better job, and I won't be in debt because I'm paying off my debts, and roller skating (laughs)—well, I guess I'll still have my sense of humor.

Therapist: And anything else you're doing now that would need to continue so you can have that feeling of being really alive in the future?

Client: Well, I don't want to get fat. So that means no bingeing.

Therapist: What will you be doing instead?

Client: Just healthy eating. And exercise, I guess.

Therapist: And what difference will that make?

Client: Feeling better and better about my body.

Therapist: Well, that can only be good. What else needs to happen for you to have that really alive feeling five, ten years from now? How would you know that you had really accomplished that, that you lived up to what you wanted?

Client: I would have found a good relationship and I would be in it on a committed basis, maybe married.

Therapist: What would be a sign to you that you were in a good relationship?

Client: Well, no drugs would be involved. And he would be someone trustworthy, and with self-respect, as well as respect for me.

Therapist: What would help you recognize that?

Client: The way he treated me, but not just that the way he was around other people. And whether he showed any signs of abusing drugs. It would show if I really paid attention.

Therapist: And what difference would that make for you to be in a good relationship?

Client: I'd feel good. I'd really know it could be different for me from what I grew up with.

Therapist: And over time, knowing it can be different for you from what you grew up with, what difference does that make over time?

Client: (very seriously, and with emphasis) It makes all the difference in the world. The difference between life and death.

Therapist: And how will you know you're doing that and continuing to do it?

Client: Just the kinds of things I've been saying. I can do it if I put my mind to it. I'm already doing the G.E.D., so I know I can do it.

Therapist: You really can.

Five years later, the above client is in college, still free from drugs, and dating someone who appears very healthy and nurturing. She is maintaining a normal weight, and is not bingeing or purging. She has required occasional follow-up appointments approximately twice a year, which she uses to identify what she needs to continue and what she needs to add to her current activities.

Sexual abuse survivors often initially lack the ability to envision, much less live out, a healthy, satisfying future. The process of finding out what they "wouldn't be doing" (usually these are the self-destructive behaviors stemming from the sexual abuse) as part of a satisfying, healthy future, and then finding out what they would be doing instead (the most important part), provides them with a concrete map that they can then follow to make their future vision a reality.

A Million Dollars

Occasionally, sexual abuse survivors present idealized versions of the future they want, which may subsequently seem to them to be too big of a step to even attempt. This response seems to occur more often with teenagers than adults. The following dialogue

shows how to translate the larger, more daunting goal into concrete steps that the client knows she can take.

Therapist: What would allow you to say that you were living out
  a satisfying future five years from now?
Client: I would have made a million dollars.
Therapist: And what difference will that make for you?
Client: Well, I'd have money and I could do whatever I wanted,
  and I would have security. And that would give me peace of
  mind.
Therapist: (looking for another exception to the problem of an
  unsatisfying future/present) Are there any times now when
  you experience that security and peace, even in small doses,
  even in glimpses, the smallest bit?
Client: (nonchalantly) Not really.
Therapist: And anything else? Anything else that will be signs to
  you that you're living a satisfying future five years from now?
Client: Not really—just some nice material possessions, like a
  nice house, and a car.
Therapist: So what would be the smallest sign that you were just
  a little closer to having the money for that house and car,
  even the smallest sign?
Client: I'd have a job.
Therapist: And what, for you, would be the smallest sign that
  you were moving closer to having a job?
Client: I'd have applied for one somewhere.
Therapist: And what difference would that make?
Client: At least I'd have the chance of getting one.
Therapist: And what would be the smallest sign right now that
  you were going to be in that position of applying for one?
Client: (laughing) I'd buy a copy of the paper on the way home
  and look at the ads.
Therapist: And what difference would that make?
Client: I could put in some applications on Thursday.
Therapist: And how would that affect you?
Client: Well, once it was done and I got a job, I wouldn't be as
  worried about money.
Therapist: And what difference would that make, to not be so
  worried about money?

Client: I would be in a better mood, and I suppose I would be easier to live with, and I'd get along better with my roommate, maybe.

Therapist: And how would getting along better affect you?

Client: I'd be happier.

Therapist: Seems like you figured out what you need to do this week.

Client: Yeah—get a paper and put in some job applications.

Utilizing Solely Affective Responses

Occasionally there are clients who, in response to solution-focused questions, repeatedly have an affective rather than behavioral response, such as, "I'd be feeling better about myself." Even when asked how others might recognize by observing their behavior that they were feeling better about themselves, some clients can come up with only another affective response, e.g. "I'd just *feel* better. There would be no way they could tell from how I was acting, but I'd know because I'd *feel* it."

An effective way to utilize this solely affective response is to ask the client how she and others around her would know that she was feeling this way, what would she be doing differently that would indicate these positive feelings. The identified behaviors can then be used by the client to develop the affect state she has associated with them in her description.

Another way to utilize the affective description of the solution as a "feeling state" is to ask the client, "What will you be telling yourself when you are feeling that way?" The client can then write these words down on a piece of paper and carry them around with her, practicing saying them to herself whenever the words would be helpful.

In the final stage of treatment, after the abuse issues have been addressed and the client has identified what she needs to do in small enough steps, she can accomplish her definition of a satisfying future. It is very important that the therapist communicate a sense of confidence that the client does have the inner resources to accomplish the practical goals she has set. Living out a positive future allows the client to be much more than a survivor of sexual abuse.

Developing an Image of the Adult Self She Would Have Been Without the Effects of the Abuse

A client once asked me to put her into a trance to find out what she would have been like if she hadn't been molested as a child. For some clients, going into a trance and exploring an inner image of what they would have been like without the abuse is a valuable reclaiming of the self. One client said, "It's like getting back my birthright."

Specifically, this can be accomplished in the following steps:

1. Identify the client's symbol for the present and associational cue for comfort and security (Chapters 2 and 6). Direct the client to focus on the symbol for the present and then the associational cue for comfort and security.
2. Ask the client to let her unconscious give an ideomotor signal when ready to get some help understanding what she would be like if the abuse had not occurred. (See Chapter 9 for a discussion of development of ideomotor signals.)
3. When the ideomotor signal is evidenced, ask the client's unconscious to access a meaningful image of herself apart from the abuse, as if it had never occurred.
4. Ask the client to "feel free to learn what you need to understand for now from that inner image, in order to live a really satisfying life, knowing that you can again return and explore that inner image at any appropriate time that would be helpful . . . in the next ten minutes of clock time [or whatever time is realistic for therapist and client]." Ask that she again give an ideomotor signal when she has learned what she needed to learn today.
5. Reorient the client by mentioning that she return her full focus to the symbol for the present, "becoming refreshingly awake, and consciously aware, and bringing back with you any useful information and feeling free to forget anything best left unconscious."

Once the image of herself as she would have been without the abuse has been described and explored and any feelings associated with the implied losses acknowledged and validated, the resulting information can guide the client in planning for the future.

She can choose what she wants to incorporate from that imagined personality and, in so doing, identify the gifts she developed in order to survive and cope with the abuse, thereby developing a more positive and accurate appreciation of herself both apart from the abuse and in the context of the abuse. The parts incorporated from the image of herself if she had not been abused may result in her discovering special interests and affinities of which she was not previously aware, such as, in one client, a desire to spend time outdoors in the wild. And it may also show up in such areas as like hobbies, dress, career directions, and self-esteem.

The above technique allows the client to integrate and make peace with the discrepancy between who she might have been and who she is. Not every client will find this process meaningful, but for those who feel drawn to the "self that might have been," this may afford resolution and new positive directions otherwise unavailable.

Termination

In my workshops on treating adult survivors of sexual abuse, many therapist participants have asked me, "How do you know when it is safe to terminate?" It is generally safe when the client truly feels ready and the therapist agrees. Getting to that point is the hard part. Many sexual abuse clients seem to be most comfortable terminating therapy in stages, by first lengthening the weekly time between appointments, gradually moving to monthly, and then bimonthly appointments, and then scheduling an appointment after 90 days. I have asked many of my clients how they knew that the time had come to end therapy, and several have said something like, "I knew because I wasn't having the symptoms anymore and I had run out of things I needed to talk about."

It is not uncommon for a sexual abuse survivor to call six months, a year, two years later to request an appointment to deal with a new issue or to do further work regarding the sexual abuse. While some therapists prefer in such cases to refer the client to a new therapist, because it is presumably the beginning of new work, others see the value of already knowing the client's background and context.

I routinely tell my clients that I will see them in the future if needed. I do this because of the sensitivity to real or perceived abandonment that the client may have as a result of being sexually abused. Despite this statement of availability, I have not been subject to late night phone calls or post-termination crises from my clients, even those who could be diagnosed as borderline. I believe this reassurance is the reason that I have yet to experience a problematic or even difficult termination with a sexual abuse survivor client.

One client beautifully expressed this need for reassurance upon termination, "I don't need to see you anymore if I know that I can if I ever need to." I told her she could. Her description of what she needed from me to terminate comfortably is typical. I sometimes make a joke about their telephoning this ancient, wrinkled, wizened old lady version of me and coming in and wheeling me into my office so we can meet. Clients seem to find this very amusing, but no one has ever said that it definitely won't happen!

Since I routinely use solution-focused therapy techniques as part of my work, I am commonly asked if I am doing "brief" therapy with sexual abuse survivors. My answer is that I work with my clients for as long as it takes for them to experience relief from symptoms, resolution of the intrusive traumatic memories, and acquisition of a hopeful and nonsymptomatic orientation towards the future.

The resulting therapy process is definitely "briefer" than it would be without the combination of solution-focused and Ericksonian techniques. However it is not necessarily—in fact usually not—"short term." I have in a very few cases successfully treated sexually abused clients in two or three sessions (Dolan, 1989), but this has been very rare and has been accomplished, in large part I believe, because of the perpetrator's willingness to take full responsibility for the abuse and provide appropriate support and restitution. This is, unfortunately, a rare occurrence.

More often, the length of treatment ranges from several months to three years. I have seen many clients for five years or more; however, after the first year or two, they usually call only once a year for a "follow-up." I am convinced that one function of their occasional requests is simply to experience the reassurance of my statement that I would still be there for them if needed.

If the necessary work has been accomplished, and the therapist has been able to reassure the client that her needs will be respected if she requires further therapy, termination does not need to be a problem. Difficulties with termination might indicate that the client is not yet ready to leave and has more work to do.

Forced Termination

A difficult situation arises when termination occurs not because the treatment is complete but because the therapist is changing jobs or the client or therapist is moving. Referring the client to a new therapist needs to be done in a warm and sensitive manner; however, once the referral is made, it needs to be clearly communicated to the client that the new therapist is a person with whom she could work. This will prevent the client from inadvertently triangulating the two therapists and will keep the therapy moving forward. As long the client knows that the original therapist has referred her out of concern for her best interest, termination does not need to be traumatic. Sadness on parting, however, is understandable, since the client has presumably shared a significant life experience with the therapist.

Relationships With Clients After Therapy

With alarming regularity, I hear of cases of therapists' becoming involved socially or even sexually with former clients who are survivors of sexual abuse. I feel strongly that this is not in the client's best interest and consequently constitutes unethical behavior on the part of the former therapist. This switch to being "friends," — or worse "lovers" — may be particularly damaging for survivors of incestuous sexual abuse, because it may replicate the lack of boundaries and cross-generational hierarchical violation that characterized the original abuse.

Over the past several years, I have seen in therapy a number of sexual abuse survivors who were "casualties" of their former therapist's decision to become socially involved with them. This seems, in many cases, to undo the effects of the original therapy and can certainly trigger relapse of PTS symptoms, which may be particularly severe if the relationship ends.

Another kind of a relationship with a client after therapy occurs when the client continues to keep the therapist informed about her progress as the years go by. Because of the sexual abuse survivor may have experienced abandonment from significant people in her life, keeping the therapist informed through cards on holidays and little notes telling about her life milestones can be very meaningful. Supportive responses from the therapist can be kept very brief and to the point. I am not, of course, advocating continuing therapy by mail! However, I think it can be very helpful for the client to know that it is okay to maintain contact with the therapist through occasional notes.

The Rewards of Completion

Watching a client move through the treatment process and begin to actually live out a satisfying future that defies the abuse she once suffered is probably the most compelling and meaningful reward a therapist can experience as a result of working with this complex, difficult and demanding client population. Each client's triumphs as she works to limit, overcome, and "outsmart" the effects of the past abuse have been a continuing source of profound joy for me.

As therapists we can always learn by watching our clients. Sexual abuse survivors have a lot to teach us about the human capacity to transcend seemingly impossible situations and ultimately heal. I have been inspired by their struggles, their determinations, and their successes.

13

SPECIAL CONCERNS
FOR THE THERAPIST

HERE I WILL focus on various concerns regarding the therapist's use of self both within and outside of the therapy setting. Included will be a discussion of gender issues and self-disclosure, considerations for therapists who are sexual abuse survivors, and suggestions for what to do if the client triggers the therapist's own issues. In addition, this chapter will focus in detail on symptoms of secondary post-traumatic stress and will offer the therapist practical suggestions for preventing and overcoming the stress implicit in providing treatment to trauma survivors.

Gender Issues

A respected colleague once told me, "Ideally, with a really professional therapist, the gender should not matter." This is not so simple when treating survivors of sexual abuse. If the therapist is the same sex as the offender, the client may feel very frightened and have good reason to request to see a therapist of the opposite sex. This is particularly common in the early stages of therapy.

Even if the client does not request a therapist who is a different sex from the perpetrator, the therapist should be sensitive to this issue. If a therapist of a different gender than the perpetrator would appear to allow the client to address issues more completely and efficiently, a referral should be discussed with the client. I would like to emphasize, however, that sexual abuse survivors often have little ability to trust or feel safe around individuals of *either* gender. The therapist's implied values and attitude toward sexual aggression, as well as gender discrimination, may be far more important than whether the therapist is male or female.

Most likely to need to see a therapist of the same gender are clients who have been so severely damaged by their physical and sexual abuse that they cannot discriminate enough to know that someone of the same sex as the actual perpetrator (rather than the complicitous parent) could potentially be trustworthy. It is my belief that this is most likely true of clients who have never experienced a non-abusive relationship, particularly those who suffer from multiple personality disorder, severe dissociative disorders, and/or acute flashbacks of such duration as to resemble psychotic states.

While this is certainly not always the case, in some instances the therapist who is the same sex as the offender may provide a powerful healing context in which the client can receive needed therapeutic messages. The therapist who is the exception to the client's learned mistrust may help the client to learn to make discriminations that allow for both self-protection and appropriate trust of other members of that gender. This will probably not occur until the later stages of therapy.

Male Therapist/Female Victim/Male Perpetrator

John Briere (1989) points out that while many female clients have been helped by male therapists, in most of these cases the client "had not been severely damaged by her abuse" (p.161). Briere emphasizes that, even in such cases, the male therapist should be aware that he may have to do extra work with the client to achieve the same level of rapport with which a female therapist would begin. If it is obvious that treatment would be greatly enhanced by a female therapist, a referral should be made.

It is important that the therapist be sensitive to the female sexual abuse survivor's possible learned tendency to placate males to her own detriment. If he is not sensitive to these issues, the therapist may fall into the role of using the client for his own emotional gratification, rather than creating a context that truly addresses her treatment needs.

Male therapists treating female clients should also be aware of a tendency for the therapist initially to identify with the male perpetrator (Courtois, 1988). They need to guard against communicating in any way that invalidates the client's feelings or directly or indirectly minimizes her past victimization.

In my workshops on sexual abuse treatment, I have been heartened by both male and female therapists' expressions of concern about gender issues, as well as their obvious desire to work in the client's best interest. The phenomenon that I have seen most often with male therapists and female sexual abuse survivors is a tendency for the therapist to overcompensate for the potentially difficult gender dynamics by distancing from the client. This may be due to a realistic fear on the part of the male therapist that the client will displace her rage onto him (Courtois, 1988).

The problem with the male therapist's distancing from the client is similar to the problems created by the therapist's experiencing the secondary PTS symptom of "numbing" that will be described later in this chapter. The client may view the therapist's lack of emotional involvement as abandonment and perceive his distance as further "proof" that she is bad and deserving of only negative attention. This will serve to reinforce her inner sense of shame and an image of herself as having "bad sexuality"; further, she may be confirmed in her belief that she is unworthy of emotionally positive and nurturing relationships, especially with males.

Even though it is recognized to be a serious ethical and professional conduct violation, sexual involvement between female clients and male therapists has been found to occur with alarming regularity. Significantly, there is some evidence that incest survivors may be sexually abused in therapy by male therapists in disproportionate numbers to other clients (de Young, 1981).

While sexual interaction between a therapist and client is in general potentially very damaging, when the client has a history of sexual abuse the effects are particularly disastrous. Courtois (1988) points out the damaging effects inherent in such situations, in that they comprise a reenactment the original abuse and are experienced by the client both as a betrayal and as "additional proof of the untrustworthiness of men and her own evil eroticism" (p.241).

This should not be interpreted to mean that male therapists should never see female sexual abuse survivors in treatment. I have seen many successful therapy outcomes involving this dyad. Rather, the male therapist needs to pay close attention to transference and countertransference dynamics to ensure that the client does not experience any aspect of therapy as a symbolic or actual reenactment of her victimization.

Female Therapist/Female Survivor/Male Perpetrator

In general, the female therapist treating a female survivor of sexual abuse who was abused by a male perpetrator is apt to have an easier role than her male colleague, especially in the early stages of therapy. In the treatment of sexual dysfunction, the female client is likely to feel far more comfortable discussing her issues with a female therapist.

On the other hand, the female therapist may, because of her gender, become a symbolic target for the client's rage at her mother for failing to protect her or, in some cases, for being complicitous in incestuous relations with the perpetrator or, more rarely, for being a perpetrator. When she is the object of the client's rage, the female therapist needs to guard against distancing that makes the client feeling abandoned. The client needs to be empowered to examine the aspects of the mother-daughter relationship, as well as all other aspects of her victimization.

Female Perpetrator

We should not overlook the fact that clients seeking therapy for sexual abuse include those who were directly abused by female perpetrators. In such cases, the female therapist may encounter some of the same sort of issues encountered by male therapists treating clients abused by males. Male therapists seeing clients abused by females may have some of the advantages experienced by females treating clients who were abused by males. On the other hand, the female therapist who successfully works with a female client abused by a female perpetrator is in a powerful position to provide a corrective learning for the client. She may find that females are not, by virtue of their gender, dangerous or "bad," and this can have very important ramifications for her sense of herself as a female. If the client and therapist both happen to be lesbian, the therapist's positive role modeling may also be helpful for the client in establishing a healthy sense of identity as a lesbian. However, if the lesbian therapist encounters homophobia in her community, she may feel compelled to keep her sexual identity private.

Several of my male clients have disclosed that they had been sexually victimized in childhood by female perpetrators. Based on my own clinical experience and colleagues' descriptions of their caseloads, I believe that sexual victimization of male and female children by female perpetrators is not as rare as the current research would suggest.

Female Therapist/Male Victim

The female therapist seeing a male client must, as in other dyads, guard against her own "numbing" and distancing, particularly in the area of the client's expression of rage. By virtue of cultural upbringing, some female therapists may have been conditioned to be less comfortable or accepting than males of emotions associated with anger.

There is a tendency in some cases for male clients to try to control the therapy session by treating the female therapist in a verbally abusive, discounting, sexist, or sexualizing manner (Briere, 1989). If this is occurring, the female therapist needs to clearly communicate that such treatment is not acceptable or useful and will not be tolerated. To allow the client to continue this behavior in such a way as to prevent treatment from occurring is a waste of both the therapist's and the client's time. Presumably, this behavior stems from feelings of fear associated with the client's vulnerability or displaced feelings about the perpetrator if the perpetrator was female. If the behavior continues after the issue is raised, or if the client was abused by a female perpetrator, a referral to a male therapist may well be advantageous for the client.

Male Therapist/Male Victim

Briere (1989) points out that male clients seen by male therapists often attempt to play out power and trust issues by being either "one down" or "one up" with the therapist. If good treatment is to occur, the trust issues must be addressed. If the male client was abused by a male perpetrator, the therapist needs to consider early on whether treatment would be facilitated by a referral to a female therapist.

As in other gender dyads, the therapist needs to guard against distancing because of fear of being at the receiving end of the client's displaced anger.

As in the case of the female therapist a seeing client abused by a female perpetrator, the male therapist seeing a client abused by a male perpetrator may provide a powerful corrective emotional experience for the client, who is able to learn that not all males are untrustworthy.

If both the client and therapist are gay, the therapist may also provide a valuable model of a healthy sense of self as gay. This implicit healthy role modeling may be especially helpful if, as a consequence of the abuse or because of societal prejudices, the client has been conditioned to suffer from shame or guilt regarding his sexual preferences. However, as in the case of lesbian therapists, societal prejudices may also exert pressure on the therapist to keep his own homosexuality a secret.

Clients Seen Sequentially by Male and Female Therapists

Ideally, the client should have the choice of seeing male and female therapists at various stages of therapy. Seeing a therapist of the same sex as the perpetrator can be particularly healing in the later stages of therapy. As one former client told me, "I wasn't ready to see a male therapist at first, but just as I got things from you that I could never have gotten from a man because I couldn't have told those things to a man at the time, I got things from him because he is a man, and knowing him made me realize that being a male doesn't necessarily mean that he's bad, or that all males are bad. He really did a lot to make it possible for me to relate totally differently to men now."

In all gender combinations of therapist and client, countertransference and transference need to be carefully monitored, and supervision for the therapist is strongly recommended.

Maintaining Good Boundaries

When working with a survivor of sexual abuse, it is especially important to maintain good boundaries between the therapist and client. If the client feels the relationship is sliding into a social context, she may become frightened. One way the boundaries can become blurred is through excessive self-disclosure on the part of the therapist.

This is tricky, because the sex abuse survivor is probably quite adept at "taking care" of others and may feel most comfortable when putting her own needs aside. She may try over and over again to shift the focus of the session onto the therapist rather than on herself. Early in her therapy with me, one survivor of sexual abuse actually apologized for talking too much about herself during our session! When I assured her that it was quite appropriate and desirable for her to talk about herself in our sessions, she commented, "Really? With my last therapist, it was usually more balanced—half the time I would talk and half the time she would talk about herself and what had happened to her in her victimization."

It was not surprising to me that the client later confided that she had been unable to disclose the full extent of the abuse while working with her previous therapist. When I asked the client why she had withheld information, she said, "Well, no offense intended, but she was more like a friend, and I didn't want to upset her. With you, I know you care about me but it doesn't feel as personal—like I don't feel like I have to worry about your getting personally upset if I tell you something really bad that happened." The client then worried aloud that she was being "selfish" by not thinking of my needs. She had to be reassured several times over the course of her treatment that using our time together for herself was not selfish, but healthy and appropriate.

While I suspect the former therapist had good intentions behind her self-disclosure, it unfortunately reenacted the client's learned childhood role of putting her own needs aside to take care of the adult from whom she should rightfully expect care-taking. Care must be taken to gently redirect clients back to their own issues, reminding them that "this time is for you."

Another way the client-therapist boundary can become blurred is if appointment times and session limits are not adhered to. The session should begin promptly at the scheduled time; if the client is late, the session should still end at the scheduled time. This is necessary for the client's sense of security. If the client is in crisis and the therapist has an extra half-hour or so available, this should be directly negotiated at the end of the hour by telling the client, "I have an extra half an hour available today if you would like to continue this session." The session should not continue without this acknowledgment of the scheduled agreement.

I am not advocating abruptly and insensitively "kicking clients out the door" at the end of the session. Rather, I am suggesting that sticking to a previously agreed upon schedule helps give the client a sense of predictability and security that was so often missing in childhood, and also prevents her from becoming overwhelmed by the issues she is dealing with in the therapy session.

Self-Disclosure

It is my experience as a psychotherapist and a supervisor of psychotherapists treating survivors of sexual abuse that self-disclosure is best used very selectively, if at all. It should be used only in contexts that are clearly in the interest of the client. These contexts are those in which the therapist's self-disclosure clearly and powerfully communicates a message of hope or empathy or both.

Furthermore, the self-disclosure should be made only in cases where it appears to be the only truly effective, or at least the most effective, way of expressing empathy or communicating a much-needed message of hope to the client. I believe this is particularly important because of the survivor's boundary issues and security needs and because of hierarchical considerations. Since the family hierarchy was violated in childhood sexual abuse, it particularly needs to be maintained in treatment; otherwise the therapist risks reenacting aspects of the hierarchical confusion present in the original abuse situation by "acting like another client" with the client.

The therapist who is also survivor of sexual abuse presents special concerns regarding self-disclosure. Specific self-disclosure regarding details of abuse that the therapist experienced is risky. In the first place, if the therapist is spending part of the session talking about her own experiences of victimization, it is possible that the client has succeeded in "taking care" of the therapist, rather than focusing on her own needs.

Secondly, the client may get caught in a no-win self-comparison. Even in classic cases of incestuous abuse, no two experiences are alike. The client is at risk for feeling very inadequate, since she may view the disclosure in this way: "My therapist had it a lot worse than I did as a kid, and she dealt with it—years ago. I feel really inadequate that after all these years I'm still having problems and my abuse was so minor compared to what she went through." Or, conversely, "My therapist thinks she understands because her brother fondled her once, but that is absolutely nothing compared to what I went through. How can she think she knows how I feel?"

Therapists Who Are Survivors of Sexual Abuse

According to recent studies, about one-third of women and one-tenth of men in North America are sexually victimized before they reach their mid-teens (Finkelhor, 1984; Peters, Wyatt, & Finkelhor, 1986; Russell, 1983). It is therefore not surprising that there are many therapists who are also former victims of childhood sexual abuse.

Being both a psychotherapist and a survivor of sexual abuse has both advantages and disadvantages. If the therapist has worked through her own victimization, she is likely to have an advantage of being more able to readily recognize and understand the client's issues from "having been there." She is also likely to communicate an implicit confidence to the client that "you really can get through this and come out at the other side okay." This is communicated implicitly in the therapist's general attitude toward the client. One client described it well when upon ending therapy she said to the therapist (a survivor), "I just want to tell you that all along I could tell that you knew I could get over this stuff—even at first when I couldn't believe I could—and that really made a big difference to me."

There are potential complications involved in being a survivor of sexual abuse working as a therapist treating others who were abused. There is the danger, even if your issues are resolved, that old traumatic memories will be re-elicited and you may suffer from flashbacks that presumably would not occur if you worked in a different area. And when such flashbacks occur, there is the danger that the therapist will unfairly blame herself for not having worked through her own abuse to the extent that all flashbacks are preventable. All flashbacks are *not* preventable. Because of the very nature of a flashback, it is not a phenomenon subject to rigid conscious control. The techniques in this book are reliable and helpful ways to lessen the likelihood of a flashback's occurring and minimize the impact of flashbacks when they do occur, but they are not foolproof.

Too often I have seen therapists as clients who mentally beat themselves up when they have a flashback or experience other symptoms such as dissociation. In so doing they are berating themselves for being victimized in the first place, rather than compassionately recognizing the flashback or other symptoms as a classically conditioned response to an evocative stimulus. One therapist I saw clearly summed up this self-abusive interpretation: "I get so mad at myself, I just hate myself for still having these feelings come up after all these years. I ask myself, 'Why the hell haven't you dealt with it?' What am I avoiding and I didn't even know I was avoiding? I should be over this by now and I'm not and I feel terrible about myself because of that."

Being "over it" for the sexual abuse survivor/psychotherapist may not mean never having a PTS symptom. In some cases, that just may not be realistic because of the nature of PTS and the nature of the victimization. However, being over it can mean being in control in such a way as to minimize the duration and impact of symptoms so that they are not allowed to interfere with personal relationships, good feelings about oneself, and in particular, work with clients.

Another problem is that the therapist may project unresolved issues onto the client. Having a history of the same sort of abuse may put therapists at a higher risk for getting their issues mixed up with the client's. The therapist who is a survivor of sexual abuse has to monitor herself constantly to make sure that her issues are kept distinct and separate from the issues with which she is assisting her client in therapy.

Whether the therapist is or is not a survivor of sexual abuse herself, she is likely eventually to encounter another therapist who is a survivor in the role of a client. In treating a therapist who is a survivor of sexual abuse, one must take care not to give the perception, however inadvertently, of criticizing her for having her own symptoms of the abuse. Because of her history of victimization, she is at risk for being overly self-critical and projecting this onto others. It is crucial that she not be allowed to blame and further abuse herself for needing therapy.

For example, the therapist who is a survivor, particularly if her abuse was dissociated for many years, may initially feel in retrospect like a "phony" because "I had my own issues and didn't even know about them, much less deal with them, and here I was trying to help other people." Strong reassurance is important. I suggest telling her the "glass in the knee" story (see Chapter 11) or a similar metaphor.

What To Do If Client Issues Bring Up Therapist Issues

Working with survivors of sexual abuse is often an intense emotional experience because of the content of the sessions. Good therapists are compassionate people, and it is not surprising that working with a client who is dealing with powerful past experiences sometimes triggers the therapist's own issues. Having one's own issues come up is not a bad thing for the therapist as long as the therapist's issues and needs do not get confused with the client's issues and treatment needs.

The most obvious sign that the therapist's own issues are coming up are vivid memories of times in the past when the therapist experienced feelings or events similar to what the client is currently describing. If such memories are distracting the therapist from the client's problem, and if they carry an intense negative emotion, it is likely that the therapist is dealing with old unresolved issues. Feeling very emotional during or afterwards when thinking about a session, in addition to possibly being a sign of secondary post-traumatic stress, may also be a signal that the therapy with clients is evoking the therapist's own unresolved issues.

Signs that the therapist's own issues are coming up may also include a strong investment in the client's taking some particular action for which she is not ready or even interested.

For example, one therapist I supervised sought help in sorting out difficulties he was having with a client who refused to "deal with" her parents. The parents had been clearly abusive over many years, and the client had chosen not to have contact with them for the past decade.

The therapist kept urging the client to write and mail them a letter detailing her feelings about them. The client was not willing to do this. Arguably, the act of sorting out feelings in a letter might have been helpful in the client's further resolution of any issues with her parents, and the letter would not have to be mailed. However, the client was unwilling to do this task, and the therapist was so invested in it that an impasse developed between them.

Reading this, you probably accurately predicted that the therapist had issues with his own parents that needed attention. Since his parents had died several years ago, writing a letter was the feasible solution. Once he gave himself the option of this therapeutic ritual, he could move beyond the impasse with the client.

If feeling overinvested in some area, the therapist might ask if there is anything going on with the client that is in some way indirectly or directly reminiscent of his or her own life experiences. Sometimes it helps to just list the general themes the client is dealing with, such as abandonment, betrayal, unresolved anger, sadness, and loneliness. Asking oneself if these recall events in one's own life will not only help the therapist separate personal issues from client issues, but also provide a good opportunity for the therapist to heal in ways that may not have been available or possible before.

Identifying that the therapist's own issues are coming up means that one is continuing to grow as a person and as a therapist. Here are some techniques for resolving issues that come up from doing therapy with others:

1. Lefthand/righthand dialogue to resolve old developmental issues. Write out all your concerns with your nondominant hand. Now "answer" with your dominant hand. You can then switch back to your nondominant hand and see it you have any other ideas to add to your solution-focused "answer." Continue until you feel comforted and your concerns are in a state of resolution. (The nondomi-

nant hand writing is used to access unconscious process. The technique is derived from writing exercises found in *The Power of Your Other Hand* by Lucia Capacchione.)

2. Write out your concerns, read them and then write down (or just imagine) what you would say to a client who was feeling that way.

3. See a therapist yourself and give yourself the luxury of really talking it over with another professional.

4. Make a list of all the ways your situation is like your client's and then write down how you feel about what happened back then or, if the issue is current, about what is happening in your life right now. Now write down how your situation is different from the client's. Now, if it still feels emotionally charged for you, give yourself some ideas about how to deal with it using one of the above techniques.

Secondary Post-Traumatic Stress

Working with survivors of sexual abuse can produce secondary symptoms of post-traumatic stress in the therapist. These may include sleeplessness, a vivid mental replaying of the client's description of the trauma after the session similar to flashbacks, lack of interest in sex or romance (Briere, 1989), "numbing," and generalized anxiety similar to that found in actual victims of sexual abuse.

In the clinical setting, there may be a tendency to see all clients as potential sexual abuse victims or perpetrators. Coworkers may find themselves indulging in fantasies of violent revenge against perpetrators, and a pervasive cynicism about the human character may begin to become the staff "culture."

One symptom of secondary post-traumatic stress in staff working with sexual abuse clients is a tendency to talk about sexual abuse all the time. This may be tricky to identify because, after a particularly intense session, it can be healthy and helpful to debrief with a colleague, and in group treatment settings it is often necessary to fill in other staff members on what has transpired in treatment that day. However, discussions of sexual abuse issues that extend well into the therapist's social time on a regular basis can perpetuate secondary post-traumatic stress, since the therapist is deprived of time that should be a break from the psychological intensity of working with trauma survivors.

This is not to say that staff members should not socialize. Some of the healthiest teams I have seen enjoy an occasional trip to a pub or restaurant together. However, they appear to be able, in these recreational settings, to focus on play and "social talk" about their lives and families as opposed to analyzing and re-analyzing their current work. If work needs discussion, this should be provided as part of supervision or in ongoing personal therapy.

"Numbing" can occur in the therapist in apparent response to the overwhelming intensity of the client's description of the abuse or, perhaps more accurately, in response to the culmination of listening to many, many grisly tales of suffering over time with little personal relief and comfort. Numbing may also be a sign that the therapist's own issues of victimization are being evoked. Signs of numbing include a flatness of affect in and out of the therapy session and a lack of humor or warmth.

The danger of the therapist's "numbing" is that it may well be experienced by the client as "coldness," and the therapist may be perceived as distant and rejecting.

Numbing is a signal that the therapist needs to take some time away from trauma and to participate in some experiences that instill comfort and hope. I have seen many therapists take comfort in retreats into nature, sports that demand full physical participation and mental attention such as skiing, gymnastics, etc., and simply "getting away from it all" for a few days.

Some therapists have reported having dreams about their clients' victimization, and it is not uncommon for therapists who are experiencing secondary post-traumatic stress to have nightmares of being themselves victimized similar to the nightmares of victims. If the therapist is a survivor of sexual abuse, he or she may be at higher risk for developing these secondary symptoms. However, I have heard of therapists with no personal history of sexual abuse experiencing these symptoms. It would appear that these therapists are deeply concerned and caring about their clients and are consequently traumatized by hearing that another person was so cruelly hurt.

If having post-traumatic stress nightmares, the therapist can benefit from the same strategies taught to clients: "Reassure yourself by looking around the room and establishing your orientation to the here and now. Your associational cue will be helpful. The nightmare needs to be appreciated as your unconscious attempt to work through and depotentiate the trauma you experienced through your client's description of victimization."

It is also common for the therapist when experiencing secondary post-traumatic stress to feel overwhelmed, even incompetent in the face of the client's history of significant trauma and extensive symptomatology. This can occur even with highly trained and well-seasoned, competent therapists. It is helpful in these cases to seek reassurance from trusted colleagues and to get some supervision, so that responsibility for treatment is a shared experience. Peer or individual supervision can provide healthy boundaries for the examination of treatment concerns, thus preventing them from invading personal time.

Perhaps the most subtle symptom of secondary post-traumatic stress is a listlessness, which I have heard staff members describe as "kind of like a low grade depression, only it's not chemical and I can't identify any cause in my personal life right now. I feel fine until I come back to work after a vacation and I fall right into the 'blahs.'" Similar to the pervasive cynicism discussed above, this form of post-traumatic stress is characterized by a tendency to see life as bleak in view of all the victimization the therapist has observed, and consequently to withdraw and isolate, not unlike victims do. Obviously one of the "cures" in this case is to reconnect to community life, doing activities with friends. It is often helpful to develop friendships outside the psychotherapy field to help regain the zest and interest that make life worth living.

Specific Effects of Secondary PTS on Staff Interaction

One of the most destructive effects of this secondary post-traumatic stress reaction on the treatment staff culture is the phenomenon of therapists' publicly analyzing other staff members in terms of whether they appear to have been victimized as children or not. In these scenarios, the staff member who is suspected of being a survivor of sexual abuse is talked about, but never in her/his presence. Her clinical opinions and treatment ideas are discounted because she is "seeing it wrong because she hasn't worked through her own victimization."

These sorts of comments about another colleague are victimizing in their own right, dangerous to morale, and disastrous to team building. Furthermore, often there is no actual evidence that the colleague was victimized; even if the past victimization is a fact, discounting her opinions or speculating about private aspects of her life is highly unprofessional and disrespectful at best and abusive at worst.

One of the most important goals of treatment of sexual abuse is to empower the survivor to see herself as more than an abuse survivor, in fact to reclaim her vision of herself as a healthy human being capable of gradually overcoming consequences of the trauma by strengthening her life resources and focusing on the other nontraumatic aspects of her life. To view other colleagues primarily in terms of whether they were victimized or not is to depersonalize and deny them the basic respect that should be accorded to both clients and staff members—in fact to human beings in general. If this behavior is going on in a work setting, it should be compassionately identified as symptomatic of secondary post-traumatic stress, and immediate action should be taken among colleagues to discourage participation in this destructive "gossiping."

Another phenomenon I have observed among treatment staff who work with survivors of sexual abuse is a tendency to engage in "gallows humor" about bizarre and macabre ways to punish the perpetrators of sexual abuse. Since some of the perpetrators are actually the victims of past sexual abuse, the "revenge fantasies" are inconsistent with the staff's treatment philosophy. Gallows humor can be helpful in reducing staff stress level, but if "revenge fantasies" become pervasive the staff may have trouble working effectively with those (admittedly rare) perpetrators who do express remorse and a sincere desire to try to help the victim recover.

Coping With Secondary Post-traumatic Stress

Here are some ideas to prevent, mitigate, and relieve secondary post-traumatic stress:

1. Change your clothes when you come home from work. Some therapists seem to benefit especially from wearing expressive "fun" clothes after work that would not be suitable in the professional setting.
2. Develop an after work ritual that leaves no doubt that your work role is over. Drink a cup of tea, go for a walk, read the paper, or play a musical instrument. Working out can be a great stress release as well as a ritual of completion at the end of the workday.
3. Alter the balance of your caseload to include fewer victims of trauma and more clients with a variety of complaints. For instance, about half of my caseload consists of survivors of sexual abuse and trauma; the other half represents a variety of problems.

The possibilities for rituals to decompress after the stress of the workday are as varied as the personality styles of therapists. However, do not underestimate their importance. When working with sexual abuse survivors, chances are you need one, so that you have some boundaries between work and nonwork. This is due to the psychologically compelling aspects of working with trauma, which the unconscious is likely to respond to all too thoroughly. Fortunately, the unconscious will respond also to these rituals. This is particularly valuable since most secondary post-traumatic stress is an unconscious response. (If it were conscious you wouldn't have it, because being a good therapist you'd talk yourself out of it rationally.)

The Therapist as a General Role Model for Healthy Living

Keeping oneself healthy emotionally and physically is important not just personally, but also in the professional role. Clients need therapists who are role models for healthy emotional and physical living. Survivors of incest and physical abuse, in particular, have lacked healthy role models in their families. It is up to the therapist to provide an example of the what functional living looks like to the client, so it becomes a concrete and therefore more achievable construct.

Some therapists have told me that they are "too busy" to take some time each day to exercise or feel too selfish when they give themselves a recreational break from the day's stressors. Such activity is not a luxury. It is a necessity for therapists working with an intense caseload of sexual abuse survivors. If it is not done, there is a high risk of developing secondary post-traumatic stress. Of course, secondary post-traumatic stress can occur even if the therapist is doing a great job of self-nurturance, simply because of the nature of treating trauma.

Sometimes it helps to put things in perspective by remembering that each of us has only a limited time on this earth. What is really important in terms of how we spend our time? If doing some healthy activity that brings feelings of being glad to be alive or even just a little bit more "taken care of," do it! You deserve it.

REFERENCES

American Psychiatric Association. (1987). *Diagnostic and statistical manual of mental disorders* (3rd ed., rev.). Washington, DC: Author.

Bagley, C. (1984, June). Mental health and the in-family sexual abuse of children and adolescents. *Canada's Mental Health, 6*, 17–23.

Bagley, C., & Ramsay, R. (1986). Disrupted childhood and vulnerability to sexual assault. Long-term sequels with implications for counseling. *Social Work and Human Sexuality, 4*, 33–48.

Bagley, C., & Young, L. (1987). Juvenile prostitution and child sexual abuse: A controlled study. *Canadian Journal of Community Mental Health, 44*, 33–48.

Bass, E., & Davis, L. (1988). *The courage to heal: Women healing from sexual abuse.* New York: Harper & Row.

Beahrs, J. O. (1982). *Unity and multiplicity: Multilevel consciousness of self in hypnosis, psychiatric disorder and mental health.* New York: Brunner/Mazel.

Becker, J., Skinner, L., Abel, G., & Treacy, E. (1982). Incidence and types of sexual dysfunctions in rape and incest victims. *Journal of Sex and Marital Therapy, 8*, 65–74.

Benward, J., & Densen-Gerber, J. (1975). Incest as a causative factor in anti-social behavior: An exploratory study. *Contemporary Drug Problems, 4*(3): 323–340.

Berg, I. (1990). *Solution-focused approach to family based services.* Milwaukee, WI: Brief Family Therapy Center.

Bliss, E. L. (1984). A symptom profile of patients with multiple personalities including MMPI results. *Journal of Nervous and Mental Disease, 172*, 197–202.

Blake-White, J., & Kline, C. M. (1985). Treating the dissociative process in adult victims of childhood incest. *Social Casework, 66*, 394–402.

Braun, B. G. (Ed.) (1986). *Treatment of multiple personality disorder.* Washington, DC: American Psychiatric Press, Inc.

Brickman, J. (1984). Feminist, non-sexist and traditional models of therapy: Implications for working with incest. *Women and Therapy, 3*, 49–67.

Briere, J. (1984, April). The effects of childhood sexual abuse on later psychological functioning: Defining a post-abuse syndrome. Paper presented at the Third National Conference on the Sexual Victimization of Children, Children's Hospital National Medical Center, Washington, DC.

Briere, J. (1988). The long-term clinical correlates of childhood sexual victimization. In R. A. Prentky & V. Quinsey (Eds.), *Human sexual aggression: Current perspectives* (Vol. 528, pp. 327–334). New York: New York Academy of Sciences.

Briere, J. (1989). *Therapy for adults molested as children: Beyond survival.* New York: Springer.

Briere, J., Evans, D., Runtz, M., & Wall, T. (1988). Symptomatology in men who were molested as children: A comparison study. *American Journal of Orthopsychiatry, 58,* 457–461.

Briere, J., & Runtz, M. (1986). Suicidal thoughts and behaviors in former sexual abuse victims. *Canadian Journal of Behavioural Sciences, 18,* 413–423.

Briere, J., & Runtz, M. (1987). Post sexual abuse trauma: Data and implications for clinical practice. *Journal of Interpersonal Violence, 3,* 367–379.

Briere, J., & Runtz, M. (1988). Symptomatology associated with childhood sexual victimization in a non-clinical adult sample. *Child Abuse and Neglect, 12,* 331–341.

Briere, J., & Zaidi, L. (1988, August). Sexual abuse histories and sequelae in psychiatric emergency room patients. Paper presented at the annual meeting of the American Psychological Association, Atlanta, GA.

Browne, A., & Finkelhor, D. (1986). Impact of child sexual abuse: A review of the research. *Psychological Bulletin, 99,* 66–77.

Burgess, A. W., & Holmstrom, L. L. (1974). Rape trauma syndrome. *American Journal of Psychiatry, 131,* 981–986.

Butler, S. (1978). *Conspiracy of silence: The trauma of incest.* New York: Bantam Books.

Calof, D. (1987). Treating adult survivors of sexual abuse. Workshop presentation at the Family Therapy Network Symposium, Washington, DC.

Capacchione, L. (1988). *The power of your other hand.* North Hollywood, CA: New Castle Publishing.

Capacchione, L. (1979). *The creative journal: The art of finding yourself.* Athens, OH: Ohio University/Swallow Press.

Carter, P., & Gilligan, S. (1983). Personal communication in workshop setting as part of intensive six-month training in Ericksonian hypnotherapy, held in Milwaukee, Wisconsin.

Close, H. (1990). Personal communication.

Combs, G., & Freedman, J. (1990). *Symbol, story, and ceremony: Using metaphor in individual and family therapy.* New York: Norton.

Coons, P. M., & Milstein, V. (1986). Psychosexual disturbances in multiple personality: Characteristics, etiology, and treatment. *Journal of Clinical Psychiatry, 47,* 106–110.

Courtois, C. (1979). The incest experience and its aftermath. *Victimotology: An International Journal, 4,* 337–347.

Courtois, C. (1988). *Healing the incest wound: Adult survivors in therapy.* New York: Norton.

De Francis, V. (1969). Protecting the child victim of sex crimes committed by adults. Presented to the Denver Humane Association.

de Shazer, S. (1982). *Patterns of brief family therapy.* New York: Guilford.

REFERENCES

de Shazer, S. (1984). The death of resistance. *Family Process*, *23*(1): 11–17.

de Shazer, S. (1985). *Keys to solution in brief therapy*. New York: Norton.

de Shazer, S. (1987, September/October). Minimal elegance. *Family Therapy Networker*, *59*.

de Shazer, S. (1988). *Clues: Investigating solutions in brief therapy*. New York: Norton.

de Shazer S., Berg, I., Lipchik, E., Nunnally, E., Molnar, A., Gingerich, W., & Weiner-Davis, M. (1986). Brief therapy: Focused solution development. *Family Process*, *25*, 207–222.

de Young, M. (1981). Case reports: The sexual exploitation of incest victims by helping professionals. *Victimotology: An International Journal*, *1*,*4*, 91–101.

de Young, M. (1982). Self-injurious behavior in incest victims: A research note. *Child Welfare*, *62*, 577–584.

Dolan, Y. (1985). *A path with a heart: Ericksonian utilization with resistant and chronic clients*. New York: Brunner/Mazel.

Dolan, Y. (1989). Only once if I really mean it: Brief treatment of a previously dissociated incest case. *Journal of Systemic and Strategic Therapy*, Winter.

Donaldson, M. A., & Gardner, R. (1985). Diagnosis and treatment of traumatic stress among women after childhood incest. In C. Figley (Ed.), *Trauma and its wake: The study and treatment of post-traumatic stress disorder*. New York: Brunner/Mazel.

Erickson, M. H. (1954). Pseudo-orientation in time as a hypnotherapeutic procedure. *Journal of Clinical and Experimental Hypnosis*, *2*, 261–283. Also in E. L. Rossi (Ed.). (1980). *The collected papers of Milton H. Erickson* (Vol. IV, pp. 397–423). New York: Irvington.

Erickson, M. H., & Rossi, E. L. (1979). *Hypnotherapy*. New York: Irvington.

Erickson, M. H., & Rossi, E. L. (1980). The indirect forms of suggestion. In E. L. Rossi (Ed.), *Hypnotherapy* (pp. 18–53). New York: Irvington.

Erickson, M. H., & Rossi, E. L. (1989). *The February man*. New York: Brunner/Mazel.

Erickson, M. H., Rossi, E. L., & Rossi, S. K. (1976). *Hypnotic realities*. New York: Irvington.

Feldenkrais, M. (1972). *Awareness through movement*. New York: Harper & Row.

Finkelhor, D. (1979). *Sexually victimized children*. New York: Free Press.

Finkelhor, D. (1980). Sex among siblings: A survey report on its prevalence, variety, and effects. *Archives of Sexual Behavior*, *9*, 171–194.

Finkelhor, D. (1984). *Child sexual abuse: New theory and research*. Beverly Hills: Sage Publications.

Finkelhor, D. (1986). *A sourcebook on child sexual abuse: New theory and research*. Beverly Hills: Sage Publications

Gelinas, D. J. (1981). Identification and treatment of incest victims. In E. Howell & M. Bayes (Eds.), *Women and mental health*. New York: Basic Books.

Gelinas, D. J. (1983). The persisting negative effects of incest. *Psychiatry*, *46*, 312–332.

Gilligan, S. G. (1987). *Therapeutic trances: The cooperation principle in Ericksonian hypnotherapy*. New York: Brunner/Mazel.

Goodwin, J. (1984). Incest victims exhibit post-traumatic stress disorder. *Clinical Psychiatry News*, *12*, 13.

Goodwin, J., McCarthy, T., & DiVasto, P. (1981). Prior incest in mothers of abused children. *Child Abuse and Neglect*, *5*, 87–95.

REFERENCES

Goodwin, J., Simms, M., & Bergman, R. (1979). Hysterical seizures: A sequel to incest. *American Journal of Orthopsychiatry, 49*, 698–703.

Hartmann, E. (1984). *The nightmare: The psychology and biology of terrifying dreams.* New York: Basic Books.

Herman, J. L. (1981). *Father-daughter incest.* Cambridge, MA: Harvard University Press.

Herman, J. L. (1985). Histories of violence in the outpatient population: An exploratory study. *American Journal of Orthopsychiatry, 55*, 1–4.

Herman, J. L., Russell, D. E. H., & Trocki, K. (1986). Long-term effects of incestuous abuse in childhood. *American Journal of Psychiatry, 143*, 1293–1296.

Herman, J. L., & Schatzow, E. (1987). Recovery and verification of memories of childhood sexual trauma. *Psychoanalytic Psychology, 4*, 1–4.

Hilgard, E. R. (1987). *Divided consciousness: Multiple controls in human thought and action.* New York: Wiley.

Imber-Black, E., Roberts, J., & Whiting, R. (1988). *Rituals in families and family therapy.* New York: Norton.

James, J., & Meyerding, J. (1977). Early sexual experience and prostitution. *American Journal of Psychiatry, 134*, 1381–1385.

Janoff-Bulman, R., & Frieze, I. H. (1983). A theoretical perspective for understanding reactions to victimization. *Journal of Social Issues, 39*, 1–17.

Jehu, D., Klassen, C., & Gazan, M. (1985–1986). Cognitive restructuring of distorted beliefs associated with childhood sexual abuse. *Journal of Social work and Human Sexuality, 4*, 1–35.

Johnson, C. E. (1990). Personal communication.

Johnson, L. (1989). Personal communication.

Kempe, R. S., & Kempe, C. H. (1984). *The common secret: Sexual abuse of children and adolescents.* New York: W. H. Freeman.

Langmade, C. J. (1983). The impact of pre- and postpubertal onset of incest experiences in adult women as measured by sex anxiety, sex guilt, sexual satisfaction and sexual behavior. *Dissertation Abstracts International, 44*, 917B.

Lerner, M. J. (1980). *The belief in a just world: A fundamental delusion.* New York: Plenum Press.

Lindberg, F. H., & Distad, L. J. (1985a). Post-traumatic stress disorder in women who experienced childhood incest. *Child Abuse and Neglect, 9*, 329–334.

Lindberg, F. H., & Distad, L. J. (1985b). Survival responses to incest: Adults in crisis. *Child Abuse and Neglect, 9*, 521–526.

Lipchik, E., & de Shazer, S. (1986). The purposeful interview. *Journal of Strategic and Systemic Therapies, 5* (1–2): 88–89.

Lipchik, E. (1988). Purposeful sequences for beginning the solution focused interview. In E. Lipchik (Ed.), *Interviewing* (pp. 105–117). Rockville, MD: Aspen.

Maltz, W. (1988). Identifying and treating the sexual repercussions of incest: A couples therapy approach. *Journal of Sex and Marital Therapy, 14*, 145–163.

Maltz, W., & Holman, B. (1987). *Incest and sexuality: A guide to understanding and healing.* Lexington, MA: Lexington Books.

McCann, L., Pearlman, L. A., Sackheim, D. K., & Abramson, D. J. (1985). Assessment and treatment of the adult survivor of childhood sexual abuse within a schema framework. In S. M. Sgroi (Ed.), *Vulnerable populations* (Vol. 1). Lexington, MA: Lexington Books.

McCord, J. (1985). Long-term adjustment in female survivors of incest: An exploratory study. *Dissertation Abstracts International, 46*, 650B.

Meiselman, K. C. (1978). *Incest: A psychological study of causes and effects with treatment recommendations*. San Francisco: Jossey-Bass.

Miller, D. T., & Porter, C. A. (1983). Self-blame in victims of violence. *Journal of Social Issues, 39*, 139–152.

Morris, F. (1979). *Hypnosis with friends and lovers*. New York: Harper & Row.

O'Hanlon, W. H., & Weiner-Davis, M. (1989). *In search of solutions*. New York: Norton.

Peters, S. D., Wyatt, G. E., & Finkelhor, D. (1986). Prevalence. In D. Finkelhor and associates, *A sourcebook on child sexual abuse*. Beverly Hills: Sage.

Proust, M. (1928). *Swann's way*. New York: Modern Library.

Putnam, F. W., Post, R. M., Guroff, J. J., et al. (1983). *One hundred cases of multiple personality disorder* (New Research Abstract #77). Washington, DC: American Psychiatric Association.

Reich, J. W., & Gutierres, S. E. (1979). Escape/aggression incidence in sexually abused juvenile delinquents. *Criminal Justice and Behavior, 6*, 239–243.

Rossi, E. L. (1986). *The psychobiology of mind body-healing: New concepts of therapeutic hypnosis*. New York: Norton.

Rossi, E. L., & Cheek, D. (1988). *Mind-body therapy: Methods of ideodynamic healing in hypnosis*. New York: Norton.

Runtz, M. (1987). The psychosocial adjustment of women who were sexually and physically abused during childhood and early adulthood: A focus on re-victimization. Unpublished masters thesis, University of Manitoba. Cited in Briere, J. (1989), *Therapy for adults molested as children: Beyond survival*. New York: Springer.

Runtz, M., & Briere, J. (1986). Adolescent "acting out" and childhood history of sexual abuse. *Journal of Interpersonal Violence, 1*, 326–334.

Russell, D. E. H. (1983). The incidence and prevalence of intrafamilial and extrafamilial sexual abuse of female children. *Child Abuse and Neglect, 7*, 144–146.

Russell, D. E. H. (1986). *The secret trauma: Incest in the lives of girls and women*. New York: Basic Books.

Schaub, R. (1989). Personal communication.

Sedney, M. A., & Brooks, B. (1984). Factors associated with a history of childhood sexual experiences in nonclinical female population. *Journal of the American Academy of Child Psychiatry, 23*, 215–218.

Sgroi, S. M., Blick, L. C., & Porter, F. S. (1982). A conceptual framework for child sexual abuse. In S. M. Sgroi (Ed.), *Handbook of clinical intervention in child sexual abuse*. Lexington, MA: D.C. Heath.

Shengold, L. (1963). The parent as sphinx. *Journal of American Psychoanalytic Association, 11*, 735–751.

Shengold, L. (1979). Child abuse and deprivation: Soul murder. *Journal of the American Psychoanalytical Association, 27*, 533–559.

Shengold, L. (1989). *Soul murder: The effects of childhood abuse and deprivation*. New Haven, CT: Yale University Press.

Silbert, M. H., & Pines, A. M. (1981). Sexual child abuse as an antecedent to prostitution. *Child Abuse and Neglect, 5*, 407–411.

REFERENCES

Summit, R. (1983). The child sexual abuse accommodation syndrome. *Child Abuse and Neglect, 7*, 177–193.

Trepper, T. S., & Barrett, M. J. (1989). *Systemic treatment of incest.* New York: Brunner/Mazel.

Tsai, M., Felman-Summers, S., & Edgar, M. (1979). Childhood molestation: Variables related to differential impacts on psychosocial functioning in adult women. *Journal of Abnormal Psychology, 88*, 407–417.

Van der Kolk, B. (1987). The psychological consequences of overwhelming life experience. In B. van der Kolk (Ed.), *Psychological trauma.* Washington, DC: American Psychiatric Press, Inc.

Weiner-Davis, M., de Shazer, S., & Gingerich, W. (1987). Building on pretreatment change to construct the therapeutic solution: An exploratory study. *Journal of Marital and Family Therapy, 13*(4): 359–363.

Wheeler, B. R., & Walton, E. (1987, December). Personality disturbances of adult incest victims. *Social Casework, 597*–602.

White, M. (1986). Negative explanation, restraint and double description: A template for family therapy. *Family Process, 25*(2).

White, M. (1988). The process of questioning: A therapy of literary merit? Dulwich Centre Newletter, Winter.

White, M., & Epston, D. (1990). *Narrative means to therapeutic ends.* New York: Norton.

INDEX

identify supports
- people
- past people

object of safety ← _ p 92
if feels ≠ safe — move _ 1st to notice
                           calls 7h